Dialogue for Intercultural Understanding

Fiona Maine · Maria Vrikki
Editors

Dialogue for Intercultural Understanding

Placing Cultural Literacy at the Heart of Learning

Springer

Editors
Fiona Maine
Faculty of Education
University of Cambridge
Cambridge, UK

Maria Vrikki
Department of Education
University of Nicosia
Nicosia, Cyprus

ISBN 978-3-030-71780-3 ISBN 978-3-030-71778-0 (eBook)
https://doi.org/10.1007/978-3-030-71778-0

This Springer imprint is published by the registered company Springer Nature Switzerland AG
The registered company address is: Gewerbestrasse 11, 6330 Cham, Switzerland

Acknowledgments

This project has received funding from the European Union's Horizon 2020 research and innovation Programme under grant agreement No 770045.

The sole responsibility of this publication lies with the author. The European Union is not responsible for any use that may be made of the information contained therein.

Contents

Contributors

Michael J. Baker Centre National de La Recherche Scientifique, Télécom Paris, Paris, France

Lucas M. Bietti The Norwegian University of Science and Technology, Trondheim, Norway

Benjamin Brummernhenrich University of Münster, Münster, Germany

Talli Cedar The Hebrew University of Jerusalem, Jerusalem, Israel

Maria Chatzianastasi Department of Education, University of Nicosia, Nicosia, Cyprus

Françoise Détienne Centre National de La Recherche Scientifique, Télécom Paris, Paris, France

Lilija Duoblienė Faculty of Philosophy, Institute of Educational Sciences, Vilnius University, Vilnius, Lithuania

Maria Evagorou Department of Education, University of Nicosia, Nicosia, Cyprus

Riikka Hofmann Faculty of Education, University of Cambridge, Cambridge, UK

Regina Jucks University of Münster, Münster, Germany

Sandra Kairė Faculty of Philosophy, Institute of Educational Sciences, Vilnius University, Vilnius, Lithuania

Aino-Kaisa Koistinen University of Jyväskylä, Jyväskylä, Finland

Tuuli Lähdesmäki University of Jyväskylä, Jyväskylä, Finland

Fiona Maine Faculty of Education, University of Cambridge, Cambridge, UK

Elisabeth Mayweg-Paus Faculty of Humanities and Social Sciences, Department of Education Studies, Digital Knowledge Management, Humboldt University of Berlin, Berlin, Germany

Beci McCaughran Faculty of Education, University of Cambridge, Cambridge, UK

Erez Nir The Hebrew University of Jerusalem, Jerusalem, Israel

Gabriel Pallarès Centre National de La Recherche Scientifique, Télécom Paris, Paris, France

Chrysi Rapanta NOVA University, Lisbon, Portugal

Marina Rodosthenous-Balafa Department of Education, University of Nicosia, Nicosia, Cyprus

Stéphane Safin Télécom Paris, Paris, France

Baruch B. Schwarz The Hebrew University of Jerusalem, Jerusalem, Israel

Ben Zion Slakmon Tel Aviv University, Tel Aviv, Israel

Agni Stylianou-Georgiou Department of Education, University of Nicosia, Nicosia, Cyprus

Susana Trovão NOVA University, Lisbon, Portugal

Maria Vrikki Department of Education, University of Nicosia, Nicosia, Cyprus

Irena Zaleskienė Faculty of Philosophy, Institute of Educational Sciences, Vilnius University, Vilnius, Lithuania

Maria Zimmermann Faculty of Humanities and Social Sciences, Department of Education Studies, Digital Knowledge Management, Humboldt University of Berlin, Berlin, Germany

List of Figures

List of Tables

Chapter 1
An Introduction to Dialogue for Intercultural Understanding: Placing Cultural Literacy at the Heart of Learning

Fiona Maine and Maria Vrikki

1.1 The DIALLS Project Aims and Overview

This book is a result of an extensive, ambitious and wide-ranging pan-European project focusing on the development of children and young people's cultural literacy and what it means to be European in the twenty-first century, prioritizing intercultural dialogue and mutual understanding. The book explores themes underpinning this unique interdisciplinary project, drawing together scholars from cultural studies, civics education and linguistics, psychologists, socio-cultural literacy researchers, teacher educators and digital learning experts. This chapter sets the context for the book by introducing the DIALLS project (Dialogue and Argumentation for cultural Literacy Learning in Schools) and its core aims and themes. It sets the tone of interdisciplinarity and its importance for an educational future where issues of living together, social responsibility and sustainable development transcend traditional categories of learning. DIALLS is seen as an opportunity for a synthesis of thinking, but our book allows each author to explore the goals of the project from their own interdisciplinary angle.

The three-year long DIALLS project has included ten partners from countries in and around Europe. The project was developed in response to a call from the European Commission (EC) Horizon 2020 scheme to gain a greater understanding of cultural literacy as a non-normative concept covering relevant culture-related knowledge, skills and competences and how young people in particular acquire it. The call argued that,

F. Maine (✉)
Faculty of Education, University of Cambridge, Cambridge, UK
e-mail: flm27@cam.ac.uk

M. Vrikki
Department of Education, University of Nicosia, Nicosia, Cyprus
e-mail: vrikki.m@unic.ac.cy

F. Maine and M. Vrikki (eds.), *Dialogue for Intercultural Understanding*,
https://doi.org/10.1007/978-3-030-71778-0_1

> Cultural diversity is one of Europe's most valuable assets and European educational and cultural systems need to cater for diversity and enable all citizens to build the skills and competences needed for effective inter-cultural dialogue and mutual understanding. The challenge is about understanding how young people make sense of Europe and its differing cultures. The influences on young people are wide ranging including formal education, family and cultural background and media. (European Commission 2017, 89)

The EC challenge was to create a project that could address how children and young people might develop the knowledge, skills and competencies needed for intercultural dialogue and mutual understanding.

The DIALLS project has met this challenge by working with teachers in different educational settings (pre-primary, primary and secondary) to create cross-curricular resources and activities. A Cultural Literacy Learning Programme (CLLP) was developed to teach children dialogue and argumentation as core skills needed for meaningful interactions where cultural values, identities and heritages could be explored in authentic discussions. The program, developed by teachers and researchers working together across several European countries, drew on Cultural Texts from Europe as stimuli for classroom discussion. One innovation of the project was that these were short films and texts that contained no words, so not only could they be used across all countries with no translation, but their non-verbal nature potentiated rich dialogues as children worked together to explore their meanings. This co-construction gave authentic opportunities for students to practice their skills of dialogue and argumentation to explore their ideas and move beyond interpretations of the text into rich, philosophical discussions about living together and social responsibility. In a further innovation and to enable intercultural dialogue in action, the project developed an online platform as a tool for engagement across classes.

1.2 Reconceptualizing Cultural Literacy

The DIALLS project centralizes co-constructive dialogue as a main cultural literacy value, with the aim of promoting tolerance, empathy and inclusion as key dispositions underpinning it. This aim has been achieved through teaching children in schools from a young age to engage together in discussions in the CLLP where they may have differing viewpoints or perspectives, to enable a growing awareness of their own cultural identities, and those of others.

As a term, Cultural Literacy has traditionally been used to describe knowledge about a list of significant cultural facts. Hirsch, who coined the phrase in 1988, even created a list of 5000 cultural items that 'Every American should know'. Whilst there has been significant debate about what should be on the list, few authors have challenged the notion of having a list in the first place, a problem that we address in the project. DIALLS moves beyond a concept of cultural literacy as being about knowledge of culture (through exploration of literature and art for example) into a consideration of the disposition to explore different interpretations of it. Thus, DIALLS reconceptualizes *cultural literacy* as a social practice that is inherently dialogic and based on learning and gaining knowledge through empathetic, tolerant and inclusive interaction with others (Maine et al. 2019). In other words, for our project we see cultural literacy as at the heart of intercultural dialogue and mutual understanding. The concept of 'literacy' itself has changed over time, from normative expectations about reading and writing print, into concepts about 'social practice' (Street 1984) and 'reading the world' (Freire and Macedo 1987). This view of literacy embraces multi-modality, a key feature of the DIALLS project as children are supported not only to co-construct meaning from visual and moving image texts but represent their responses through artwork in multiple non-verbal modes. For example, in one of the CLLP lessons, young children (five and six year-olds) created soundscapes for busy market scenes, in another lesson eight and nine year-olds responded to themes of inclusion by creating physical tableaus of themselves enacting inclusive behaviors.

We apply this evolution to the term 'cultural literacy' as we consider it to be 'dialogic' and by that we turn to Buber and his theories to explain how individuals view the world, their place in it and their relationship with it. Buber (1958) describes two positions in relation to a world view. An 'I-it' relationship views that world and its people as 'other' to the self. This position sets individuals as just that—a distinction between oneself and everyone else. However, he also describes an 'I-Thou' mode of being, that instead focuses on relationships. Through this an intersubjectivity is created, as 'we' exist together and our experience is present and mutual. 'My *Thou* affects me, as I affect it' Buber (1958, 12) argues. Through this lens, culture is a fluid and 'dynamic co-construction, lived in the present and not solely rooted in the past' (Maine et al 2019, 389).

In the European Network of Cultural Literacy in Europe, cultural literacy is described as:

> an attitude to the social and cultural phenomena that shape and fill our existence – bodies of knowledge, fields of social action, individuals or groups, and of course cultural artefacts, including texts – which views them as being essentially *readable*. This legibility is defined by the key concepts of textuality, rhetoricity, fictionality and historicity ... which are understood as properties both of the phenomena themselves and of our ways of investigating them. (Segal 2014, 3)

Crucially this European definition uses 'attitude' as an indicator rather than just considering knowledge about culture only. It is more liberal, more open to global problems, cultural innovations and inventions, and critical skills. It works with the fields of cultural memory, migration and translation, electronic textuality, biopolitics and the body.

From this position, the underpinning dispositions of tolerance, empathy and inclusion take on particular significance and these three dispositions are key to Buber's concept of genuine dialogue (Shady and Larson 2010). We consider these dispositions together. Tolerance is at the center of the 2014 UNESCO report on Learning to Live Together, and more than merely 'putting up with' alternative views we view it as an by "an absence of prejudice, racism or ethnocentrism" (Rapp and Freitag 2015, 1033) and a capacity "to maintain ongoing relationships of negotiation, compromise, and mutuality" (Creppel 2008, 351). However, following Shady and Larson's interpretation of Buber's work (2010) we recognize that tolerance might still present more of an 'I-It' perspective (1947) and so look to empathy and inclusion as deeper commitments to living together. Buber (1957) takes an interesting perspective on the issue of empathy. He argues that in empathizing with other viewpoints, it is crucial that one's own position is not lost (1957), and he turns to the concept of inclusion to promote 'genuine dialogue' 'where each of the participants really has in mind the other or others in their present and particular being and turns to them with the intention of establishing a living mutual relation between himself and them' (1947, 22).

1.3 Dialogue and Argumentation in DIALLS

Dialogue in DIALLS then pertains to a wider concept of engagement with cultures, values, heritages and identities of both self and other people. This engagement opens up a 'dialogic space' where an 'I-Thou' relationship builds towards acceptance of multiple viewpoints. Wegerif writes:

> People always have irreducibly different perspectives on the world because we have different bodies and histories. Even when we think that we agree about concepts we inevitably understand those concepts differently. This is not to suggest that achieving 'common ground' is not important in dialogues but that it is one moment in a larger flow of meaning that is more fundamentally described as the tension between different perspectives held together in proximity around a dialogic gap. If there is no gap then there is no dialogue and if there is no dialogue then there is no meaning. (Wegerif 2011, 182)

Dialogue means more than this in DIALLS and we embrace dialogue and argumentation as involving key skills that young people can learn to enable them to talk together across their diversity. These skills include listening carefully, building on and being sensitive to each other's viewpoints, critiquing perspectives thoughtfully and thinking about shared values and ideas. Careful positioning of ideas, respectful disagreements and acknowledgements of changes of mind are all part of participating in a pluralistic society and the CLLP lessons focus on two types of learning objective in parallel: to learn how to engage meaningfully in genuine dialogue and to discuss themes around living together, social responsibility and sustainable development.

1.4 An Interdisciplinary Project

We follow the principles of genuine dialogue espoused in the make-up of our project itself. We are interdisciplinary researchers and each chapter of our book explores a theme that is common to the project; we celebrate our interdisciplinarity by exploring these themes through different lenses.

The chapters in the book start with broader reflections on how education policy has embraced the notion of 'intercultural dialogue' and realized core concepts within different curricula, in addition to examining citizenship education and cultural literacy and their place in schools. In Chapter 2, researchers from Portugal start us off by asking whether and how educational research has changed its conception of "intercultural" in the face of the current fluid cultural realities around the world and the need for a continuously adapting and adaptive education. To address the question, they conducted a systematic review of empirical research with the goal to reveal the most predominant objectives, methods, contents, and risks that teaching and learning interculturally has faced in the last two decades. They end with recommendations regarding the most predominant current mandates of contemporary educational systems struggling with the challenges of globalization and inclusion.

In Chapter 3, Lithuanian researchers explore how the concept of Social Responsibility develops in educational research discourse and how it relates to the concepts of Citizenship and Cultural literacy. All of these concepts are defined and reflected in the contemporary research literature considering the challenging world issues such as multiculturalism, inclusion, climate change and they are discussed in consideration within a framework of Cultural Literacy Analysis framework developed as part of the DIALLS project. In the empirical part of the chapter the authors present, analyse and compare research data on how some of the interrelated concepts are reflected in different national education policy documentation. Finally, the chapter ends with the conclusions from the theoretical and empirical data, which are strongly conditioned by the research: Social Responsibility serves as a key ground stone for cultural literacy learning.

In Chapter 4, our Finnish colleagues look more closely at how intercultural dialogue has been defined as a policy and practice in policy discourses and research literature since the establishment of the concept in the Council of Europe's White Paper on Intercultural Dialogue (2008). Besides agreeing with its importance, recent research includes criticism of its implicit meanings and uses in policy discourses, as well as its implementation in practice. They summarize this criticism and discuss what kind of challenges scholars have identified from policy discourses and the implementation of intercultural dialogue. The chapter ends by discussing how art may function as an arena and instrument to overcome some of these challenges.

In Chapter 5 colleagues from Cambridge look closely at Cultural Texts in the project and how collaborative meanings can be made as teachers and children engage together in reading wordless picturebooks. Whilst similar in their wordlessness, the reading pathways of these narratives can vary considerably, offering different affordances for the oral co-construction of narratives. Case studies of children engaging together with their teachers are presented to illustrate how teachers can mediate these texts and support children in their dialogic co-construction. The chapter explores how the themes underpinning cultural literacy as defined in the DIALLS project can be realized in talk and through talk with young children. The data demonstrate how the language modelled by teachers and their careful guidance allows independent sense-making and enables collaborative co-construction.

The book stays with the Cultural Texts as researchers from Cyprus investigate some of the texts that were used in the DIALLS project in Chapter 6. The authors present several creative ways to analyze and teach the theme of "diversity", as this is approached in various ways across age groups (i.e. pre-primary, primary and secondary education). The wordless picturebooks that are comparatively examined both in terms of illustration and teaching are *Saturday* by Sasjua Halfmouw, *To the Market* by Noëlle Smit.

Chapter 7 investigates the potential of digital tools to support children's development skills around dialogue and argumentation and how these can ensure challenge and extension of ideas. Researchers from France and Israel describe the process of designing the 'DIALLS platform', a new Internet-based platform for supporting cultural literacy and understanding of European values based on collaborative and teacher-led reflection on wordless texts. They present the multistage process adopted for the designing of the platform. Firstly, a systematic and critical review of existing tools supporting the co-creation and sharing of cultural resources (e.g., multimodal texts, images, videos) was undertaken. Secondly, several co-design workshops with researchers, teachers and students were conducted aimed at contextualizing and further specifying the functionalities of the existing tools. Thirdly, multiple usability studies where teachers in five European countries tested different versions of the platform as well as the set of blended online pedagogical scenarios were organized. To conclude, the complexities and challenges involved in the development of an online platform aimed at supporting the objectives of a large European research project in Education are discussed.

Chapter 8, written by members of the teams in Israel and France, presents a theoretical overview of historical and philosophical approaches to moral development. Then, it introduces the researchers' methodology, which focuses on a microgenetic approach for analysis meant to examine two aspects of moral development existing in the DIALLS framework: dialogue on ethics (DoE) and ethics of dialogue (EoD). This methodology lends itself to the settings in DIALLS, as teachers direct the children to interact and create a dialogue following the textless narratives they are presented with. These discussions include both talking about certain values that appear in those narratives and conceptualizing them, and the children's conduct towards each other within the interaction, executing—or not—moral/ethical values expressed in the interaction. The researchers' approach is presented through an illustrative example taken from a DIALLS lesson at an Israeli primary school.

Chapter 9 stays with themes of social interaction, written by researchers from Münster, Germany, and France. Here, a hypothesis is developed about how social relations influence how students argue with each other. Building on findings about how relations develop in small student groups, the researchers focus on perceived psychological safety as an antecedent of sophisticated argumentation. Feeling safe and valued should benefit risk-taking, in the sense that students should be more willing to contribute diverse, and maybe unusual, perspectives. However, strong social cohesion could also lead groups to converge too readily on simple, non-challenging ideas. After building a theoretical model, the authors operationalize central communicational dimensions: social aspects such as supportive behavior and facework, and cognitive aspects such as deepening and broadening. Excerpts from discussions recorded in a German classroom serve as examples for variations on these dimensions. Finally, the chapter describes how the multi-lingual discussion corpus and additional data gathered during the DIALLS project will enable testing this hypothesis.

Moving from students to their teachers, authors from Cyprus and England discuss in Chapter 10 the importance of offering a teacher professional development (PD) program in DIALLS in order to support teachers in the implementation of the CLLP. Focusing on the PD offered in Cyprus and Cambridge, the authors explore how theories of effective teacher professional learning were incorporated in the development of the PD. It then proceeds to discuss how teachers were supported in promoting dialogue and argumentation with their students. The chapter ends by presenting teacher reflection data on the PD and its benefits.

We stay with teachers in Chapter 11 as researchers from Berlin, Germany, consider communities of practice for teachers. With respect to the sustainable impact of educational programs, teachers need to be able to deal with the open educational resources of a program efficiently and appropriately. The chapter outlines how digital collaboration among teachers who are aiming to work with the open educational resources of DIALLS in their classrooms may support them in (1) using the materials and (2) building a long-lasting 'community of practice'. As part of an ongoing community of practice, teachers can share their own knowledge and experiences as a basis of their professional development. In this sense, the exchange of support and feedback also may give future teachers the opportunity to become confident and self-determined in teaching cultural literacy with the materials of DIALLS. In the chapter, the advantages and challenges of engaging in digital communities are discussed by considering the specific affordances of DIALLS.

1.5 An International Project in the Time of COVID 19

Normally, the specific time and place of a project is placed in the background of writings about it, yet the unprecedented crisis that the world found itself in during the Spring of 2020 inevitably had an impact on DIALLS and our engagement with teachers in and across countries. Initially planned innovations to engage children in actual intercultural dialogues through our designed platform were impeded by the closures of schools and then stringent social distancing measures on their return. As this book goes to press, schools are still in turmoil with a generation of children and young people affected by the pandemic and resultant societal actions. As children gradually return to school after months of being socially distant from their peers, the importance of a project like DIALLS is significant. If the goals of the project are to listen to and learn about and from each other, then the skills to enable this need to be centralized.

References

Buber, M. 1947. *Between man and man* (R.G. Smith Trans.). London: Routledge.
Buber, M. 1957. *Pointing the way: Collected essays* (M. Friedman, Trans.). New York: Harper & Brothers.
Buber, M. 1958. *I and thou* (2nd ed., R. G. Smith, Trans.). Edinburgh: T and T Clark Ltd.
Creppel, I. 2008. Toleration, politics, and the role of mutuality. In *Toleration and its limits*, ed. M.S. Williams and J. Waldron, 315–359. New York and London: New York University Press.
European Commission. 2017. Europe in a changing world—Inclusive, innovative and reflective Societies. https://ec.europa.eu/research/participants/data/ref/h2020/wp/2016_2017/main/h2020-wp1617-societies_en.pdf. Accessed June 2020.
Freire, P., and D. Macedo. 1987. *Literacy: Reading the word and the world*. London: Routledge and Kegan Paul.
Hirsch, E.D. 1988. *Cultural Literacy: What every American needs to know*. New York: Vintage Books.
Maine, F., V. Cook, and T. Lähdesmäki. 2019. Reconceptualizing cultural literacy as a dialogic practice. *London Review of Education* 17 (3): 384–393.
Rapp, C., and M. Freitag. 2015. Teaching tolerance? Associational diversity and tolerance formation. *Political Studies* 63 (5): 1031–1051.
Segal, N. 2014. Introduction. In *From literature to cultural literacy*, ed. N. Segal and D. Koleva. London: Palgrave Macmillan.
Shady, S., and M. Larson. 2010. Tolerance, empathy or inclusion? Insights from Martin Buber. *Educational Theory* 60 (1): 81–96.
Street, B. 1984. *Literacy in theory and practice*, vol. 9. Cambridge: Cambridge University Press.
Wegerif, R. 2011. Towards a dialogic theory of how children learn to think. *Thinking Skills and Creativity* 6 (3): 179–190.

Fiona Maine is a Senior Lecturer in literacy education at the University of Cambridge. Her research focusses on the responses of children as they read multimodal texts together. She is the principal Investigator of DIALLS.

Maria Vrikki is a Postdoctoral Researcher at the University of Nicosia. Her research interests focus on educational dialogue, teacher professional learning and professional development.

Chapter 2
Intercultural Education for the Twenty-First Century: A Comparative Review of Research

Chrysi Rapanta and Susana Trovão

2.1 Introduction

Based on the assumption that globalization should not imply homogenization, it is important for education to promote dialogue and intercultural understanding. The first appearance of the term 'intercultural education' in Europe dates back to 1983, when European ministers of education at a conference in Berlin, in a resolution for the schooling of migrant children, highlighted the intercultural dimension of education (Portera 2008). One of the mandates of intercultural education is to promote intercultural dialogue, meaning dialogue that is "open and respectful" and that takes place between individuals or groups "with different ethnic, cultural, religious and linguistic backgrounds and heritage on the basis of mutual understanding and respect" (Council of Europe 2008, 10). Such backgrounds and heritages form cultural identities, not limited to ethnic, religious and linguistic ones, as culture is a broader concept including several layers such as "experience, interest, orientation to the world, values, dispositions, sensibilities, social languages, and discourses" (Cope and Kalantzis 2009, 173). As cultural identities are multi-layered, so is cultural diversity, and therefore it becomes a challenge for educators and researchers to address it (Hepple et al. 2017). Referring to Leclercq (2002), Hajisoteriou and Angelides (2017, 367) argue that "intercultural education aims to stress the dynamic nature of cultural diversity as an unstable mixture of sameness and otherness." This challenge relates to the dynamic concept of culture itself, as socially constructed, and continuously shaped and reshaped through communicative interactions (Holmes et al. 2015).

Faced with this fluidity of cultural identities, several European research initiatives, such as DIALLS, have focused on intercultural dialogue as a vivid experience not limited to *knowing about* other ethnical/religious/linguistic identities, but including the engagement in a *being with* relationship with any other person having their own

C. Rapanta (✉) · S. Trovão
NOVA University, Lisbon, Portugal
e-mail: chrysi.rapanta@fcsh.unl.pt

F. Maine and M. Vrikki (eds.), *Dialogue for Intercultural Understanding*,
https://doi.org/10.1007/978-3-030-71778-0_2

cultural identities. This twofold consideration of otherness and engagement forms the basis of the approach adopted by DIALLS with regard to intercultural dialogue and informs the project's place within the European context of intercultural education. The goal of this chapter is to analyze the intercultural education research literature, investigating its most salient theoretical operationalizations throughout the years, and identifying challenges and gaps that still need to be addressed by current and future projects.

2.2 Theoretical Operationalizations of Intercultural Education Research

2.2.1 Intercultural Learning

Under a broad understanding, intercultural learning is about "how we come to understand other cultures and our own through *interaction*, how we learn and communicate in *cultural contexts*, and how we learn *culturally*" (Jin and Cortazzi 2013, 1; emphasis added). Of the three key concepts mentioned, i.e. 'interaction', 'cultural context' and 'learning culturally', the first relates to means (dialogue), the third to consequences (culturally learning competence), while understanding and awareness of the cultural context is most related to intercultural learning understood strictly. Such cultural context awareness is mainly subjective, i.e. based on and including one's own world views (Bennett 2009). In this sense, an important related concept to intercultural learning is "cultural self-awareness," i.e. recognizing the ways in which one's "own worldview is reflective to some extent of the group of people with whom they interact" (Bennett 2009, S4).

Another related concept to cultural awareness is cultural sensitivity. According to the Developmental Model of Intercultural Sensitivity (DMIS) (Bennett 1993), people seem to move through six possible orientations while learning culturally: three ethnocentric orientations (Denial, Defense, Minimization), where one's own culture is experienced as central; and three ethnorelative orientations (Acceptance, Adaptation, Integration), where one's culture is experienced in the context of other cultures. The underlying assumption of the DMIS model is that as one's experience of cultural diversity becomes more sophisticated, in the movement from ethnocentrism towards ethno relativism, one's potential for demonstrating intercultural competence also increases (Hammer et al. 2003). To further highlight this passage from sensitivity to competence, Hammer et al. (2003) use the term intercultural sensitivity to refer to "the ability to discriminate and experience relevant cultural differences", and the term intercultural competence to mean "the ability to think and act in interculturally appropriate ways" (p. 422). The latter is further explained below.

2.2.2 Intercultural Competence

According to Otten (2003), intercultural learning leads to intercultural competence. Intercultural competence is largely associated with social, culturally learnt competence, such as the ability for empathy and perspective taking (Busse and Krause 2015). It can be defined as "the ability to interact effectively and appropriately in intercultural situations, based on one's intercultural knowledge, skills and attitudes" (Deardorff 2006, 247). To these components, Deardorff (2006) and others (e.g. Busse and Krause 2015) add the ability for reflection, which includes the display of flexibility and empathy. Deardorff's definition of intercultural competence is different from the Intercultural Communicative Competence (ICC) which mainly refers to the ability of communicating effectively in a foreign language (Byram 2012).

In its initial conceptualization by Byram (1997), intercultural competence (IC) comprised a diverse set of skills and attitudes, including the knowledge of contents about the others' cultures (*savoirs*), the skills to interpret and relate (*savoir comprendre*), the skills to discover and/or interact (*savoir apprendre/faire*), the attitudes of being with others (*savoir être*), and the attitude of critical cultural awareness (*savoir s'engager*), which refers to "relativisation of one's own and valuing of others' meanings, beliefs and behaviours" (p. 35). However influential this description of intercultural (communicative) competence has been, it should not be ignored that it was proposed in the field of foreign language teaching to describe effective social interaction with someone from a different country. From this perspective, especially meaningful for foreign language education contexts, the differences between IC and ICC are difficult to identify, rendering Byram's proposal limited as regards the '*savoirs*' or know-what aspects of intercultural communication, which need to refer to a particular culture or cultures. This limitation is overcome with an 'etic' view of intercultural dialogue, as explained below.

2.2.3 Intercultural Dialogue

Intercultural dialogue is broadly defined as "the exchange of views and opinions between different cultures" (European Commission n.d.). In this broad definition, a distinction between the *emic* (i.e. culture-specific) and *etic* (i.e. culture-general) aspects (Triandis 1994) of cultural awareness or sensitivity is implied, with a clear focus towards the latter. Moreover, cultures are perceived as 'containers' and intercultural dialogue "as the interaction of stable and cohesive units which mutually accept and appreciate one another but which remain closed to mutual influences" (Gropas and Triandafyllidou 2011, 413). Therefore, a focus on the 'etic' aspects of culture as implied in the general definitions of intercultural dialogue often found in European policy documents (Lähdesmäki et al. 2020) weakens, if not cancels, the 'inter' (Portera 2008) dynamics of dialogue and their implied transition of knowledge and learning as part of an emic negotiation (Allmen 2011).

A culture-specific approach to intercultural dialogue must take into consideration both individuals' *objective* and *subjective* cultures. Objective culture, also known as 'Big-C' culture, refers to "the set of institutional, political and historical circumstances that have emerged from and are maintained by a group of interacting people" (Bennett 2009, S3). Subjective culture, also known as 'little-c' culture, refers to the "worldview of people who interact in a particular context" (Bennett 2009, S3). The importance of taking into consideration both types of culture when teaching or engaging in intercultural dialogue is explained by educational researchers O'Connor and Michaels (2007, 275), commenting on Wells (2007):

> in the process of language acquisition, children acquire their culture's implicit sign system. As signs are internalized, so is the 'dialogicality' or meaning-making stance of the home culture internalized. In this way, children from different cultures, different social classes, or different school environments take on more than language; they take on different values or 'meaning potentials' and expectations relating to making meaning in dialogue with others or in thinking on one's own.

Based on the above, we cannot speak of intercultural dialogue without taking into consideration the meaning negotiation dynamics between at least two individuals representing different, both objective and subjective, cultural backgrounds at that moment of interaction. Further extending this assumption, it is those interaction dynamics, and their analysis, that define whether a dialogue is *inter*-cultural, and not any a priori definition of individuals' static characteristics before entering the dialogue. This view is adopted by the recently developed field of intercultural pragmatics, where culture is seen "as a socially constituted set of various kinds of knowledge structures that individuals turn to as relevant situations permit, enable and usually encourage" (Kesckes 2014, 4). These knowledge structures can be of various types, as previously explained, comprising specific culture knowledge (know-what), skills (know-how), attitudes (know-to-be) and behaviors (know-to-engage), all of which are also important components of intercultural competence (Byram 1997; Barrett 2012). A common paradox in the sociocognitive learning literature (Sfard 2008) emerges: from an *acquisition* perspective, intercultural competence is a prerequisite for engaging in intercultural dialogue; from a *participation* perspective, intercultural dialogue fosters intercultural competence.

For DIALLS researchers (e.g. Maine et al. 2019) and other educational researchers, the dialogue participation and engagement perspective prevails. Following Buber's (1955) perspective on genuine dialogue, a 'simple' conscious awareness of the other or others and "the intention of establishing a living mutual relation between himself and them" (p. 22) is enough for someone to engage in intercultural dialogue in its broader emic sense. Nonetheless, as dialogue analysts would counter-argue, such awareness of the others and their intentions in dialogue are not at all simple to develop, from the participants' point of view, and to detect, from the analysts' point of view. As Kesckes (2014, 11) points out:

> To interpret an utterance properly, the interlocutor has to arrive at an understanding not only of its communicative function of utterances but also of the communicative agenda of his/her dialogue pattern, i.e., what s/he really wants to achieve in the dialogue.

Thus, since understanding of the content but also and especially of the communicative function of the others' utterances is highly problematic to achieve and to analyze, the study of intercultural dialogue *in action*, and not as a pre-defined or taken-for-granted entity, is itself a good starting point.

To summarize this theoretical introduction, the basis of intercultural education is intercultural dialogue (UNESCO 2009), which, in its turn, may or may not satisfy the intercultural education standards and goals, depending on the degree, depth or quality of participants' intercultural learning which leads to the so-called intercultural competence. At the same time, intercultural competence perceived as sensitivity and adaptability to different cultural contexts may be enhanced through people's engagement in dialogue and learning with and from each other. The three interrelated concepts, namely dialogue, learning and competence are important pillars of intercultural education, as policy documentation analysis shows (Lähdesmäki et al. 2020; see also Chapter 4 in this volume). However, it is not yet clear how the three concepts have thus far been operationalized and assessed by empirical educational studies.

2.3 The Present Study

In the face of the current fluid cultural realities the world over, and the need for a continuously adapting and adaptive education, the question of whether and how educational research has changed its conception and operationalization of intercultural education emerges as highly relevant. To address this question, a systematic review of empirical research is presented, aiming to reveal the predominant objectives, methods, contents, and risks of teaching and learning interculturally in the last two decades. Another aim shall be to identify whether there are any emerging differences by comparing research conducted in the beginning, middle, and end of the studied period (2000–2019). The chapter ends with recommendations regarding the facing challenges of contemporary educational systems struggling with the challenges of globalization and inclusion.

2.3.1 Research Questions

The following aspects/questions were taken into account when looking at intercultural education research initiatives described in the selected literature:

a. Which are the main explicit goals of intercultural education when operationalized through concrete programs, interventions or research initiatives? Have those goals changed over the years?

b. Do those programs, interventions, initiatives include students *interacting with* different objective or subjective cultures or do they limit themselves to students *learning about* different cultures?
c. Do those programs, interventions, initiatives include a clear qualitative and/or quantitative assessment of such culture or intercultural learning? If yes, what is being assessed and how?

2.3.2 Sampling

The search for sources was carried out in the Scopus database by Elsevier for its strictness regarding quality criteria of published research. The first search performed had as unique criterion the inclusion of "intercultural education" or "intercultural learning" in the title of the document (Note: the terms "intercultural competence" and "intercultural dialogue" were not selected as keywords due to the specific meaning intended for the first, i.e. related to foreign language contexts, and the broad meaning of the second, i.e. as a general policy and not as educational praxis). This search resulted in 514 documents. After limiting the search to (a) documents published between 2000 and 2019, (b) the subject areas of Social Sciences, Arts and Humanities, and Psychology, and (c) documents written in English, search results were limited to 370 documents including journal articles, books, book chapters, and conference proceedings.

After this initial search, three screening phases followed. The first was an "abstract only" screening, during which 220 documents referring to theoretical studies and not reporting on applied or empirical research were excluded. The 150 documents left went through a second, "full text" screening, during which documents not reporting directly on the study of intercultural education/learning/competence either as a process or as an outcome (e.g. studies focusing on the need for intercultural education as a policy without describing its practice) were excluded. This second screening phase resulted in 80 documents. Finally, a third screening focused only on journal articles, due to the difficulty in finding the full texts of several book chapters and conference proceedings papers. The main exclusion criterion for this final screening was studies carried out in the general context of intercultural/multicultural education but without defining the goals and/or scope in terms of dialogue and/or learning and/or intercultural competence development (e.g. studies exclusively focusing on foreign language learning, or studies describing intercultural education in general without defining any concrete aspects, or studies only describing students' or teachers' perceptions of a course or policy). Moreover, as the focus of this study is on the experience of intercultural education defined as intercultural dialogue, learning, competence or similar, we were not interested in what international educational systems offer. We were rather interested in identifying how intercultural education is operationalized in terms of its goals, methods, and contents, and whether this operationalization has changed throughout the years. The result of

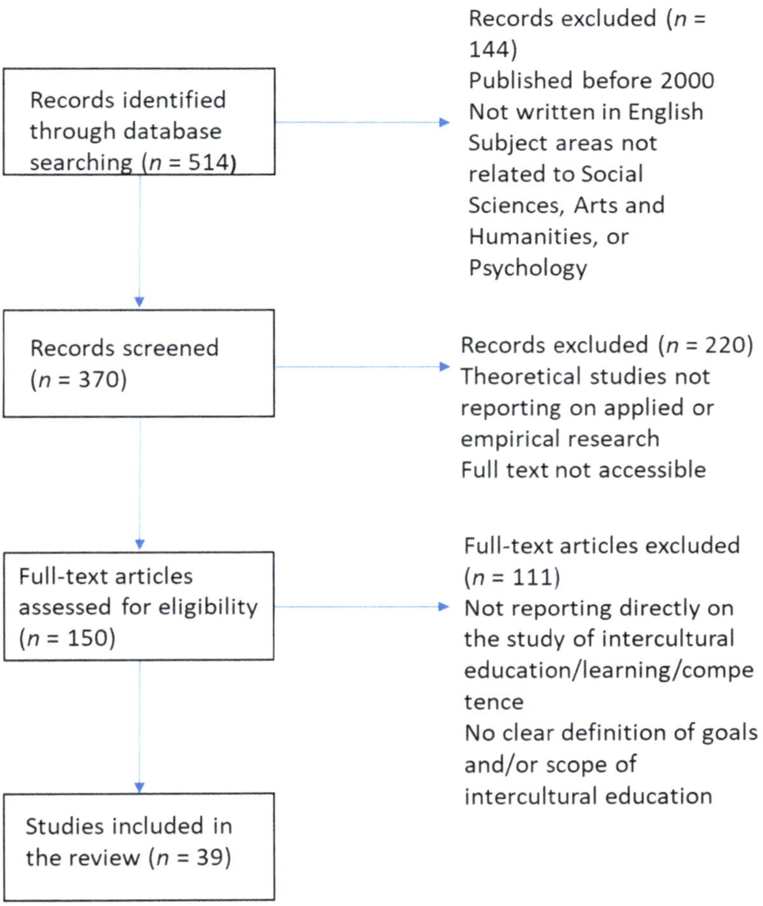

Fig. 2.1 The review sample selection process

this final screening was 39 journal articles, which formed the final review sample. Figure 2.1 shows the search and screening process.

2.4 Findings

2.4.1 Demographic Characterization of the Sample

Of the 39 studies included in the literature review, eight focused on Australia, either as host or as guest country, six on the United Kingdom, six on the United States of America, four on Germany, four on Italy, and the rest on other countries such as Spain,

China, the Netherlands, and Canada. Five studies focused on primary school students, six on secondary school, 24 on university students, and the remaining four focused on post-graduate/professional education. Among the studies focusing on university students, five had pre-service teachers as participants, whereas another five of the rest of the studies focused on both students and teachers. Finally, regarding the studies' context, the largest number (eleven studies) took place as part of an international exchange/mobility/work abroad program, ten implemented a particular intervention aimed at enhancing participants' intercultural communication/learning skills such as film watching or dramatic performance, eight were carried out in "natural" classroom environments with a multicultural or intercultural focus, five focused on transnational higher education classrooms, and five implemented some type of telecollaboration between countries. The details of the reviewed studies are presented in Fig. 2.2.

2.4.2 Chronological Progress in the Conceptualization of Intercultural Education

The first research question was about identifying the concrete goal(s) through which intercultural education was operationalized in the reviewed studies, and whether there was any change in this operationalization throughout the years. A first observation pertains to the number of studies in the review and their chronological arrangement. A main criterion of inclusion in the sample was the degree to which intercultural education goals were somehow operationalized in the studies, and not remaining vague, undefined or even left implicit, which was quite often the case. It was also common that the studies focused on theoretical or policy-making aspects of intercultural education without any interventional or empirical aspect of assessing its components and goals. This led to quite a reduced sample of 39 studies published after the year 2000. It is noteworthy that the vast majority (36 out of 39 studies) were published from 2010 onwards, and the number of publications doubled after 2015. These differences in the number of studies focusing on some type of operationalization and assessment or improvement of intercultural education goals and outcomes probably reveal an increase in the felt need for this type of focus in recent years.

Of the 16 studies published between 2000 and 2015, 56% operationalized intercultural education goals in terms of intercultural competence, mainly influenced by Michael Byram's theory of ICC. The other 44% opted for the use of intercultural learning, with one study (Martin and Griffiths 2014) adopting Mezirow's (2000) transformative learning theory as main reference and six other studies focusing on different aspects/factors of learning such as cultural dissonance (Allan 2003), intercultural adaptation (Gill 2007), and (self-)reflexivity (Donelan 2010; Holmes et al. 2015). Studies published after 2016 present a different image, as shown in Table 2.1. A large majority (44%) of these focus on intercultural learning, sometimes equated to intercultural dialogue, whereas the rest is divided between intercultural competence (26%) and other definitions (30%), as follows: intercultural (self-)awareness (Brooks

Authors & Date	Country	Students' Grade	Target group	Context
Allan (2003)	Netherlands	secondary	students	Multicultural classroom
O'Dowd (2003)	Spain & UK	university	students	International telecollaboration
Gill (2007)	China (UK)	university	students	Transnational higher education
Donelan (2010)	Australia	secondary	students	*use of drama as an instrument for intercultural sensibilization*
Baraldi (2012)	Italy	secondary	both	Italian as a Second Language classroom
Lee (2012)	Spain (USA)	university	students	*use of blogs and ethnograhic interviews to native speakers*
Chao (2013)	Taiwan	university	students	*use of films as part of an EFL course*
King & al. (2013)	USA	university	students	not a particular context - the authors were interest in cultural identities and experiences in their broac
Ari & Laron (2014)	Israel	university	students	Transnational higher education
Martin & Griffiths (2014)	UK (Gambia & India)	beyond university	teachers	Work abroad
Santos et al. (2014)	Portugal	primary	both	Intercultural communication course
Borghetti et al. (2015)	Italy	university	students	International exchange/mobility program
Busse & Krause (2015)	Germany	university	students	Intercultural communication course
Campbell & Walta (2015)	Australia	pre-service teachers	students	Work abroad
Holmes et al. (2015)	UK & Italy	university	both	International exchange/mobility program
Lau (2015)	Canada (Taiwan)	primary	students	International telecollaboration
Brooks & Pitts (2016)	USA (Singapore)	university	students	International telecollaboration
Tonkin & Coudray (2016)	Australia (Germany)	university	students	International exchange/mobility program
Wilbur (2016)	USA (Italy & Estonia)	university	students	International exchange/mobility program
Frimberger (2016)	Scotland	university	students	*use of drama as a method for "strangeness" experiences narration and reflection*
Bedekovic (2017)	Croatia, Serbia, Bosnia-Herzegovina,	pre-service teachers	students	Development of an intercultural curriculum
Cloonan & al. (2017)	Australia	beyond university	teachers	*autobographical storytelling*
Grimminger-Seidensticker & Möhwald (2017)	Germany	secondary	students	*physical education lessons including experiences of strangeness (e.g playing soccer with different objec*
Hernandez-Bravo et al. (2017)	Spain	primary	students	Development of an intercultural curriculum
Chan et al. (2017)	Hong Kong & Sweden	beyond university	students	International telecollaboration project
Hajisoteriou & Angelides (2017)	Cyprus	primary	both	*collaborative art-making*
Hepple et al. (2017)	Australia	pre-service teachers	students	International exchange/mobility program
Bozdag (2018)	Australia (Malaysia)	secondary	both	International telecollaboration project
Mitchell & Paras (2018)	Canada (India)	university	students	Transnational higher education
Senyshyn (2018)	USA	university	students	Transnational higher education
Varga-Dobai (2018)	USA	pre-service teachers	students	*cultural selfie: arts-based self-potrtait*
Mesker et al. (2018)	Netherlands (UK, South Africa,	pre-service teachers	students	Work abroad
Dai & Garcia (2019)	China (Australia)	university	students	Transnational higher education
Piipponen & Karlsson (2019)	Scotland, Europe)	primary	students	*storycrafting method (use of narrative scenarios)*
Borhaug & Weringer (2019)	Europe	secondary	students	Multicultural summercamp
Dorsett & al. (2019)	Australia	university	students	International exchange/mobility program
Hyett & al. (2019)	Australia	university	students	*virtual learning activity*
Hessel (2019)	Germany (UK)	university	students	International exchange/mobility program
O'Brien et al. (2019)	Ireland	beyond university	students	Work abroad

Fig. 2.2 Demographic characterization of the reviewed studies

and Pitts 2016; Bedeković 2017; Varga-Dobai 2018; Børhaug and Weyringer 2019), intercultural adjustment (Dai and Garcia 2019), and finally definitions referring to a broader sense of intercultural competency, literacy or even education, often defined as a 'transcultural' competence (Frimberger 2016; Tonkin and Coudray 2016; Hajisoteriou and Angelides 2017; Hyett et. al. 2019). The Fisher's exact text of independence between year of publication (i.e. before or after 2015) and main intercultural education goal (i.e. intercultural competence, learning, or other) was significant ($p = 0.03$). See Table 2.2 for the corresponding cross-tabulation.

Table 2.1 A synthetic presentation of how intercultural education goals have been defined throughout the years

Main concepts	Main influences				
Studies 2000–2015	*Byram*	*Bennett*	*Deardorff*	*Mezirow*	*Other*
Intercultural competence	O'Dowd (2003), Lee (2012), Chao (2013), Lau (2015)	Ari and Laron (2014), Busse and Krause (2015)	King et al. (2013), Busse and Krause (2015)		Intercultural sensitivity (Campbell and Walta 2015)
Intercultural learning				Martin and Griffiths (2014)	Cultural dissonance (Allan 2003), intercultural adaptation (Gill 2007), (self-)reflexivity (Donelan 2010; Holmes et al. 2015), positive intercultural relations (Baraldi 2012), interculturality/intercultural encounters (Borghetti et al. 2015)
Studies 2016–2019					
Intercultural competence	Wilbor (2016), Hessel (2019)	Perspective shifting (Mitchell and Paras 2018)	Hernandez-Bravo et al. (2017), Hessel (2019)	Dorsett et al. (2019)	
Intercultural learning/dialogue	Hepple et al. (2017)	Bozdag (2018)	O'Brien et al. (2019)	Mesker et al. (2018), Senyshyn (2018)	Cloonan et al. (2017), intercultural encounters: Chan et al. (2017), Grimminger-Seidensticker & Möhwald (2017), Piipponen & Karlsson (2019)
Intercultural (self-)awareness		Bedekovic (2017), Varga-Dobai (2018)			Brooks & Pitts (2016), Børhaug & Weringer (2019)
Intercultural competency/literacy/education					Frimberger (2016), Tonkin & Coudray (2016), Hajisoteriou & Angelides (2017), Hyett & al. (2019)
Intercultural adjustment					Dai & Garcia (2019)

Table 2.2 Cross-tabulation of year of publication and main operationalized goal

Year	Intercultural competence	Intercultural learning	Other	Total
2000–2015	9	7	0	16
2016–2019	6	10	7	23
Total	15	17	7	39

2.4.3 Ways of Operationalizing Intercultural Education

As an answer to the second research question, i.e. whether authors have focused on *learning about* versus *interacting with* other cultures, the latter was predominant in the analyzed sample, although manifested in different forms, as explained below.

Cultural self-awareness or 'cultural sensitivity' refers to the degree to which individuals are able and disposed to reflect on their own cultural identities, to identify any dissonances between them, and to understand the origins of the same (i.e. whether consciously or unconsciously acquired). In the analyzed sample, cultural self-awareness was studied both as an intra-personal and as an inter-personal process. Examples of studies that adopted the former include Varga-Dobai's (2018) study with pre-service teachers applying the 'cultural selfie' technique as a way of exploring their own 'funds of knowledge', and Mesker et al.' s (2018) study, again with pre-service teachers, where personal biographies and visual metaphors of intra-personal development helped reveal their learning mechanisms of identification, reflection and transformation. When applied in inter-personal contexts, cultural self-awareness can easily be replaced by interpersonal/intercultural awareness and reflexivity. Indeed, several studies showed that this type of reflective experience usually takes place through encounters with others. For instance, Hepple et al. (2017) describe the critical cultural self-examination and 'multicultural awakening' stimulated by the immersion experience of ten Australian pre-service teachers in Malaysian culture. Mitchell and Paras (2018) describe how the experience of intercultural encounters between Canadian and Indian university students caused the former to shift cultural perspective and to question their values, beliefs, and self-concept. In another study, with secondary school students, Børhaug and Weyringer (2019) describe how European summer-camp activities led participants to an indirect experience of the stigmatized position of the other and stimulated critical and empathic reflections on social justice and to greater awareness. Thus, reflecting on the experience of others and with others often comes hand-in-hand with cultural self-awareness and is, as Bennett (2009) argues, the precursor of intercultural learning.

For such a personal experience to be transformed into knowledge, an active/reflective dialectic between *intention* and *extension* of experience is necessary, as Kolb (2015) argues. Intention refers to the internal reflection preceding or accompanying action, whereas extension refers to the action itself, i.e. the active external manipulation of the external world (Kolb 2015, 67). This dynamic, dialectical basis of knowledge creation also applies to intercultural learning, which also explains why some authors have characterized it as *transformative* learning (Martin and Griffiths 2014; Mesker et al. 2018; Senyshyn 2018; Dorsett et al. 2019). During the process of transformation, which follows reflection, the individual "experiences profound changes in their existing practices", which usually results in "a new role or new identity" (Mesker et al. 2018, 56). Therefore, from this perspective, for individual competence or learning to be achieved, a manifestation of transformation is necessary in how individuals perceive themselves, others, and the world as a whole. For some authors in the analyzed sample, this transformation is manifested simply as a change of perspective from a more ethnocentric towards a more ethnorelativist worldview, following Bennett's (1993, 2009) theory. For others, transformation is or can be even more holistic, and includes a continuous adaptation to new realities, new perspectives, and new 'others' and 'otherness/-es' encountered both outside and within oneself. For instance, Frimberger (2016) uses drama as a method to stimulate 'strangeness' experiences with university students and help them acquire a collective understanding of the "transcultural, in-flux and subjective dimensions of intercultural encounters" (p. 133). Hajisoteriou and Angelides (2017) present a method of collaborative art-making as a way for primary school students to empathize with each other's emotions, within a context of civic efficacy, democratic agency, and friendship promotion.

2.4.4 Main Methods Used, Findings and Considerations

Regarding the third research question, i.e. the studies' main methods and findings, the analysis showed that a large majority of the sample (34 out of 39 studies) used qualitative methods of data collection and analysis, three used mixed methods (questionnaire and interview), and only two opted for quantitative methods (closed-ended questionnaires). From the studies that implemented qualitative methods, seven used ethnographic and narrative research methods, 13 used interviews, either alone or in combination with other methods, three used some type of transcribed classroom interaction analysis, and 11 studies used other qualitative analysis methods such as analysis of diaries, blog entries, written reflection or fieldnotes.

In terms of the main findings of the reviewed studies, only two of them (Santos et al. 2014; O'Brien et al. 2019) report an increase of culture-specific knowledge among their main outcomes. Most studies focus on the experiential aspects of intercultural learning, mentioning the value of: 'embodied' experiences (Donelan 2010; Tonkin and Coudray 2016; Frimberger 2016), 'immersion', 'boundary' and 'belonging' experiences (Hepple et al. 2017; Mesker et al. 2018; Dai and Garcia 2019), or even the concrete experience of the 'stigmatised position of the other' (Børhaug and Weyringer 2019). Other experiential and affective aspects were also highlighted: cultural/cognitive dissonance (Allan 2003; Mitchell and Paras 2018), non-essentialist engagement (Holmes et al. 2015), enacted understanding of the Other (Gill 2007), and mutual enrichment (Bedeković 2017). For such experiential or even transformative learning to take place, a disorienting dilemma (Senyshyn 2018), contradiction (Baraldi 2012), or out-of-comfort-zone experiences (Hyett et al. 2019) are often necessary, while Martin and Griffiths (2014) stress the value of dialogue and critical reflection on those same experiences. The teachers' role (Piipponen and Karlsson 2019) and tension/discomfort balance (Grimminger-Seidensticker and Möhwald 2017; Mitchell and Paras 2018) are also reported as essential for successful intercultural learning.

When it comes to findings related to intercultural competence, such as acquisition of knowledge, skills, and attitudes, several studies identify a gradual acquisition and improvement of skills (Chao 2013; Santos et al. 2014; Wilbur 2016) and attitudes, namely ethnorelativism (Campbell and Walta 2015), empathy (Hernandez-Bravo et al. 2017), or understanding of cultural diversity (Busse and Krause 2015). However, other studies revealed problems in the development of students' intercultural competence. For instance, Ari and Laron (2014) found that encounters with 'others' during mixed-education (Arab–Jewish) college experience positively influenced the multicultural attitudes of participants, but only at a low percentage (11%). Another not-so-positive finding is reported by Lau (2015), who mentions the difficulty of disrupting children's ingrained stereotypes of migrants/refugees, and their tendency to be attracted more by the 'exotic' customs and festivals rather than deeper understandings. Students' superficial understanding of culture which remained at a traditions-sharing level is also reported by Bozdağ (2018) in his study with adolescents.

Finally, when it comes to the main challenges identified by the reviewed studies, several authors have considered the influence of national culture on education, especially on policy makers' intercultural perceptions (Allan 2003; Bedeković 2017; Hernandez-Bravo et al. 2017; Bozdağ 2018). Other studies highlight limitations in the use of the concept 'culture' to refer only to a national identity, and its consequences on students' intercultural learning outcomes (Bozdağ 2018; Hessel 2019). Studies also highlight the teachers' role within intercultural education initiatives, notably the need for educational support for cross-system transitions (Dai and Garcia 2019) and the importance of teacher education (Senyshyn 2018). Cloonan et al. (2017) further argue that teachers' exposure to intercultural learning techniques does not guarantee an increase in their capacity to deal with interculturality in their classrooms. Finally, regarding intercultural education projects mediated by the use of technologies, Tonkin and Coudray (2016) warn that students' concentration on online interaction may disconnect them from the very experiences which educators wish them to reflect on.

2.5 Conclusion

The goal of this review was to track the progress, if any, in the use and operationalization of the term 'intercultural education' in representative literature of the last two decades (2000–2019). The most salient finding was that there is a significant tendency towards different operationalizations of intercultural education after 2015, not limited to static concepts such as intercultural competence, but expanded towards learning and dialogue as dynamic and interdependent constructs: the more one engages in meaningful interaction with others, the more (s)he learns about oneself and the others; and the more one learns and reflects about his/her own learning, the more eager (s)he is to engage in genuine intercultural dialogue (with a focus on the 'inter' aspects of the interaction, such as mutuality, reciprocity, and responsiveness). This marked shift from a static, de facto view of intercultural education as a competence to deal with other cultures, towards a more dynamic, etic, culture-transcending perspective of intercultural education is highly significant. First, it shows how the recent reality of the new waves of immigration due to the Middle East crisis is reflected on actual challenges that educational systems face, in particular when it regards an 'always-in-the-making' citizenship education (Rapanta et al. 2020). Second, it highlights the importance of cultural literacy as "an indispensable tool for transcending the clash of ignorances (…) as part of a broad toolkit of worldviews, attitudes and competences that young people acquire for their lifelong journey" (UNESCO 2009, 118).

This new conceptualization of intercultural education based on an awareness development during intercultural learning experiences places attention on the fact that cultural diversity and internationalization per se are not enough for intercultural learning and dialogue to occur (Otten 2003). On the contrary, as our review showed, many times it is the national educational system, and with that, the way teaching and learning is perceived, that poses obstacles for authentic dialogue to occur. To add to this challenge, adopting an action-oriented perspective to interculturalism further implies that all education is potentially intercultural, when it addresses interaction, inclusion, or integration (Faas 2010). This tension between the official discourse about intercultural education, on one hand, and its actual implementation and operationalization in the classroom practice, on the other, is not to ignore, and, in fact, it emerged from the present review as well, as explained below.

First, the transformational aspects of experiential, intercultural learning are mainly assessed through self-reporting methods (e.g. reflective narratives, interviews), and not through more dynamic ways of assessment, such as interactional analysis over a period of time. This limitation is also observed by Borghetti et al. (2015) who argue that when intercultural learning is explored through interviews or questionnaires after a particular event (e.g. a class, a stay abroad, an intercultural encounter), there is the risk that participants forget or tend to justify what they have been doing and why during their interaction with the objective or subjective cultures. The second major space of improvement for intercultural education research is related to this distinction between cultures, still limited to the national level, when what is supposed to be studied are the "different and multiple identity subjectivities" (Trovão 2012, 263) that every individual carries with them. Although a few studies focus on the intra-personal aspects of cultural literacy development (e.g. Bedekovic 2017; Børhaug and Weringer 2019; Brooks and Pitts 2016; Varga-Dobai 2018), a gap in the study of the dynamic aspects of cultural literacy and how it is developed through dialogue with *any* others is observed. Moreover, addressing otherness only in relation to differences in ethnical identities entails the risk of reinforcing stereotypes and prejudices (Catarci 2014; Muller-Mirza 2011).

This gap in existing intercultural education initiatives is addressed by the DIALLS project. Rather than drawing on definitions about what intercultural education and dialogue should look like, DIALLS promotes the view of cultural literacy as an always-in-the-making dialogue praxis (Maine et al. 2019; Rapanta et al. 2020). This is achieved through the implementation of a pedagogy that promotes genuine dialogue and constructive argumentation, where all viewpoints, and subsequently the cultural subjectivities expressed within, are equally welcome and encouraged to be expressed.

References

Allan, M. 2003. Frontier crossings: Cultural dissonance, intercultural learning and the multicultural personality. *Journal of Research in International Education* 2: 83–110.

Allmen, M.R.-V. 2011. The intercultural perspective and its development through cooperation with the Council of Europe. In *Intercultural and multicultural education: Enhancing global interconnectedness*, ed. C.A. Grant and A. Portela, 33–48. New York: Routledge.

Ari, L.L., and D. Laron. 2014. Intercultural learning in graduate studies at an Israeli college of education: Attitudes toward multiculturalism among Jewish and Arab students. *Higher Education* 68: 243–262.

Baraldi, C. 2012. Intercultural education and communication in second language interactions. *Intercultural Education* 23: 297–311.

Barrett, M. 2012. Intercultural competence. *EWC Statement Series, 2nd issue* (23–27). Oslo: European Wergeland Centre.

Bedeković, V. 2017. Intercultural education in the function of the European values promotion. *Informatologia* 50: 74–86.

Bennett, M. 1993. Towards ethnorelativism: A development model of intercultural sensitivity. In *Education for the intercultural experience*, ed. M. Paige, 21–71. Yarmouth: Intercultural Press.

Bennett, M. 2009. Defining, measuring, and facilitating intercultural learning: A conceptual introduction to the Intercultural Education double supplement. *Intercultural Education* 20: S1–S13.

Borghetti, C., A. Beaven, and R. Pugliese. 2015. Interactions among future study abroad students: Exploring potential intercultural learning sequences. *Intercultural Education* 26: 31–48.

Børhaug, B.F., and S. Weyringer. 2019. Developing critical and empathic capabilities in intercultural education through the VaKE approach. *Intercultural Education* 30: 1–14.

Bozdağ, Ç. 2018. Intercultural learning in schools through telecollaboration? A critical case study of eTwinning between Turkey and Germany. *International Communication Gazette* 80: 677–694.

Brooks, C.F., and M.J. Pitts. 2016. Communication and identity management in a globally-connected classroom: An online international and intercultural learning experience. *Journal of International and Intercultural Communication* 9: 52–68.

Buber, M. 1955. *Between man and man*, trans, by Ronald Gregor Smith. Boston: Beacon Press.

Busse, V., and U.M. Krause. 2015. Addressing cultural diversity: Effects of a problem-based intercultural learning unit. *Learning Environments Research* 18: 425–452.

Byram, M. 1997. *Teaching and assessing intercultural communicative competence*. Clevedon: Multilingual Matters.

Byram, M. 2012. Conceptualizing intercultural (communicative) competence and intercultural citizenship. In *The Routledge handbook of language and intercultural communication*, ed. J. Jackson, 85–98. London: Routledge.

Campbell, C.J., and C. Walta. 2015. Maximising intercultural learning in short term international placements: Findings associated with orientation programs, guided reflection and immersion. *Australian Journal of Teacher Education*. https://doi.org/10.14221/ajte.2015v40n10.1.

Catarci, M. 2014. Intercultural education in the European context: Key remarks from a comparative study. *Intercultural Education* 25: 95–104.
Chan, E.A., T. Lai, A. Wong, S. Ho, B. Chan, M. Stenberg, and E. Carlson. 2017. Nursing students' intercultural learning via internationalization at home: A qualitative descriptive study. *Nurse Education Today* 52: 34–39.
Chao, T.C. 2013. A diary study of university EFL learners' intercultural learning through foreign films. *Language, Culture and Curriculum* 26: 247–265.
Cloonan, A., B. Fox, S. Ohi, and C. Halse. 2017. An analysis of the use of autobiographical narrative for teachers' intercultural learning. *Teaching Education* 28: 131–144.
Cope, B. and M. Kalantzis. 2009. "Multiliteracies": New literacies, new learning. *Pedagogies: An International Journal* 4: 164–195.
Council of Europe. 2008. *White paper on intercultural dialogue: Living together as equals in dignity*. Strasbourg: Council of Europe.
Dai, K., and J. Garcia. 2019. Intercultural learning in transnational articulation programs: The hidden agenda of Chinese students' experiences. *Journal of International Students* 9: 362–383.
Deardorff, D.K. 2006. Identification and assessment of intercultural competence as a student outcome of internationalization. *Journal of Studies in International Education* 10: 241–266.
Donelan, K. 2010. Drama as intercultural education: An ethnographic study of an intercultural performance project in a secondary school. *Youth Theatre Journal* 24: 19–33.
Dorsett, P., S. Larmar., and J. Clark. 2019. Transformative intercultural learning: A short-term international study tour. *Journal of Social Work Education* 55: 565–578.
European Commission. n.d. Intercultural dialogue. https://ec.europa.eu/culture/policy/strategic-framework/intercultural-dialogue_en. Accessed 22 June 2020.
Faas, D. 2010. *Negotiating political identities: Multiethnic schools and youth in Europe*. Farnham: Ashgate.
Frimberger, K. 2016. A Brechtian theatre pedagogy for intercultural education research. *Language and Intercultural Communication* 16: 130–147.
Gill, S. 2007. Overseas students' intercultural adaptation as intercultural learning: A transformative framework. *Compare* 37: 167–183.
Grimminger-Seidensticker, E., and A. Möhwald. 2017. Intercultural education in physical education: Results of a quasi-experimental intervention study with secondary school students. *Physical Education and Sport Pedagogy* 22: 445–458.
Gropas, R., and A. Triandafyllidou. 2011. Greek education policy and the challenge of migration: An 'intercultural' view of assimilation. *Race Ethnicity and Education* 14: 399–419.
Hadjisoteriou, C., D. Faas, and P. Angelides. 2015. The Europeanisation of intercultural education? Responses from EU policy-makers. *Educational Review* 67: 218–235.
Hajisoteriou, C., and P. Angelides. 2017. Collaborative art-making for reducing marginalisation and promoting intercultural education and inclusion. *International Journal of Inclusive Education* 21: 361–375.
Hammer, M.R., M. Bennett, and R. Wiseman. 2003. Measuring intercultural sensitivity: The intercultural development inventory. *International Journal of Intercultural Relations* 27: 421–443.
Hepple, E., J. Alford, D. Henderson, D. Tangen, M. Hurwood, A. Alwi, ... and A. Alwi. 2017. Developing intercultural learning in Australian pre-service teachers through participating in a short term mobility program in Malaysia. *Teaching and Teacher Education* 66: 273–281.
Hernández-Bravo, J.A., M.C. Cardona-Moltó, and J.R. Hernández-Bravo. 2017. Developing elementary school students' intercultural competence through teacher-led tutoring action plans on intercultural education. *Intercultural Education* 28: 20–38.
Hessel, G. 2019. The role of international student interactions in English as a lingua franca in L2 acquisition, L2 motivational development and intercultural learning during study abroad. *Studies in Second Language Learning and Teaching* 9: 495–517.
Holmes, P., L. Bavieri, and S. Ganassin. 2015. Developing intercultural understanding for study abroad: Students' and teachers' perspectives on pre-departure intercultural learning. *Intercultural Education* 26: 16–30.

Hyett, N., K. Lee, R. Knevel, T. Fortune, M. Yau, and S. Borkovic. 2019. Trialing virtual intercultural learning with Australian and Hong Kong allied health students to improve cultural competency. *Journal of Studies in International Education* 23: 389–406.
Jin, L., and M. Cortazzi. 2013. *Researching intercultural learning*. Hampshire: Palgrave Macmillan.
Kesckes, I. 2014. *Intercultural pragmatics*. Oxford: Oxford University Press.
King, P.M., R.J. Perez, and W.J. Shim. 2013. How college students experience intercultural learning: Key features and approaches. *Journal of Diversity in Higher Education* 6: 69–83.
Kolb, D.A. 2015. *Experiential learning*, 2nd ed. New Jersey: Pearson Education.
Lähdesmäki, T., A.K. Koistinen, and S. Ylönen. 2020. *Intercultural dialogue in the European education policies: A conceptual approach*. Cham: Palgrave Macmillan.
Lau, S.M. 2015. Intercultural education through a bilingual children's rights project: Reflections on its possibilities and challenges with young learners. *Intercultural Education* 26: 469–482.
Leclercq, J.M. 2002. *The lessons of thirty years of European co-operation for intercultural education*. Strasbourg: Steering Committee for Education.
Lee, L. 2012. Engaging study abroad students in intercultural learning through blogging and ethnographic interviews. *Foreign Language Annals* 45: 7–21.
Maine, F., V. Cook, and T. Lähdesmäki. 2019. Reconceptualizing cultural literacy as a dialogic practice. *London Review of Education* 17: 383–392.
Martin, F., and H. Griffiths. 2014. Relating to the 'other': Transformative, intercultural learning in post-colonial contexts. *Compare* 44: 938–959.
Mesker, P., H. Wassink, S. Akkerman, and C. Bakker. 2018. Differences that matter: Boundary experiences in student teachers' intercultural learning. *International Journal of Intercultural Relations* 64: 54–66.
Mezirow, J. 2000. *Learning as transformation—Critical perspectives on a theory in progress*. San Francisco: Jossey-Bass.
Mitchell, L., and A. Paras. 2018. When difference creates dissonance: Understanding the 'engine' of intercultural learning in study abroad. *Intercultural Education* 29: 321–339.
Mirza, N.M. 2011. Civic education and intercultural issues in Switzerland: Psychosocial dimensions of an education to "otherness." *Journal of Social Science Education* 10: 31–40.
O'Brien, B., D. Tuohy, A. Fahy, and K. Markey. 2019. Home students' experiences of intercultural learning: A qualitative descriptive design. *Nurse Education Today* 74: 25–30.
O'Connor, C., and S. Michaels. 2007. When is dialogue 'dialogic'? *Human Development* 50: 275–285.
O'Dowd, R. 2003. Understanding the "other side": Intercultural learning in a Spanish-English e-mail exchange. *Language Learning & Technology* 7: 118–144.
Otten, M. 2003. Intercultural learning and diversity in higher education. *Journal of Studies in International Education* 7: 12–26.
Piipponen, O., and L. Karlsson. 2019. Children encountering each other through storytelling: Promoting intercultural learning in schools. *The Journal of Educational Research* 112: 590–603.
Portera, A. 2008. Intercultural education in Europe: Epistemological and semantic aspects. *Intercultural Education* 19: 481–491.
Rapanta, C., M. Vrikki, and M. Evagorou. 2020. Preparing culturally literate citizens through dialogue and argumentation: Rethinking citizenship education. *The Curriculum Journal*. https://doi.org/10.1002/curj.95.
Santos, M., and H. Araújo e Sá, and A. Simões . 2014. Intercultural education in primary school: A collaborative project. *Language and Intercultural Communication* 14: 140–150.
Senyshyn, R. 2018. Teaching for transformation: Converting the intercultural experience of preservice teachers into intercultural learning. *Intercultural Education* 29: 163–184.
Sfard, A. 2008. On two metaphors for learning and the dangers of choosing just one. In *Knowledge and practice: Representations and identities*, ed. P. Murphy and R. McCormick, 30–45. Milton Keynes: The Open University.

Tonkin, K., and C.B.D. Coudray. 2016. Not blogging, drinking: Peer learning, sociality and intercultural learning in study abroad. *Journal of Research in International Education* 15: 106–119.
Triandis, H.C. 1994. *Culture and social behaviour*. New York: McGraw-Hill.
Trovão, S. 2012. Comparing postcolonial identity formations: Legacies of Portuguese and British colonialisms in East Africa. *Social Identities* 18: 261–280.
UNESCO. 2009. World report: Investing in cultural diversity and intercultural dialogue. Paris: UNESCO. Available at: https://en.unesco.org/interculturaldialogue/resources/130.
Varga-Dobai, K. 2018. Remixing selfies: Arts-based explorations of funds of knowledge, meaning-making, and intercultural learning in literacy. *International Journal of Multicultural Education* 20: 117–132.
Wells, G. 2007. Semiotic mediation, dialogue and the construction of knowledge. *Human Development* 50: 244–274.
Wilbur, G. 2016. The staying power of intercultural learning through reflective inquiry. *Reflective Practice* 17: 59–71.

Chrysi Rapanta (PhD Communication Sciences, University of Lugano, Switzerland) is a Senior Researcher at NOVA University Lisbon, Faculty of Social and Human Sciences, where she also teaches Intercultural communication and Social science methods courses. She has experience in the field of Argumentation and Education.

Susana Trovão (PhD Anthropology, Universidade Nova, Portugal) is a Full Professor of Anthropology at NOVA University Lisbon, Faculty of Social and Human Sciences. Her areas of research and expertise comprise Migrations, Inter-Ethnicities and Transnationalism.

Chapter 3
Social Responsibility Through the Lens of an Agenda for Cultural Literacy Learning: Analyses of National Education Policy Documentation

Sandra Kairė, Lilija Duoblienė, and Irena Zaleskienė

3.1 Introduction

The contemporary world is marked by numerous new challenges: growth of inequality, migration, development of new technologies, climate change. All of them create tensions among nations, social groups or cultures. In the face of growing multiculturalism and need for dialogue, social responsibility as a concept in the educational field has received due attention. For instance, Berman (1990, 1997, 2011) emphasized the importance of education for social responsibility in school and classroom and defined it as personal investment in the well-being of others. Vallaeys (2014) discussed social responsibility as a matter of university mission and function. Berman (2011) related the concept of social responsibility to the development of social consciousness that meant balancing on personal self-realization and personal achievement with equal focus on social self-realization and collective achievement. In particular, a person becomes conscious that personal development (i.e. How will I lead my life?) is interrelated with the development of others (i.e. What does the way I lead my life mean for the life of others?). In this case, social responsibility embraces cultural values and creates empowerment, cooperation, compassion, and respect.

Some researchers looked at different meanings of social responsibility (Dahlsrud 2008; Vallaeys 2018) and found that most of them attempt to take a social and citizenship approach to social responsibility as a meaningful action towards society. The United Nations (2013) highlight education for social responsibility at school level as a value-driven way for school development that encourages students to become more effective and compassionate individuals, prepared for the challenges of leadership and responsibility beyond their school environment. In the context presented above, we see *education* for social responsibility as a creation of a bridge

S. Kairė (✉) · L. Duoblienė · I. Zaleskienė
Faculty of Philosophy, Institute of Educational Sciences, Vilnius University, Vilnius, Lithuania
e-mail: sandra.kaire@fsf.vu.lt

F. Maine and M. Vrikki (eds.), *Dialogue for Intercultural Understanding*,
https://doi.org/10.1007/978-3-030-71778-0_3

of communality which connects people from different stakeholders, diverse activities, diverse cultures, different personalities, etc. Education for citizenship, which is of the same importance as education for social responsibility, is seen as a creative way for every personality willing and able to participate in building this type of bridge which leads to a socially responsible, more coherent and sustainable social environment for everyone, especially those who are different in times of multiculturalism. This understanding deepens and adds more value to understanding the extended cultural literacy concept which helps to disclose that people feel involved in co-creating and supporting lives not only for themselves but for others as well.

We argue that social responsibility is an important attitude and action used to support the concept of citizenship. Strengthening education for active participation in schools could provide a much stronger framework for developing sustainability, and also intercultural cooperation for seeking common purposes in a rapidly changing and multicultural world. Thus, we raise the research question: What is the role of social responsibility in education for cultural literacy and how the concept of "social responsibility" is manifested in education policy documents?

To answer this research question, we used data from the DIALLS project. The authors of the paper, who are members of the DIALLS research team at Vilnius University, consider education for citizenship and education for social responsibility to be strongly interconnected with cultural literacy learning as it is understood and presented by the DIALLS project. It should help young people in schools to build up more dialogic, friendlier, more active, more respectful, and responsible communities and civic societies through empathy, tolerance and inclusion.

3.2 Social Responsibility in the Contexts of Cultural Literacy Learning and Education for Citizenship

Social responsibility is one of the cornerstones in the Cultural Literacy conceptual structure, composed by the DIALLS group (see Chapter 1 for overview). At present, due to the possibility to study abroad and be part of a more globalized educational network, students live in multicultural societies and have not only the opportunity, but also the responsibility of communicating with people from cultural and national backgrounds that differ from theirs. Accordingly, they need adequate education. The concept of literacy nowadays is changing rapidly and is understood not as singular and autonomous skill progression of learning to read and write, but it is in its essence "social practice" (Street 1984; Carter 2006). The concept of cultural literacy is also changing, and its understanding has radically turned from Hirsch (1980, 1989), who was the pioneer of the concept, to becoming much more sensitive towards communication, dialogue and social responsibility (Maine et al. 2019). Moreover, the first Cultural Literacy Education CLE conference (April 16–18, 2015, London) concluded that cultural literacy is a key societal challenge for now and the future and that social and cultural issues are seen side by side through the lens of literary thinking, employing communication, comparison and critique.[1] The concept of cultural literacy has been transformed partly using Freire's (2017) ideas towards critical and dialogic thinking, existential perception of action and events, and growth of reflection by turning attention to social responsibility. Presenting the ideas and purposes of the CLE, Segal (2015) stresses contemporary contexts of cultures that face migration, biopolitics, biosociality and unequal body treatment in different societies, and growth of new types of problems, which is why it is important to foster human rights and social responsibility.

Education for social responsibility started being perceived neither as a way to ensure higher professional prestige among companies, as it was around the nineteenth and twentieth centuries (Crave et al. 2014), nor as a way to increase power, which was treated as foundation given the development of Corporate Social Responsibility in 1960 (Davis 1960). In discussing the concept of "social responsibility", some contemporary researchers (Hussain and Gonen 2017) point to the emotional approach which is generated from love, care and empathy. Thus, responsibility incorporates the emotional ability to empathize with others and understand their otherness, which means to put oneself in the place of another. Attention to social responsibility in education increased following Levinas' (1998) philosophy of dialogue, in which he outlined openness to unfamiliar others. He directed the existentialist's care for the world towards the care for the other, in that way giving priority to the social aspect. Practice caring as the main moral value in Levinas' view leads towards a socially sustainable world. Empathy to the "Unfamiliar Other" in the perspective of Levinas has been broadly reflected in those times and later, for example by Levin (1998), Biesta (2003) and Strhan (2012), and it is even more important to discuss it nowadays (Baranova and Duobliene 2019), when cultural diversity in the world is growing and provoking unpredictable encounters.

The main authors (Putnam 2002; Tonge et al. 2012; Martinache and Gobert 2020) researching citizenship education, cooperation, civic participation and engagement strengthen different forms of civic activism. However, most of these forms and actions are related to cognitive and practical approaches. Analysis of the works of mentioned authors showed that, theoretically, education for citizenship does not necessarily incorporate an emotional approach that represents the cornerstone of "social responsibility".

Looking into tendencies shifting educational perspectives, the outcome document of the Technical Consultation on global citizenship education "Global Citizenship Education—An Emerging Perspective" (2013) appears to shift the educational perspective and leads to the main competences of global citizenship, partly trying to cover the emotional dimension in the developmental process of learner skills, including: non-cognitive social skills (empathy and conflict resolution), communicative skills and aptitudes for networking and interacting with people of different backgrounds, origins, cultures and perspectives; behavioral capacities to act collaboratively and responsibly, and to strive for collective good. It is clear that even global

[1]The CLE Forum was established on the basis of LCS (Literary and Cultural Studies). More information: https://cleurope.eu/.

citizenship cannot be avoided by *supervision* of *social responsibility*. Furthermore, we found the importance of social responsibility versus citizenship in the UNESCO Strategy "Education 2030 Incheon Declaration and Framework for Action for the Implementation of Sustainable Development Goal 4" (2015). Target 4.7 of this document reads that all learners should promote sustainable development through education, sustainable lifestyles, human rights, gender equality, promotion of a culture of peace and non-violence, global citizenship and appreciation of cultural diversity and cultural contribution to sustainable development. Social responsibility then becomes a particularly important concept for the understanding of the Global Citizenship and Cultural Literacy.

Theoretical and education policy discourse analysis shows that social responsibility is undoubtedly significant for teaching cultural literacy across European schools and all over the world. In the time of rapid changes, imbalances in nature and an aggressive human relationship with it, new waves of human migration, robotization of organic life, and the high speed of IT development and flows of information, humanity is facing injustice, insensibility and manipulation in social and cultural life, especially in social networks. Responsibility becomes one of the most important values in multicultural communication as well as in dealing/living with others, especially those who are different. As Segal claims (2011, 275), "nature may give us the basic tools to be empathic and socially responsible, but we need social guidance to do so collectively on an ongoing basis" and that cannot work out of the context. The authors of this paper would argue that it cannot work out of the cultural context and based on cultural literacy, which is also emphasized by DIALLS.

That is why "social responsibility" occupies a significant part and has a special role in the composition of other elements of culture-related concepts united within the Cultural Analysis Framework developed as part of the DIALLS project.

3.3 Methodology

The examination of national policy documentation was conducted as a qualitative conceptual analysis, extended with a quantification of the chosen concepts. This methodological choice is motivated by a constructivist perspective on concepts, emphasizing their contested, controversial, and transforming nature (e.g. Koselleck 2002; Guzzini 2005). According to Guzzini (2005), a constructivist conceptual analysis not only enables analytical assessment (i.e. what exactly it is meant by the concept that is used), but also encourages understanding of the performative aspects of the concepts (i.e. what does the concept might do). Therefore, the chosen approach not only enables clear understandings of the concepts and its variables, but also stimulates reflection on their performative nature, i.e. what particular concept can achieve in educational politics and practice. Based on a constructivist perspective, concepts are considered as a part of language that is also performative (Guzzini, 2005). The performative view of language makes meaning of words and signs in relation to reality, humans and artifacts (Guzzini 2005; Barinaga 2009). From this perspective, the concepts used in the national policy documentation are also seen as a performative part of educational policy language.

The analysis of the national policy documentation in this chapter encompasses five selected countries from nine participant countries of the DIALLS project—Cyprus, the United Kingdom, France, Finland, Germany, Lithuania, Spain, and Portugal. Firstly, the selection of countries was based on accessibility of the national policy documentation for the qualitative concept analysis in the English language. The latter criterion was essential for selecting countries and at the same time the most challenging one, as often national policy documents in each country are primarily written in the official language. Thus, based on these two criteria, five countries have been selected. It was possible to get access to the national policy documentation in English for Finland, Lithuania, the England and Spain, while Portugal has been selected following consultations and translation support from a Portuguese university participating in the DIALLS project.

The selection of the national education policy documents was carried out using the following criteria: (a) official documents that are applicable for the entire school system in the chosen country; (b) official documents that are the same or as similar as possible among all the selected countries; (c) official documents that are available in English. Based on these criteria, the chapter concentrates on 14 national policy documents that are relevant.[2] The selected documents provide an equivalent comparative analysis of these five countries.

The conceptual analysis of the education policy documentation in this chapter focuses on origin and performance of the concept of social responsibility. The concept analysis of the data was guided by theoretical views on constructivist perspectives on concepts, performativity of language and context. Therefore, the analysis not only focused on the concept of social responsibility, but also of the established overlap or relation of social responsibility concept with other culture-related concepts.[3] The analysis included the following questions: (a) How are the concepts defined: explicitly or implicitly? (b) What is the conceptual context of these concepts? (c) What is their cultural/societal context to which they are connected in the documents? (d) What is their relationship with the concept of social responsibility? The findings in the chapter are discussed in order to answer these questions.

The conceptual analysis of the national documents was carried out using MAXQDA18 software for qualitative and mixed methods data that can be used for data coding and retrieving coded segments. The MAXQDA software incorporates various data management features as well as various visual tools for data analysis.

[2]The list of all selected documents appears after the list of references.

[3]The culture-related concepts were identified in the planning phase of the project as a key for intercultural dialogue and cultural literacy. This list is based on the previous experience and expertise of team members from the University of Jyväskylä and Vilnius University representing different scholarly approaches, also the list is based on the literature review and the development of the notion of cultural literacy. The key culture-related concepts that address different aspects of cultural literacy have been listed in the DIALLS Grant Agreement (2018). The concepts are *cultural literacy, culture, value/values, cultural heritage, identity, inclusion, empathy, tolerance, multiculturalism, intercultural dialogue, citizenship, participation and cooperation* (Lähdesmäki et al. 2018).

The relation between social responsibility and other culture-related concepts in the national policy documents at issue are visualized using Code Maps.

Code Maps reveal an overlap of different concepts (coded segments) in the national policy documentation. In particular, the more similar the concepts are in terms of their use in a particular national policy document, the closer they are placed together on the map. The circles symbolize the concepts with the distances between two concepts representing how similarly the concepts have been applied in the document. The larger the circles are, the more assignments have been made with the particular concept. The connecting lines between different concepts indicate which codes overlap or co-occur in the document. The thicker the connection lines are displayed, the more coincidences there are between two concepts. The connection line between two concepts appears if there are at least two frequencies between these concepts in one segment of the document.

3.4 Findings: Manifestation of Social Responsibility Through Citizenship, Cooperation and Participation

There are other scientific analyses about the significance of the social responsibility concepts for the educational systems in the selected countries. For instance, Rauhansalo and Kvieska (2017) analyzed the significance of social studies and social subjects in the Finnish educational system and revealed that the Finnish National Board of Education identifies social studies as a critical element for the basics of democracy education, like equality, respect for human rights, social responsibility and freedom of opinions. Another example is the Teaching Personal and Social Responsibility model proposed by Hellison (2003). It represents one of the most consistent intervention programs that can be applied in physical education classes, and which has been widely explored in the Spanish education context (e.g. Escartí et al., 2010; Carbonero et al. 2017). However, surprisingly, social responsibility as a single two-term concept does not appear in the analysed national policy documentation of any of the five countries. Moreover, looking into the national policy documentation, it is difficult to identify clear reasons why the term of social responsibility (or social and responsible) does not appear there.

Having analysed Finland's national documents, we found the closest relation between *social* and *responsible* in the statement of national goals of the Finnish education. Specifically, the first national goal of education that steers the preparation of the National Core Curriculum is identified as *Growth as a human being and membership in society* (The Core Curriculum of Basic Education 2014). The description of this goal specifically states that "supporting the pupils' growth as human beings and into ethically responsible members of society is a central goal" (The Core Curriculum of Basic Education 2014, 25). We could grasp another close occurrence of *social* and *responsible* in the profiles of social studies curricular subjects. However, in all these cases the relation between *social* and *responsible* is more implicit than explicit as co-occurrences of the terms *social* and *responsible* are barely linked to each other. The co-occurrences presuppose close relation between society and individual's responsibility. However, *social* and *responsibility* more often occur as two separate terms or concepts in the Finnish documents.

Similarly, in the national documentation of Lithuania, the co-occurrences of the terms *social* and *responsible* are not used as united, but rather as supplementary or separate elements. For example, there is an obvious distinction between two concepts in the Lithuanian Law on Education (2016) where responsibility is related to the formation of a human being, while the social element is exceptionally significant for modern social competence of an individual. These two terms also occur in the Curriculum Framework of Primary and Basic Education of Lithuania (2008) where educating a *responsible citizen* is related to pupils' *social integration and lifelong learning.*

In the education policy documentation of the England and Spain, *social* and *responsible* basically occur in the descriptions of citizenship education. The England's Secondary Education Curriculum (2013) explicitly states that citizenship should "equip pupils with the skills and knowledge to explore political and social issues critically [--] and should also prepare pupils to take their place in society as responsible citizens" (59). These two terms are also incorporated in the aim of education where educating a responsible citizen is related to pupils' *social integration* and *lifelong learning.* Similarly, in the case of Spain, it is explicitly indicated that "[--] education is the most effective way of guaranteeing the exercise of democratic, responsible, free and active citizenship, which is essential for the constitution of an advanced, dynamic and equitable society (the Spanish Law on Education 2006, 13). Yet, in both countries the concepts of responsible citizens and social issues generally occur not as a single element, but as complementary principles of citizenship education.

The concept of social responsibility in Portugal's Law on the Education System (1986, 2009) is also implicitly related to social or civic citizenship. The Portuguese Students' Profile at the End of Compulsory Education (2017) also repeatedly states that the conceptual framework of a pupil orients towards training of autonomous, responsible and engaged citizens who are not only self-aware, but also conscious of others and the world and become active participants in society.

The analysis reveals that, in general, social responsibility as a singular concept occasionally occurs in the national documents. These two concepts are regularly considered as complementary or separate aspects in school education. In generalizing the dominant meaning of social responsibility among all the selected countries, we could state that being socially responsible means being a human and a natural member of society. In this case, social responsibility is interlinked with individual responsibility. However, such a rare reference to the concept of social responsibility in the national policy documentation of all five countries inevitably minimizes its significant contribution to promoting and practicing cultural literacy and making sense of Europe. Yet, this concept manifests in the national policy documentation through other culture-related concepts that will be analysed below. Meanwhile, the

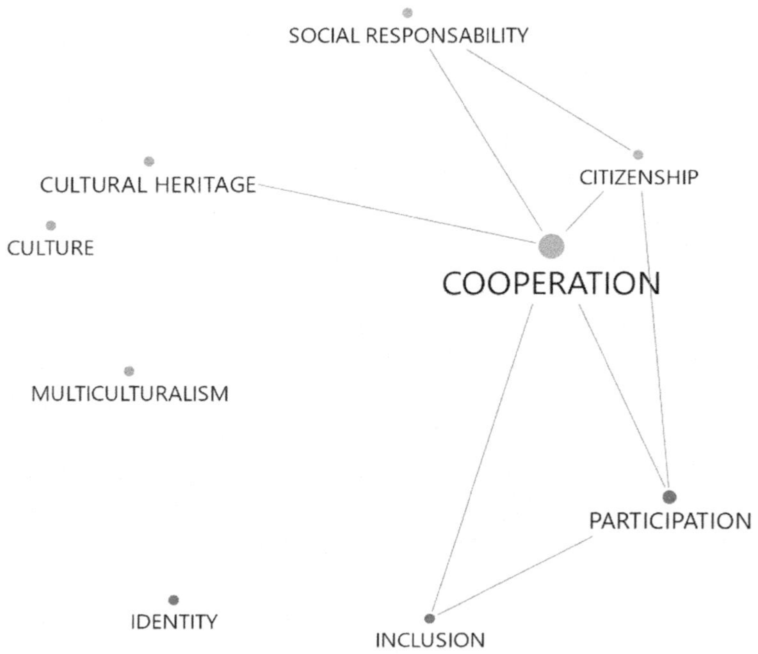

Fig. 3.1 Code map of the Core Curriculum of Basic Education (Finland, 2014)

concept of cultural literacy is rarely visible in the analysed documents of all countries and, therefore, is hardly related to social responsibility.

Looking into the overlap of social responsibility with other culture-related concepts in the National Curriculum (or Curriculum Framework) of the selected countries, we can see a variety of combinations. For example, in the National Curriculum of Finland, the concept of *cooperation* is the most frequent among all the analysed concepts (588)[4] and, therefore, could be considered a core concept that forms relations with various other concepts (see Fig. 3.1).

It can be clearly seen in the code map that social responsibility also overlaps with cooperation. In particular, social responsibility together with cooperation and citizenship establish a cluster (i.e. *light grey* concept cycles in the Fig. 3.1) that shows the closest co-occurrence of these three concepts in the National Curriculum of Basic Education of Finland. We can also see other clusters: the cluster of cultural heritage, culture and multiculturalism, and the cluster of participation, inclusion and identity. However, these two clusters do overlap only with the dominant concept of cooperation, while social responsibility co-occurs only with two concepts in the same cluster.

[4]In the analysis, the quantitative frequency of the particular concept is given in the brackets.

Interestingly, the concept of cultural literacy does not appear in the code map of Finland. Generally, the concept of cultural literacy is mentioned only twice in this document and is related to another concept that does not belong to any of the analysed culture-related concepts, i.e. to *multiliteracy*. Specifically, the concept of cultural literacy is mentioned both times as one of literacies (together with analytic and critical literacies) integrated into multiliteracy. As cultural literacy relates to multiliteracy, the meaning of this concept is related to producing, interpreting, and analyzing oral, written or visual cultural (or culture-related) texts. Thus, cultural literacy is rarely related to any of the cluster of concepts that we see on the concept map.

The National Plan of Education and Citizenship of Portugal (see Fig. 3.2) also shows similar co-occurrences of social responsibility and other culture-related concepts.

The code map demonstrates that social responsibility occurs in a cluster (light grey colour) together with many other culture-related concepts—*cooperation, identity, citizenship, inclusion* and *cultural dialogue*. In the documents at issue, social responsibility is placed closely to identity and cooperation, yet, the closest co-occurrence of social responsibility is seen only with the particular meaning of the citizenship concept (a connecting line between these two concepts)—*citizenship as a subject of the Citizenship and Development curricular unit*. The content of this curricular subject is based on three main axes: personal civic attitude (identity as a citizen, individual autonomy, human rights); interpersonal relations (communication, dialogue); social and intercultural relations (democracy, sustainable human development, globalization and interdependence, peace and conflict management). Social responsibility

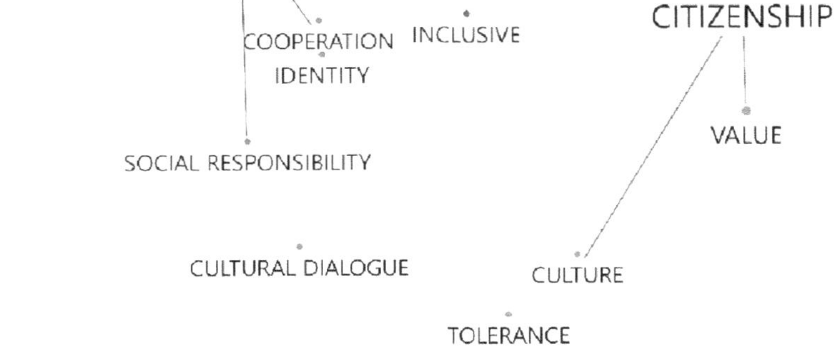

Fig. 3.2 Code map of Education and Citizenship. National Plan (Portugal, 2017)

implicitly manifests through all three axes, but especially, through the third one—*social and intercultural relations*. However, the overlap of these two concepts in the document is predictive as the concept of citizenship is the most visible concept (104) in the analysed document that focuses on citizenship education. Thus, citizenship becomes an umbrella concept that co-occurs with other concepts, including social responsibility.

At the same time, cultural literacy does not appear in the Portuguese National Plan for Education for Citizenship. Cultural literacy as a term appears only in the Student's Profile at the End of Compulsory Education (2017). The document states that after school education every pupil should become

> …a citizen endowed with cultural, scientific and technological literacy, able to critically question reality, to assess and select information, to make assumptions, and capable of making decisions based on the daily experience. (The Student's Profile at the End of Compulsory Education, 10)

However, it is a single segment that refers to cultural literacy; we could hardly grasp any manifestation of this particular concept in any other part of this national policy document of Portugal.

Likewise, the relationship between social responsibility and citizenship clearly manifests in the curricula documents of Lithuania and Spain. Interestingly, in both cases social responsibility forms a cluster only with this particular concept, i.e. these two concepts are placed closely to each other, yet they do not intersect. It suggests that both concepts supplement each other in the analysed documents, especially in the case of Spain, as the occurrence of both concepts is displayed in a similar position (Figs. 3.3 and 3.4).

The code maps reveal other similarities shared by these two countries. We do see occurrences of analogous concepts and there are three clusters in each case that hardly overlap with each other (no connecting lines among any of the concepts). Furthermore, in both cases there is no manifestation of cultural literacy. In the case of Lithuania, the concept of cultural literacy marginally manifests (2) only in the Law on Education (1991/2016) as socio-cultural maturity or general literacy. Both times the concept is mentioned for the purpose of (basic and secondary) education, but it is not explicitly defined:

> The purpose of basic education shall be to provide an individual with the basics of moral, sociocultural and civic maturity, general literacy, the basics of technological literacy, to cultivate national consciousness, to foster an intent and ability to make decisions and choices and to continue learning. (1991/2016, 12)

As seen from the stated purpose of basic education, sociocultural maturity is mentioned in relation to the concepts of morality and citizenship, whereas general and technological literacies here are mentioned separately. In the case of Spain, however, the concept of cultural literacy does not appear in any of the analysed national documents.

Finally, in the case of the England, we found only one cluster that encompasses three concepts—*social responsibility, citizenship, and participation*, whereas other analysed culture-related concepts do not form any intersections. However, the close

Fig. 3.3 Code map of the Curriculum Framework for Primary and Basic Education (Lithuania, 2008)

placement of all three concepts in the National Curriculum Framework of Secondary Education (2013) is a specific one. The concept of citizenship is an umbrella concept that encompasses participation and social responsibility. In particular, the latter two concepts appear in the profile of the citizenship education curricular subject. Here social responsibility and participation are related to one of the concrete activities—*volunteering*—that stimulates the formation of an active citizen.

> The national curriculum for citizenship aims to ensure that all pupils:
>
> [--] develop an interest in, and commitment to, participation in volunteering as well as other forms of responsible activity, that they will take with them into adulthood develop an interest in, and commitment to, participation in volunteering as well as other forms of responsible activity, that they will take with them into adulthood. [--] (The National Curriculum Framework of Secondary Education 2013, 59)

Interestingly enough, the England's National Curriculum of Secondary Education (2013) is the only document where social responsibility is in close placement with the concept of participation. Nevertheless, participation also manifests in the code maps of other countries (except Spain). In the cases of Finland and Portugal, we can see an obvious intersection of participation and citizenship. The latter concept is

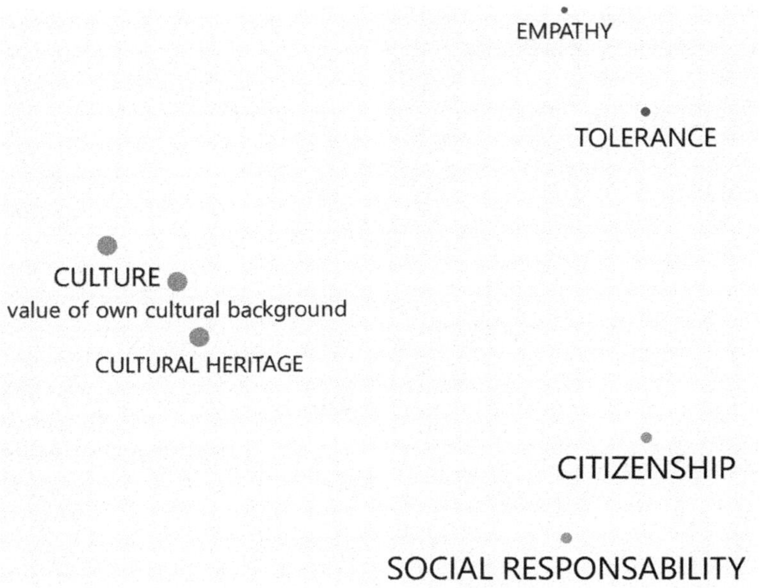

Fig. 3.4 Code map of the Basic Curriculum for Compulsory Secondary Education (Spain, 2013)

the dominant one in relation to social responsibility in all selected countries; thus, it clearly manifests in relation to social responsibility. As citizenship is in close placement with participation, we could also relate social responsibility to participation more closely than to cooperation. The concept of cooperation occurs only in the code map of Finland and could be considered in a more fragmental intersection than participation.

3.5 Conclusions

Education policy discourse and literature analysis demonstrates the crucial role of the change of understanding of "social responsibility" in the contemporary world. Social responsibility builds bridges between different cultures and keeps their communication alive, transforming passivity into activity and creating conditions for living and working together for well-being in the future. Although social responsibility is one of the most important components of cultural literacy, the interrelation between cultural literacy and social responsibility is not clearly defined in educational policy discourse and literature. That is because understanding of cultural literacy is changing very fast, depending on changes in the world, the appearance of new social, cultural and economic challenges. If cultural literacy was first introduced and understood as a set of knowledge, later regarded as the skills for cultural communication, today it would be much more related to social actions towards implementation of common understanding for living together with those "who are different", creating culture of dialogue and empathy.

Even though the significance of social responsibility for education is obvious, the conceptual analysis showed that this particular concept is hardly visible and present in the national education policy documentation of the selected EU countries. Surprisingly, the performance of social responsibility as a single two-term concept is sporadic in the national policy documentation of all five analysed countries. Moreover, looking into the national policy documentation, it is difficult to identify clear reasons why the term of social responsibility (or social and responsible as two separate, but inter-related concepts) does not appear. The analysis captured only some possible manifestations of social responsibility that mainly refers to being a human and a mature member of society. Therefore, it raises question: what this concept can achieve in educational politics and practice? The analysis of the relationship between social responsibility and other culture-related concepts demonstrated that the latter concept in one way or another tends to relate to three other concepts—*citizenship, cooperation and/or participation.* The qualitative analysis revealed that all four concepts are often overlapping, porous, and supplementing each other. However, the relations between all concepts are not equivalent.

Commonly, citizenship and social responsibility have a solid interconnection. Citizenship becomes the dominant concept in the selected national policy documentation of the five countries that comprises other culture-related concepts and social responsibility. Specifically, citizenship refers to the formation or growth of an active, responsible and democratic citizen who also actively participates as a responsible member of society. However, the relation between social responsibility and cooperation and participation is more porous. On the one hand, it is possible to state that active membership of a responsible citizen undoubtedly manifests through a person's actual participation and cooperation in school life and afterwards in social as well as civic life. Yet, on the other hand, the concepts of *social* and *responsible* in the national policy documentation of the five countries frequently appear not as united, but as two supplementary elements that are not necessarily interrelated. Besides, cooperation and participation usually manifest not as equivalents, but as components of active citizenship. Therefore, the relation between social responsibility and these two concepts is unstable.

In comparison with *citizenship*, the qualitative analysis revealed that *cultural literacy* is rarely visible in the national policy documentation of the selected countries. Other concepts occurring in the documents—*participation* and *cooperation*—are not relevant to the cultural literacy concept. Such a rare appearance of cultural literacy inevitably minimizes the significant contribution of this concept not only to social responsibility, but also to other culture-related concepts. The discourse in education policy documentation utilized a broad variety of possible meanings of the analysed concepts that might have crucial importance for cultural literacy and citizenship. However, the analysis revealed that the education policy documentation in the countries at issue seeks to guide education administration and teachers through the concepts, the meanings of which are rarely defined, explained or related to cultural literacy or such concepts as culture or cultural heritage. Therefore, it is hard to confirm that social responsibility is actually on the agenda for cultural literacy learning. The analysis revealed how the education policy documentation seeks to guide education administration and teachers through extremely broad and ambiguous concepts, the meanings of which varied even within the same document.

Responding to the findings of the presented research study, we would recommend that national education policy makers, researchers and practitioners reflect on analytical and performative aspects of the concept of social responsibility, i.e. how it appears in the national policy documentation, what it means and what these meanings can do in practice. Moreover, social responsibility is the bedrock of cultural literacy learning, development and usage of citizenship participatory skills in everyday life emphasizing not only rational, but also strong emotional dimensions.

References

Baranova, J., and L. Duoblienė. 2019. Meeting with the 'unfamiliar other' in multimodal education. *Ethics and Education* 15 (1): 33–47. https://doi.org/10.1080/17449642.2019.1700446.

Barinaga, S. 2009. A performative view of language—Methodological considerations and consequences for the study of culture. *Forum Qualitative Sozialforschung/Forum: Qualitative Social Research* 10 (1): Art. 24, n.p. https://nbn-resolving.de/urn:nbn:de:0114-fqs0901244.

Berman, S. 1990. Education for social responsibility. *Educational Leadership*, November: 75–80. https://www.ascd.org/ASCD/pdf/journals/ed_lead/el_199011_berman.pdf.

Berman, S. 1997. *Children's social consciousness and the development of social responsibility*. New York: University of New York Press.

Berman, S. 2011. Leading for social responsibility. In *Leadership for social justice and democracy in our schools*, ed. P. Houston, A. Blankstein, and R. Cole, 123–144. Thousand Oaks, CA: Corwin Press.

Biesta, G. 2003. Learning from Levinas: A response. *Studies in Philosophy and Education* 22 (1): 61–68. https://doi.org/10.1023/A:1021137611436.

Carbonero, M., L. Martín-Antón, L. Otero, and E. Monsalvo. 2017. Program to promote personal and social responsibility in the secondary classroom. *Frontiers in Psychology* 8: 809. https://www.ncbi.nlm.nih.gov/pmc/articles/PMC5439012/.

Carter, S. 2006. Redefining literacy as a social practice. *Journal of Basic Writing* 25 (2): 94–125.

Crave, A., D. Matten, and L. Spence (eds.). 2014. *Corporate social responsibility. Readings and cases in the global context.* London: Taylor & Francis, Routledge.

Dahlsrud, A. 2008. How corporate social responsibility is defined: An analysis of 37 Definitions. *Corporate Social Responsibility and Environmental Management* 15: 1–13. https://doi.org/10.1002/csr.132.

Davis, K. 1960. Can business afford to ignore social responsibilities? *California Management Review* 2 (3): 70–76. https://doi.org/10.2307/41166246.

Escartí, A., M. Gutiérrez, C. Pascual, and R. Lopis. 2010. Implementation of the personal and social responsibility. *International Journal of Psychology and Psychological Therapy* 10 (3): 387–402.

Freire, P. 2017. *Pedagogy of the oppressed*. New York: Continuum.

Guzzini, S. 2005. The concept of power: A constructivist analysis. *Journal of International Studies* 33 (3): 495–521. https://doi.org/10.1177/03058298050330031301.

Hellison D. 2003. Teaching personal and social responsibility in physical education. In *Students learning in physical education: Applying research to enhance instruction,* ed. J. Silverman and C. Ennis, 269–286. Champaign, IL: Human Kinetics.

Hirsch, E.D. 1980. Culture and literacy. *Journal of Basic Writing* 3 (1): 27–47.
Hirsch, E.D. 1989. *A first dictionary for cultural literacy: What our children need to know*. Boston and New York: Houghton Mifflin Company.
Hussain, J.A., and S. Gonen. 2017. Education for social responsibility. In *Beyond bystanders: Educational leadership for humane culture in a globalised reality*, ed. N., Aloni and L. Weintrob: 269–282. London: Springer.
Koselleck, R. 2002. *The practice of conceptual history: Timing history, spacing concepts*. Stanford: Stanford University Press.
Lähdesmäki, T., A. Koistinen, S. Ylönen, I. Zaleskiene, L. Duobliene, S. Kaire, F. Maine, and V. Cook. 2018. *Cultural analysis framework*. https://dialls2020.eu/wp-content/uploads/2019/09/resubmitted-cultural-analysis-framework-with-coversheet-.pdf.
Levinas, E. 1998. *Entre Nous: On thinking-of-the-other*. New York: Columbia University Press.
Levin, D. M. 1998. Tracework: Myself and others in the moral phenomenology of Merleau—Ponty and Levinas. *International Journal of Philosophical Studies* 6 (3): 345–392. https://doi.org/10.1080/096725598342037.
Maine, F., V. Cook, and T. Lähdesmäki. 2019. Reconceptualizing cultural literacy as a dialogic practice. *London Review of Education* 17 (3): 384–393. https://doi.org/10.18546/LRE.17.3.12.
Martinache, I., and C. Gobert. 2020. The merchant, the scientist and the citizen The competing approaches of social science education in the French high school. *Journal of Social Science Education* 19 (1): 10–26. https://www.jsse.org/index.php/jsse/article/view/1617/3542.
Putnam, R.D. 2002. *Democracies in flux: The evolution of social capital in contemporary society*. New York: Oxford Press.
Rauhansalo, T., and V. Kvieska. 2017. Finnish education system in integrated social education context. *Social Education* 46 (2): 24–39. https://socialinisugdymas.leu.lt/index.php/socialinisugdymas/article/view/194.
Segal, E.A. 2011. Social empathy: A model built on empathy, contextual understanding, and social responsibility that promotes social justice. *Journal of Social Service Research* 37 (3): 266–277. https://doi.org/10.1080/01488376.2011.564040.
Segal, N. 2015. From literature to cultural literacy. *Humanities* 4: 68–79. https://doi.org/10.3390/h4010068.
Street, B. 1984. *Literacy in theory and practice*, vol. 9. Cambridge: Cambridge University Press.
Strhan, A. 2012. *Levinas, subjectivity, education: Towards an ethics of radical responsibility*. West Sussex: Wiley-Blackwell.
Tonge, J., A. Mycock, and B. Jeffery. 2012. Does citizenship education make young people better-engaged citizens? *Political Studies* 60: 578–602. https://doi.org/10.1111/j.1467-9248.2011.00931.x.
UNESCO. 2013. *Outcome document of the technical consultation on global citizenship education: Global citizenship education—An emerging perspective*. Programme and Meeting Document. https://unesdoc.unesco.org/ark:/48223/pf0000224115. Accessed 13 January 2019.
UNESCO. 2015. *Education 2030 Incheon Declaration and Framework for Action for implementation of Sustainable Development Goal 4*. Programme and Meeting Document. https://unesdoc.unesco.org/ark:/48223/pf0000245656. Accessed May 2020.
United Nations. 2013. *Education for social responsibility*. https://sustainabledevelopment.un.org/partnership/?p=2418. Accessed 22 January 2019.
Vallaeys, F. 2014. University social responsibility: A mature and responsible definition. *GUNI Report of Higher Education in the World* 5: 88–96. https://doi.org/10.13140/2.1.2121.1523.
Vallaeys, F. 2018. *Defining social responsibility: A matter of philosophical urgency for universities*. International Network, Supported by UNESCO: https://www.guninetwork.org/articles/defining-social-responsibility-matter-philosophical-urgency-universities.

Documents Analyzed

England

Department of Education (England). *The Education Act 2011.* https://www.legislation.gov.uk/ukpga/2011/21 Accessed 1 September 2018.
Department for Education (England). *The National Curriculum in England. Key Stages 1 and 2 Framework Document (Primary Education)*, 2013. https://assets.publishing.service.gov.uk/government/uploads/system/uploads/attachment_data/file/425601/PRIMARY_national_curriculum.pdf. Accessed 1 September 2018.
Department for Education (England). *The National Curriculum in England. Key Stages 2 and 4 Framework Document (Secondary Education)*, 2013. https://assets.publishing.service.gov.uk/government/uploads/system/uploads/attachment_data/file/381754/SECONDARY_national_curriculum.pdf. Accessed 1 September 2018.
Department for Education (England). *Teachers' Standards. Guidance for School Leaders, School Staff and Governing Bodies*, 2011 (Introduction Updated 2013). https://assets.publishing.service.gov.uk/government/uploads/system/uploads/attachment_data/file/665520/Teachers__Standards.pdf Accessed 15 September 2018.

Finland

Finnish National Board of Education. 2014. *Core Curriculum of Basic Education*. Helsinki: Next Print Oy.
Ministry of Education, Finland. *Basic Education Act 628/1998. Amendments up to 1136/2010*, 2010. https://ncee.org/wp-content/uploads/2017/01/Fin-non-AV-2-Finland-Basic-Education-Act-1998.pdf. Accessed 18 September 2018.

Lithuania

Ministry of Education and Science of the Republic of Lithuania. *Curriculum Framework for Primary and Basic (Lower Secondary) Education. Resolution*, no. ISAK–970 (2008). https://www.sac.smm.lt/wp-content/uploads/2016/01/18en-vertimas-SAC-2008-Bendrosios-programos-08-09-22_Anglu-k.pdf. Accessed 10 September 2018.
Parliament of the Republic of Lithuania. Republic of Lithuania. *Law on Education*, no. I-1489 (1991/2016). https://e-seimas.lrs.lt/portal/legalAct/lt/TAD/df672e20b93311e5be9bf78e07ed6470?jfwid=rivwzvpvg. Accessed 10 September 2018.

Spain

Ministerio de Educación y Ciencia. *The Organic Law of Education*. Madrid: MEC, 2006.
Ministerio de Educación y Ciencia. *Organic Law 8/2013 of 9 December For Improving Educational Quality* (2013, published 2018). https://www.global-regulation.com/translation/spain/1447540/royal-decree-1105---2014%252c-of-26-december%252c-which-establishes-the-basic-curriculum-of-compulsory-secondary-education-and-secondary-education.html. Accessed 30 September 2018.

Portugal

Assembleia da República. 1986. *The Education System Framework Law*. 46/86, October 14. https://dre.pt/web/guest/pesquisa/-/search/222418/details/normal?p_p_auth=D688OvBC. Accessed 3 October 2018.
Direcção Geral da Educação. *Perfil dos Alunos à Saída da Escolaridade Obrigatória* [Student's Profile at the End of Compulsory Education]. Despacho n.º 6478/2017, 26 de Julho. Portugal: Ministério da Educação, 2017. https://dge.mec.pt/sites/default/files/Curriculo/Projeto_Autonomia_e_Flexibilidade/perfil_dos_alunos.pdf. Accessed 3 October 2018.

Sandra Kairė PhD in Education, Assistant Professor at the Institute of Educational Sciences, Faculty of Philosophy at Vilnius University. Her research field covers intercultural learning and interactions among different cultural groups in the educational context.

Lilija Duoblienė PhD in Education, Professor, Head of the Department of Education Theory and Culture at the Institute of Educational Sciences, Faculty of Philosophy at Vilnius University. Her research field is philosophy, multimodality and visuality in education.

Irena Zaleskienė Professor, PhD in Education, Senior Researcher at the Institute of Educational Sciences, Faculty of Philosophy at Vilnius University; DIALLS local co-coordinator. Her research field encompasses citizenship and social responsibility.

Chapter 4
Explorations of Linkages Between Intercultural Dialogue, Art, and Empathy

Tuuli Lähdesmäki and Aino-Kaisa Koistinen

4.1 Introduction: What is intercultural dialogue?

In the 2000s, European societies have transformed quickly due to the networked global economy, deepening a European integration process, forced and voluntary movement of people to and within Europe, and influence of social media on culture, communication, and society. Europe has become an increasingly diverse and pluricultural continent where many people simultaneously identify with multiple different cultural and social groups. In such "super-diversified" (Vertovec 2007) European societies diversity itself is broad, multidimensional, and fluid (ibid.; Blommaert and Rampton 2011). Different social locations and identities intersect within them—whether cultural, ethnic, national, social, religious, or linguistic. At the same time, however, European societies have faced the rise of diverse populist and radical right-wing movements promoting profoundly monoculturalist views and cultural purism. What are the means to confront this polarization of views and attitudes in Europe?

In this chapter, we examine the concept of intercultural dialogue in the context of the objectives of the DIALLS project (Chapter 1), focusing on the interconnections of intercultural dialogue, art, and empathy. We explore how intercultural dialogue has been defined as a concept, policy, and practice to tackle the various challenges that 'super-diversified' societies may face if cultural encounters within them are not based on mutual respect and aspiration to understand differences. We emphasize a core aspect in the definitions of intercultural dialogue, namely empathy. Besides agreeing that intercultural dialogue is important in today's societies, recent research includes criticism of its implicit meanings and uses in policy discourses and its implementation in practice. We continue our chapter by summarizing this criticism

T. Lähdesmäki (✉) · A.-K. Koistinen
University of Jyväskylä, Jyväskylä, Finland
e-mail: tuuli.lahdesmaki@jyu.fi

A.-K. Koistinen
e-mail: aino-kaisa.koistinen@jyu.fi

F. Maine and M. Vrikki (eds.), *Dialogue for Intercultural Understanding*,
https://doi.org/10.1007/978-3-030-71778-0_4

and discussing the challenges scholars have identified in policies and practices of intercultural dialogue. Various previous studies have emphasized 'shared space' as a prerequisite for successful intercultural dialogue. Later in our chapter, we expand this idea using feminist scholarship. In addition to 'shared space', we argue that intercultural dialogue needs 'safe space' to overcome hierarchical positions that may hinder equal and emphatic encounters of people with different backgrounds. We end our chapter by discussing how art has been perceived in academia as "an evocative and emotionally drenched expression that makes it possible to know how others feel" (Barone and Eisner 2012, 7) and as offering a form of knowledge that deals with empathy (Eisner 2008, 11). As a result, we suggest that art offers a flexible arena and instrument to set up non-hierarchical 'safe shared space' for practising intercultural dialogue, especially through its wordless mode of expression that crosses language barriers and enables creativity that can enhance empathy.

The DIALLS project recognizes art's potential in teaching empathy and defines empathy as one of the core features of cultural literacy. The Cultural Literacy Learning Programme developed in the project utilizes art as means for teaching and learning cultural literacy. Using wordless picture books and short films—thus capable of crossing language barriers—the program encourages students to create cultural artefacts of their own, such as drawings, photographs, and collages, in order to recognize, negotiate, and empathize with cultural differences. To put it simply, art is used to teach cultural literacy defined as an individual's competence and skill to encounter cultural differences with an open mind, to become tolerant, empathetic, and inclusive of other positions and perspectives, and to gain awareness of one's own cultural identity and the identities of others (Maine et al. 2019). Moreover, teaching cultural literacy is seen as a means to promote intercultural dialogue.

Intercultural dialogue is not a new concept but has an established trajectory in academic discussions and the policy discourses of several international institutions. The dialogical approach to the encounter of cultures was included in UNESCO's discourse as early as the 1980s (Wiesand et al. 2008). A similar approach started to characterize the Council of Europe's and the European Union's initiatives during the 1990s. The concept became more deeply rooted in European policy discourses at the beginning of the 2000s when the Council of Europe started a process that resulted in various declarations on intercultural dialogue, culminating in the "White Paper on intercultural dialogue" in 2008. In the same year, the EU celebrated the European Year of Intercultural Dialogue: one of its goals to raise awareness of this concept.

The concept of intercultural dialogue and policies seeking to implement it were warmly welcomed by many leading European politicians. A decade ago, several European societies faced what scholars have called 'backlash against multiculturalism' as many European heads of state accused 'multiculturalism' of creating social problems and controversies between people rather than solving them (Bauböck 2008; Vertovec and Wessendorf 2010; Modood and Meer 2012; Barrett 2013). Also in scholarly debates, multiculturalism was criticized for encouraging members of different cultures to live separately in parallel communities without any deeper interaction, for emphasizing instead of blurring boundaries, and for focusing mainly on ethnic and national issues rather than paying attention to the intersectional diversity in societies (e.g., Rodríguez-García 2010; Taylor 2012; Barrett 2013). The critics of multiculturalism discussed contemporary intersectional diversities using the concept of interculturalism, emphasizing the need to create new opportunities across cultures and to support interaction between different cultural communities (Cantle 2013).

Intercultural dialogue as a practice is instrumental to implementing the aims of interculturalism, such as fostering understanding and empathy (Cantle 2013, 80). The Council of Europe's "Reference Framework of Competences for Democratic Culture" defines intercultural dialogue as:

> an open exchange of views, on the basis of mutual understanding and respect, between individuals or groups who perceive themselves as having different cultural affiliations from each other. It requires the freedom and ability to express oneself, as well as the willingness and capacity to listen to the views of others. Intercultural dialogue fosters constructive engagement across perceived cultural divides, reduces intolerance, prejudice and stereotyping, and contributes to political, social, cultural and economic integration and the cohesion of culturally diverse societies. It fosters equality, human dignity and a sense of common purpose. It aims to develop a deeper understanding of diverse world views and practices, to increase co-operation and participation (or the freedom to make choices), to allow personal growth and transformation, and to promote respect for the other. (CofE 2018, 74–75)

This definition does not explicitly mention empathy but deals with it implicitly by emphasizing engagement across cultural divides. In academia, empathy has been connected more directly to the concept of intercultural dialogue. Empathy has been seen as the very basis of intercultural dialogue (e.g. Ratzmann 2019, 1), an effect and outcome of this practice (e.g. Elias 2017, 270), and a particular skill and competence for practising it (e.g. Houghton 2012, 97–100; Barrett 2013, 26). For instance, Houghton (2012) discusses "intellectual empathy" as a bottom-up process and cognitive skill in intercultural dialogue helping us to focus on the information provided by the interlocutor in cultural encounters and releasing us from our assumptions and stock responses based on our prior knowledge.

The above-quoted definition does not explicitly refer to the creativity often raised in scholarly discussions on intercultural dialogue. The definition, however, does highlight the ability to express oneself, personal growth, and transformation but does not characterize intercultural dialogue through creative thinking or practices. Following Wiesand et al. (2008, xiii), we argue that intercultural dialogue requires and promotes creative abilities to encounter other people and to convert experiences from these encounters into new ideas, perspectives, and forms of expression.

4.2 Challenges of Intercultural Dialogue

Although intercultural dialogue as a concept, policy, and practice has been broadly accepted and welcomed in academia, several scholars have also expressed criticism for its discursive meanings and uses as a policy instrument. Next, we will summarize the core weaknesses and limitations of the concept addressed in academia during the past decade (see Lähdesmäki et al. 2020).

The concept of intercultural dialogue was developed to respond to increasing cultural diversity in Western societies and to promote interaction, mutual respect, and understanding between people with different cultural backgrounds. Despite these premises, the concept has been criticized in academia for treating cultures as internally homogeneous. The critics have perceived the concept as categorizing people into separate and clearly identifiable cultural units, although in 'super-diversified' societies cultural differences are intersectional and do not follow any clear demarcations (Barrett 2013, 30).

Most of the critical views on the concept of intercultural dialogue emphasize the power imbalances inherent in discourses, policies, and practices dealing with it. Intercultural dialogue has been perceived as a profoundly Western concept through which Western scholars and societies seek to deal with non-Western 'others', as Lee (2016) notes. For her, research on intercultural dialogue is Western-dominated as, irrespective of countries of origin, most researchers in the field have learned and internalized Western approaches to scholarship (Lee 2016, 240). Western interest in intercultural dialogue has also been critically related to the "Western 'civilising mission' of the past and hegemonic power over language, culture, finance and politics" (Silversti 2007, n.p.) as the concept has been utilized by European political institutions, such as the European Union, to promote European citizenship, belonging to Europe, and a 'new European narrative' as its shared basis.

Scholars have also pointed out how policy discourses on intercultural dialogue include explicit and implicit power hierarchies based on Western or Eurocentric perspectives on diversity and cultural differences. Discourses, policies, and practices of intercultural dialogue have been seen as implicitly consolidating differences between Westerners or Europeans and their 'others'—and thus constructing the positions of 'us' and 'them'—rather than bringing different subjects together (Aman 2012). As Aman (2012, 1010) notes regarding the European Union's intercultural dialogue policies:

> Europeans are portrayed as having an a priori historical existence, while the ones excluded from this notion are evoked to demonstrate its difference in comparison to the European one. [...] [S]ubjects not considered as Europeans serve as markers of the multicultural present of the space.

The research on European policy discourses regarding intercultural dialogue has also recognized power hierarchies between those who are expected to facilitate the dialogue and those expected only to participate in it (Lähdesmäki and Wagener 2015; Lähdesmäki et al. 2015). As Barrett (2013, 31) notes: "[I]t is those individuals who occupy positions of power and privilege who tend to determine the implicit rules by which dialogue occurs, and their decisions are typically based on their own cultural perspective." Even though policy discourses on intercultural dialogue might explicitly recognize the 'diversity of diversities' and seek to embrace manifold aspects of diversity in contemporary societies, these discourses often focus on migrant and minority ethnic groups, constructing them as 'others' and as the participants in intercultural dialogue. Moreover, the 'others' in these discourses often narrow to mean non-European, non-white, non-Christian, and non-educated migrants and ethnic groups (Lähdesmäki et al. 2015). As intercultural dialogue policies commonly aim to tackle various challenges related to increased cultural diversity in Western societies, their discourses can unintentionally present the coexistence of cultures as a problem and source of conflict, which is contradictory to the fundamental principle of intercultural dialogue as a concept, policy, and practice (Lähdesmäki and Wagener 2015; Lähdesmäki et al. 2015).

One criticism of the practices of intercultural dialogue is that they can be elitist. Lee (2016) notes how various projects, research reports, and data sets on intercultural dialogue, as well as educational programs aiming at increasing it, are filtered through the lenses of the educated elites. She (2016, 239) points out: "Education, indeed, exists where there is money, and it is a privilege." She also criticizes the emphasis on talk over other means of expression and finding solutions in concepts of intercultural dialogue, as this privileges those who have the capacity and 'voice' to speak. Similarly, Barrett (2013, 27) shows how disadvantages in education and employment, poverty, marginalization, and discrimination represent structural barriers to practices of intercultural dialogue as people affected by these phenomena are less able to participate in these practices.

The writers of intercultural dialogue policies have been criticized for defining the concept vaguely and explaining it indistinctly and ambiguously (Näss 2010; Lähdesmäki et al. 2015, 2020; Elias 2017). Moreover, these shapers of policy approach intercultural dialogue in a universalizing manner and poorly recognize the societal or historical differences between societies (Lähdesmäki and Wagener 2015), casting doubt on whether the policies can be applied to varying social realities (Elias 2017, 259). Scholars have also noted how policy-makers may load far-reaching expectations on practices of intercultural dialogue and thus underestimate the structural inequalities and disadvantages in Western societies that cannot be solved with intercultural dialogue alone (Barrett 2013, 30). Solving these inequalities and disadvantages requires concrete structural measures and the economic resources to deliver them (Lähdesmäki and Wagener 2015, 27).

Even though researchers in the field often mention empathy as a core aspect of intercultural dialogue, policies on intercultural dialogue emphasize it less. Our previous research on discourses of intercultural dialogue in the Council of Europe's and the European Union's education policy documents indicates how rarely the authors of these documents explicitly address empathy (Lähdesmäki et al. 2020). Yet, empathy can be perceived as a crucial competence and attitude in building inclusive relationships with other people and constructing inclusive societies based on mutual respect and understanding.

4.3 Preconditions for Intercultural Dialogue: Shared and Safe Space

Both scholars and policy-makers often discuss intercultural dialogue in relation to space: it is seen as requiring a particular kind of space and physical place to succeed. The Council of Europe's "White Paper on intercultural dialogue" (2008) makes an early case for space for intercultural dialogue. It draws special attention to urban planning and design and the management of public space through its spatial agenda, which reaches from commercial to religious and from educational to leisure spaces. The White Paper crystallizes the Council's spatial agenda as follows:

> It is essential to engender spaces for dialogue that are open to all. Successful intercultural governance, at any level, is largely a matter of cultivating such spaces: physical spaces like streets, markets and shops, houses, kindergartens, schools and universities, cultural and social centres, youth clubs, churches, synagogues and mosques, company meeting rooms and workplaces, museums, libraries and other leisure facilities, or virtual spaces like the media. (CofE 2008, 33)

The discourse of the White Paper emphasizes 'openness' as the key character of space enabling intercultural dialogue. What 'open space' actually means, however, is not specified in the document (Lähdesmäki 2014).

The idea of 'open space' resonates with other spatial discussions on intercultural ideologue. One of the societal prerequisites often emphasized as key for intercultural dialogue is 'shared space'—whether a physical place or a virtual environment (Wiesand et al. 2008, 10; Barrett 2013, 28; Wilson 2013, 61). Stemming from UNESCO's report 'Our Creative Diversity' (1996), the concept of shared space has been explained as an arena where new ideas and values can be publicly recognized in a dialogue. The ERICart report explains this as follows:

> ICD [Intercultural Dialogue] can only take place in an environment where a person is guaranteed safety and dignity, equality of opportunity and participation, where different views can be voiced openly without fear, where there are shared spaces for exchanges between different cultures to take place. (Wiesand et al. 2008, iii)
>
> The main prerequisite to establish a dialogic climate is the attitude that no part/side/partner in the dialogue stays in the center of the world or in an absolute position. On the contrary, the 'center' must be emptied for the sake of dialogue in order for the majority-minority discourse to be overcome (Wiesand et al. 2008, 10).

A non-hierarchical space emptied of power imbalances sounds like an ideal that may be difficult to achieve in practice: space is always determined by complex and transforming social relations, as the long tradition of studies in the sociology of space shows (e.g. Foucault 1984; Lefebvre 1991; Soja 1996; Massey 2005). Recent discussions on intercultural dialogue have recognized this challenge and sought to see differences in how space enables or hinders equal, non-hierarchical encounters. For instance, the European Commission's "Report on the role of public arts and cultural institutions in the promotion of cultural diversity and intercultural dialogue" (2014) categorizes shared spaces as "traditional" or "neutral". The former are determined by established social, cultural, and behavior norms, such as normative dress codes, while codes are co-created by people participating and acting in the latter (EC 2014, 62, 78). Recognizing the impact of social relations on space increases the credibility of policy discourses on intercultural dialogue. Interlocutors in these discourses still struggle to explain how spaces become 'shared' and what in fact is shared by people within these spaces.

We argue that the discussion on shared space as a precondition for intercultural dialogue should now focus on the feeling of safety in space. The concept of 'safe space' stems from the 1970s women's movement, feminism and queer activism and was originally used to refer to and discuss physical places where women and sexual minorities could meet and share their experiences in a safe environment (Flensner and Von der Lippe 2019, 276). More recently, various governmental and public institutions have adapted 'safe-space policies' to protect vulnerable and oppressed groups and minorities from discrimination, harassment, hatred, and threats (see Kyrölä 2018). The core idea of safe space is not only to delimit a place where violations are not accepted but to foster social relations between people in a place to make them feel that they can speak freely as all kinds of perspectives and positions are welcomed in the delimited place, whether physical or virtual. However, 'openness' to and 'acceptance' of perspectives and positions has to be structured by rules shared by all to make everyone in the space feel that they can safely exchange ideas and be themselves. The aim of these rules is to ensure an inclusive and respectful atmosphere in terms of civility and sensitivity (Jackson 2014, 48). In reality, these two requirements—openness and regulation—create an inherent tension in the idea of safe space (Flensner and Von der Lippe 2019, 276; see Kyrölä 2018).

Academic discourses on intercultural dialogue have often utilized the concept of safe space when dealing with encounters of religious and non-religious world views in public space and intercultural education (e.g. Jackson 2014; Knauth and Vieregge 2019; Flensner and Von der Lippe 2019). Several studies on classrooms as safe spaces have recognized challenges in making spaces safe and criticized the concept for smoothing controversies that might actually lead to learning, the development of student's world views, and personal growth (e.g. Holley and Steiner 2005; Flensner and Von der Lippe 2019; Halberstam 2018; see also Kyrölä 2018). Callan (2016, 65) has even suggested that education should make students feel "intellectually unsafe" to advance learning and critical thinking (see also Halberstam 2018). Even if this is the case, all education should be based on "dignity safe space" that is "free of any reasonable anxiety that others will treat one as having an inferior social rank to theirs" as Callan (2016, 65) describes.

Discussions on safe space rarely refer to empathy as the basis for social relations that create such spaces. We argue that empathy could be seen as the foundation and defining element of safe shared space. This space is about non-hierarchical social relations that allow agency for all who share the space. In it, individuals should be able to feel safe but they are required to try to ensure that others feel so too. In this, empathy becomes crucial. Empathy has been defined in scholarly literature as a complex concept including different modes of caring for others' viewpoints and 'feeling with' them (for different modes of empathy see e.g. Smith 2006; Aaltola and Keto 2017; Velasco 2019). These studies commonly distinguish cognitive from affective or emotional empathy: the former deals with an ability to understand others' perspectives and feelings, while the latter refers to an ability to share others' emotions based on emotional cognition. Scholars have also identified compassionate empathy that moves beyond understanding others and sharing their feelings to make people take action to help those who need it. What safe shared spaces enable empathy in all its modes? We argue that art has a capacity to function as such space (see a further discussion on psychological safety and group creativity in Chapter 9 in this volume).

4.4 Art as Safe Shared Space and Enabler of Empathy

During the last few years, various projects seeking to increase intercultural dialogue have done so using art. In their book *Art and Intercultural Dialogue*, Gonçalves and Majhanovich (2016) note how art not only crosses language barriers but is also a wordless mode to express emotions and communicate. They emphasize how doing art is a creative process that fosters imagination, innovation, and problem solving that they see as key for intercultural dialogue. For them, art "masters and joins the languages of thought and emotion" and can therefore function as "a tool to better understand otherness and to communicate with the Other" (Gonçalves and Majhanovich 2016, vii). They claim (ibid.): "In fact, art initiates, fosters and protects diversity and so it can be a universal tool to initiate, nourish and protect intercultural dialogue, while celebrating cultural diversity." Art, thus, seems to have a lot of potential to promote intercultural dialogue. However, art does not automatically offer any non-hierarchical shared space or simple tool to promote respect for the other. It may nevertheless enable creative interaction, imagination, and empathy with others: this should be better recognized in policies and practices of intercultural dialogue.

Let us look more closely at empathy as one of the key components for intercultural dialogue and art. It is often claimed that art and literature can help people to learn empathy or identify with diverse others. The understanding of art's potential to influence and transform people's views, notions, and experiences is nothing new. As Fialho (2019, 3–4) points out: "The question of the transformative purpose of the arts and of literature [...] has been present since human beings realized that they could influence others through discourse." Scholars from various fields have arg2006ued that art and literature have transformative, or even radical, qualities that raise empathy and awareness of self and others (e.g. Keen 2006; Leavy 2017, 195; Fialho 2019, 6–8) and strengthen the ability to identify with others or step into someone else's shoes, so to speak (Stout 1999; Venäläinen 2019, 255). In literature, this has often been discussed in terms of readers' engagement with characters (Keen 2006). Leavy, for example, notes that "[a]s readers engage with fiction and develop emotional connections with the characters, they are constructing intimate relationships with 'the imagined other'" (2017, 199). Discussing literary fiction, Polvinen and Sklar (2019, 11) suggest: "The possible benefits of fiction to empathy and sympathy could be seen to reside not in the characters themselves, but in readers' cognitive action in imagining those characters." Art can serve as a space in which to imagine the experiences of others (Stout 1999)—and, as we argue, function as a safe space to deal with these experiences. Moreover, it has been claimed that fictional narratives can invite us to care for nature and nonhuman animals (e.g. Weik von Mossner 2017, 1–16). In the DIALLS project, art's potential for teaching us to relate to people, the environment, and animals is also taken into account, as lessons in the Cultural Literacy Learning Programme deal with themes such as climate change and sustainable development.

Worried that the call for trigger warnings to ensure that everyone in a learning environment feels safe may hinder the teaching of difficult subjects, Halberstam (2018, 57) asks: "Can we still dare to be surprised, shocked, thrilled into new forms of knowing?" Kyrölä nevertheless reminds us that, in a safe space, discomfort does not necessarily have to be erased, but it should be safe to experience (2018, 43–44). One may also argue that the transformative and imaginative capabilities of art open "the door for multiple forms of knowing" (Eisner 2008, 5). Barone and Eisner (2012, 3) claim that "the arts make […] empathic participation possible because they create forms that are evocative and compelling." Eisner argues elsewhere that art influences our knowledge production in three ways. Firstly, art evokes awareness of the nuances of qualitative situations (Eisner 2008, 10). In other words, art can broaden our awareness of the situated nature of knowledge and the experiences of others. Secondly, "[i]mages rendered in artistically expressive form often generate a kind of empathy that makes action possible" (Eisner 2008, 11). Thirdly, art provides us with "a fresh perspective so that our old habits of mind do not dominate our reactions with stock responses" (ibid.). In this sense, art can help us understand knowledge as situated and positional, depending on one's position in a society, for instance in terms of gender, class, or ethnicity (on 'situated knowledges', see Haraway 1988). Through this emphasis on situatedness, art can also help create a (feminist) safe space where intercultural dialogue between 'us' and 'others' may flourish (see Kyrölä 2018, 37).

Art education and art-based research are often considered as dealing with teaching and learning empathy (e.g. Barone and Eisner 2012, 7; Jeffers 2009, 19). This is echoed in philosopher Martha Nussbaum's (2010) work. For her, art should be used to foster empathy, dialogue, and the understanding and acceptance of otherness in education (2010, 13–16, 95–120). Numerous empirical studies and educational experiments support the claims of art as an effective pedagogical tool for teaching empathy and respect for difference (e.g. Stout 1999; Jeffers 2009; Fialho 2019, 10; Venäläinen 2019, 42). However, the idea that art can teach empathy has also been critiqued as too simplistic. Polvinen and Sklar (2019, 12) argue that instead of evoking sympathetic or empathetic responses, "fiction may, in fact, also offer us a very different kind of cognitive-emotional benefit—one that depends on our engagement with the literary artefact as a whole, and with the fictional characters specifically as fictions."

Teaching and learning empathy through art requires rigorous attention to the pedagogical tools used (Stout 1999; Jeffers 2009; Fialho 2019). Fialho asserts that if literature is to be used to teach empathy, "a formalist, knowledge-oriented approach" needs to be supplemented by forms of education that "encourage students to explore their personal responses in dialogic interactions with and about literary texts" (2019,

10). Moreover, writing on art-based research projects, Pauwels notes that "there is nothing intrinsically or automatically empowering in using pictures", meaning that art does not automatically cause empathetic or empowering experiences in the participants, but the researcher must actively steer them towards these kinds of experiences (2015, 108). These studies establish that art should by no means be overlooked in the teaching and learning of intercultural dialogue, but emphasis must be placed on pedagogical tools.

4.5 Conclusions

In this chapter, we have discussed intercultural dialogue as a concept, policy, and practice aimed at fostering mutual understanding and empathy towards others. We have noted how empathy is often defined as a key element of intercultural dialogue in scholarly texts but it is seldom mentioned in policies on the subject (see Lähdesmäki et al. 2020). Discussion is needed to find concrete ways of implementing empathy as a core feature of intercultural dialogue. In this chapter, we have suggested artistic creation and art education as such concrete tools.

Developing previous research that has identified shared space as a precondition for successful intercultural dialogue, as well as on feminist theorizations on safe space, we claim that intercultural dialogue needs to serve as safe shared space that allows for equal and empathic encounters between people from different hierarchical positions and backgrounds. Art can bring about a greater awareness of self and others and the situated nature of knowledge, as well as fostering mutual understanding. As gaining awareness of the experiences of others is important for empathic relationships to develop, art can also help in fostering empathy towards others and thus create a safe shared space for intercultural dialogue.

Nevertheless, we need to remember that art as such does not automatically evoke empathy or function as a safe shared space to learn empathy or intercultural dialogue. As discussed in our chapter, the linkages between art and empathy have been actively addressed in recent scholarship. Some of these studies claim that engagement with art, particularly reading literature, increases receivers' or readers' social awareness (David Dodell-Feder and Diana Tamir 2018) and understanding of others' minds (Kidd and Castano 2013), and, thus, enhances their ability for empathy. Some other scholars have criticized or been more reserved for such direct causality. Currie (2020, 211) notes, for instance, that empathizing with fictional characters does not equate with the exercise of empathy in response to the plights of other, real people and that" [f]iction can spread ignorance, prejudice, and insensitivity as effectively as it provides knowledge and openness" (Currie 2020, 204).

In this chapter, we have emphasized pedagogy as a key to using art to teach empathy and intercultural dialogue. In order for intercultural dialogue to flourish in the classroom and beyond, forms of education that encourage empathic interaction should therefore supplement formalist approaches to teaching art.

A broad consortium of scholars and educators from various backgrounds have developed these pedagogical tools in the DIALLS project. The Cultural Literacy Learning Programme thus offers useful tools for teachers and researchers interested in the practice of teaching empathy and intercultural dialogue through art.

References

Aaltola, E., and S. Keto. 2017. *Empatia—myötäelämisen tiede*. Helsinki: Into.
Aman, R. 2012. The EU and the recycling of colonialism: Formation of Europeans through intercultural dialogue. *Educational Philosophy and Theory* 44 (9): 1010–1023.
Barone, T., and E.W. Eisner. 2012. *Arts based research*. London: Sage.
Barrett, M. 2013. Introduction—Interculturalism and multiculturalism: Concepts and controversies. In *Interculturalism and multiculturalism: Similarities and differences*, ed. M. Barrett, 15–42. Strasbourg: Council of Europe.
Bauböck, R. 2008. Beyond culturalism and statism: Liberal responses to diversity. *EUROSPHERE Working Paper Series* 6. https://EconPapers.repec.org/RePEc:erp:ewpxxx:p0030. Accessed 8 May 2020.
Blommaert, J., and B. Rampton. 2011. *Language and Superdiversity. Diversities* 13 (2): 1–21.
Callan, E. 2016. Education in safe and unsafe spaces. *Philosophical Inquiry in Education* 24 (1): 64–78.
Cantle, T. 2013. Interculturalism as a new narrative for the era of globalisation and super-diversity. In *Interculturalism and multiculturalism: Similarities and differences*, ed. M. Barrett, 69–92. Strasbourg: Council of Europe.
CofE (Council of Europe). 2008. White paper on intercultural dialogue. 'Living together as equals in dignity.' Strasbourg: Council of Europe.
CofE (Council of Europe). 2018. Reference framework of competences for democratic culture. Vol. 1: Context, concepts and model. Strasbourg: Council of Europe.
Currie, G. 2020. *Imagining and knowing: The shape of fiction*. Oxford: Oxford University Press.
Dodell-Feder, D., and D.I. Tamir. 2018. Fiction reading has a small positive impact on social cognition: A meta-analysis. *Journal of Experimental Psychology: General* 147 (11): 1713–1727.
EC (European Commission). 2014. Report on the role of public arts and cultural institutions in the promotion of cultural diversity and intercultural dialogue. Open Method of Coordination (Omc) Working Group of EU Member States Experts. Brussels: European Commission. https://ec.europa.eu/assets/eac/culture/library/reports/201405-omc-diversity-dialogue_en.pdf. Accessed 8 May 2020.
Eisner, E.W. 2008. Art and knowledge. In *Handbook of the arts in qualitative research*, ed. J.G. Knowles and A.L. Cole, 3–12. London: Sage.
Elias, A. 2017. Racism, anti-racism and intercultural dialogue. In *Interculturalism at the crossroads: Comparative perspectives on concepts, policies, and practices*, ed. F. Mansouri, 257–276. Paris: Unesco.
Fialho, O. 2019. What is literature for? The role of transformative reading. *Cogent Arts & Humanities* 6: 1–16.
Flensner, K.K., and M. Von der Lippe. 2019. Being safe from what and safe for whom? A critical discussion of the conceptual metaphor of 'safe space.' *Intercultural Education* 30 (3): 275–288.

Foucault, M. 1984. Of other spaces: Utopias and heterotopias. *Architecture /Mouvement/ Continuité* 5: 46–49.
Gonçalves, S., and S. Majhanovich. 2016. *Art and intercultural dialogue*. Leiden: Brill.
Halberstam, J. 2018 [2016]. Trigger happy. From content warning to censorship. In *The power of vulnerability. Mobilising affect in feminist, queer and anti-racist media cultures*, ed. A. Koivunen, K. Kyrölä, and I. Ryberg, 51–58. Manchester: Manchester University Press.
Haraway, D.J. 1988. Situated knowledges: The science question in feminism and the privilege of partial perspective. *Feminist Studies* 14 (3): 575–599.
Holley, L.C., and S. Steiner. 2005. Safe space: Student perspectives on classroom environment. *Journal of Social Work Education* 41 (1): 49–64.
Houghton, S.A. 2012. *Intercultural dialogue in practice: Managing value judgement through foreign language education*. Bristol: Channel View Publications.
Jackson, R. 2014. *Signposts—policy and practice for teaching about religions and non-religious world views in intercultural education*. Strasbourg: Council of Europe.
Jeffers, C.S. 2009. Within connections: Empathy, mirror neurons, and art education. *Art Education* 62 (2): 18–23.
Kidd, D.C., and E. Castano. 2013. Reading literary fiction improves theory of mind. *Science* 342 (6156): 377–380.
Knauth, T., and D. Vieregge. 2019. Researching religion-related dialog in schools—theoretical and methodological considerations. *Religion & Education* 46 (1): 20–39.
Keen, S. 2006. A Theory of Narrative Empathy. *Narrative* 14 (3): 207–236.
Kyrölä, K. 2018. Negotiating vulnerability in the trigger warning debates. In *The power of vulnerability. Mobilising affect in feminist, queer and anti-racist media cultures*, ed. A. Koivunen, K. Kyrölä, and I. Ryberg, 29–50. Manchester: Manchester University Press.
Lähdesmäki, T. 2014. The Role of Space in the Politics of Intercultural Dialogue. In *Cultural encounter. The mosaic of urban identities*, ed. E.-N. Burduşel, O. Matiu, D. Preda, and A. Tomuş, 28–42. Sibiu: University Network of the European Capitals of Culture.
Lähdesmäki, T., P.C.C.A. Heynderickx, A. Wagener, and S.M.F. Dieltjens. 2015. Negations and negativity as linguistic devices in policy discourse of intercultural cities. *Journal of Multicultural Discourses* 10 (3): 332–348.
Lähdesmäki, T., A.-K. Koistinen, and S. Ylönen. 2020. *Intercultural dialogue in the European education policies: A conceptual approach*. New York: Palgrave Macmillan.
Lähdesmäki, T., and A. Wagener. 2015. Discourses on governing diversity in Europe: Critical analysis of the White Paper on intercultural dialogue. *International Journal of Intercultural Relations* 44: 13–28.
Leavy, P. 2017. *Research design: Quantitative, qualitative, mixed methods, arts-based, and community-based participatory research approaches*. New York: Guilford Publications.
Lee, E.L. 2016. Intercultural dialogue in theory and practice: A review. *Journal of Multicultural Discourses* 11 (2): 236–242.
Lefebvre, H. 1991. *The production of space*. Oxford: Blackwell.
Maine, F., V. Cook, and T. Lähdesmäki. 2019. Reconceptualizing cultural literacy as a dialogic practice. *London Review of Education* 17 (3): 382–391.
Massey, D. 2005. *For space*. London: Sage.
Modood, T., and N. Meer. 2012. How does interculturalism contrast with multiculturalism? *Journal of Intercultural Studies* 33 (2): 175–196.
Näss, H. E. 2010. The ambiguities of intercultural dialogue: Critical perspectives on the European Union's new agenda for culture. *Journal of Intercultural Communication* 23. https://www.immi.se/intercultural/nr23/nass.htm. Accessed 8 May 2020.
Nussbaum, M. 2010. *Not for profit. Why democracy needs the humanities*. Princeton: Princeton University Press.
Ratzmann, N. 2019. *Intercultural dialogue. A review of conceptual and empirical issues relating to social transformation*. Paris: UNESCO.

Pauwels, L. 2015. 'Participatory' visual research revisited: A critical-constructive assessment of epistemological, methodological, and social activists tenets. *Ethnography* 16 (1): 95–117.
Polvinen, M., and H. Sklar. 2019. Mimetic and synthetic views of characters: How readers process "people" in fiction. *Cogent Arts & Humanities* 6 (1): 1–15.
Rodríguez-García, D. 2010. Beyond assimilation and multiculturalism: A critical review of the debate on managing diversity. *Journal of International Migration and Integration* 11 (3): 251–271.
Silvestri, S. 2007. *Policy brief: Islam and the EU: The merits and risks of intercultural dialogue*. Brussels: European Policy Centre.
Smith, A. 2006. Cognitive empathy and emotional empathy in human behavior and evolution. *the Psychological Record* 56 (1): 3–21.
Soja, E. 1996. *Thirdspace: Journeys to Los Angeles and other real-and-imagined places*. Oxford: Blackwell.
Stout, C.J. 1999. The art of empathy: Teaching students to care. *Art Education* 52 (2): 21–34.
Taylor, C. 2012. Interculturalism or multiculturalism? *Philosophy and Social Criticism* 38 (4–5): 413–423.
UNESCO. 1996. *Our creative diversity*. Paris: UNESCO.
Velasco, J. S. 2019. In search of empathy in prehistoric times: Evolution and revolution. In *Empathy: Emotional, ethical and epistemological narratives*, ed. R. Gutiérrez Aguilar, 7–27. Leiden: Brill.
Venäläinen, P. 2019. *Nykytaide oppimisen ympäristönä. Näkemyksiä nykytaiteesta, oppimisesta ja niiden kohtaamisesta*. Dissertation. Jyväskylä: University of Jyväskylä Press.
Vertovec, S. 2007. *New complexities of cohesion in Britain: Super-diversity, transnationalism and civil-integration*. Wetherby: Communities and Local Government Publications.
Vertovec, S., and S. Wessendorf. 2010. Introduction: Assessing the backlash against multiculturalism. In *The multiculturalism backlash: European discourses, policies and practices*, ed. S. Vertovec and S. Wessendorf, 1–31. New York: Routledge.
Weik von Mossner, A. 2017. *Affective ecologies: Empathy, emotion, and environmental narrative*. Columbus: The Ohio State University Press.
Wiesand, A., I. Heiskanen, R. Mitchell, D. Cliché, M. Fisher, and L. Marsio. 2008. *Sharing diversity. National approaches to intercultural dialogue in Europe*. Bonn: European Institute for Comparative Cultural Research.
Wilson, R. 2013. The urgency of intercultural dialogue in a Europe of insecurity. In *Interculturalism and multiculturalism: Similarities and differences*, ed. M. Barrett, 53–68. Strasbourg: Council of Europe.

Tuuli Lähdesmäki (PhD in Art History and DSocSc in Sociology) is an Associate Professor at the Department of Music, Art and Culture Studies, University of Jyväskylä, Finland (JYU). She has led JYU's consortium partnership in the DIALLS project.

Aino-Kaisa Koistinen (PhD in Contemporary Culture Studies) is a Postdoctoral Researcher at the Department of Music, Art and Culture Studies, University of Jyväskylä, Finland. Her research in the DIALLS project has focused on education policies and pupils' visual creations.

Chapter 5
Using Wordless Picturebooks as Stimuli for Dialogic Engagement

Fiona Maine and Beci McCaughran

5.1 Introduction

In this chapter we explore how collaborative meanings can be made as teachers and young children (six-year-olds) engage together in reading wordless picturebooks. The activity of talking about these visual texts was a central part of the DIALLS project as children joined together not only to make meaning from them, but also use them as stimuli for deeper philosophical thinking about themes around living together and social responsibility. The discussions gave children the opportunity to engage in 'genuine dialogue' (Buber 1947), as they co-constructed meaning from the narratives and as they then related the themes within them to their own lives, values and identities. Here we look specifically at the meaning-making process and particularly examine how the very nature of co-construction from wordless narratives is not only a dialogic process (Maine 2015, 2020) but one that undertaken with tolerance, empathy and inclusion, embodies the values of cultural literacy as a dialogic social practice (Maine et al. 2019).

The data we present in this chapter demonstrate how the language modelled by teachers and their careful guidance enables independent sense-making and collaborative co-construction as a dialogic enterprise. We examine teachers engaging their classes with two wordless narratives to understand how these can be mediated differently to enhance understanding and engagement, exploring how different reading pathways of the books affect the co-construction process. As sociocultural researchers we are deeply aware that reading events are dependent on readers, the activity and the text (Snow and Sweet 2003) and are situational occurrences (Rosenblatt 1994) that are unique to each new reading and set of readers. The teachers in

F. Maine (✉) · B. McCaughran
Faculty of Education, University of Cambridge, Cambridge, UK
e-mail: flm27@cam.ac.uk

B. McCaughran
e-mail: bm493@cam.ac.uk

F. Maine and M. Vrikki (eds.), *Dialogue for Intercultural Understanding*,
https://doi.org/10.1007/978-3-030-71778-0_5

each class approached the tasks differently of course, but the affordances we draw on are from the narrative structures themselves.

A key theme of the DIALLS project was the recognition of the multimodality of literacy and expression of culture. Wordless narratives (picturebooks which tell their stories through visuals rather than verbal means) were chosen as the stimuli for discussion not only because of the convenience of their transferability for different language users but also because of their inherent gaps of meaning (Iser 1978) that afford a dialogic space of possibility (Maine 2015) in their interpretations. In Chapter 6, Rodosthenous-Balafa, Chatzianastasi and Stylianou-Georgiou present a deep exploration of such affordances in two such wordless picturebooks from a literary perspective, whilst in this chapter we look at their use in the classroom.

5.2 The Affordances of Wordless Picturebooks

'Wordless picturebooks', 'silent books', or 'picturebooks with sparse verbal text' are all labels given to picturebooks that include few or no words at all to communicate their meaning. A common misconception might be that these texts are designed for non-readers or very young children, yet the growth of the wordless picturebook market has generated a rich resource of challenging, ambiguous texts for all ages.[1] Ghiso and McGuire (2007, 355–356) argue that "quite the opposite of watered down or simplified picturebooks they are in fact a distillation – a concise presentation of all the essential features of literature" and that, "it is precisely the brevity of the verbal text and the associated challenges to the reader that open up a space for close looking and deep discussion" (ibid.). The picturebooks in this study use language in their titles, and these could be considered to set the tone of the story. Bosch would describe them as 'almost' wordless (2014, 74) rather than 'pure' wordless, as in addition to the title, author and publisher, they contain a short blurb on the back cover. However, this then raises an interesting question about language. As part of our commitment to a wide representation of texts in our project, books were sourced from around Europe. The blurbs are in a language which the children in the classes did not speak; for them then, these *were* pure wordless texts as they could not garner extra clues about the books from their blurbs. Rather than making judgements about the categorization of wordlessness being to do with a quantity of words, Arizpe argues it is, "the degree to which readers are expected to actively engage that marks the difference between picturebooks with and without words and which enables the reader to co-construct meaning" (2014, 96–97). In previous work (Maine 2015, 19) we describe this as a "dialogic space of possibility" drawing on the work of reader response theorists such as Rosenblatt (1994) and Iser (1978) to reflect reading as a transaction of meaning. Where there are no words present then this dialogic space is enhanced by the readers' collaborative interpretations of the images.

[1]In the DIALLS project, texts for 14 and 15 year-olds often discussed challenging and sensitive issues, see https://dialls2020.eu/library-en/.

5.3 Reading Visual Narratives

We make sense of the world through the construction of narratives; storytelling is a central feature of child-(and adult-)hood and, in fact, Hardy suggests that narrative is "a primary act of mind" (Hardy 1977, 12). Stories are motivating for young children as they can represent and reflect back their lives, offering a chance for deep thinking about their worlds. Stories offering moral challenges give children a chance to explore these without being personally involved, to explore their own thinking and values and those of others.

Mackey (2004) draws on the (1987) work of Rabinowitz in her work exploring how children make sense of narratives. Rabinowitz suggests a set of rules apply; the rule of noticing (what to pay attention to); of significance (how do we use what we know to help us understand); and configuration (putting the parts together so it makes sense). Mackey notes, "we notice and signify in accordance with what kind of pattern of events we anticipate, and we put pieces together in order to make sense along the lines of a particular paradigm" (2004, 51). In wordless narratives, "the visual image carries the weight of the meaning" (Arizpe et al. 2014, 34). In his work, Serafini draws on a history of semiotic research to create a similar framework for interpreting what he calls "multimodal ensembles" (2014, 11) picking out perceptual (including noticing, navigating and naming elements), structural (looking at the grammars of narrative and the visual design) and ideological (situating understandings with a sociocultural context) layers of meaning.

Picturebooks can have different reading pathways that draw on both temporal and spatial dynamics. In some wordless picturebooks the story unfolds through the "openings" (Ghiso and McGuire 2007, 347; Serafini 2014, 77) with linear logic (Kress 2003; Kress and van Leeuwen 2006) even if on each page the images are simultaneously present, offering the challenge of determining the importance of the visuals presented.[2] Other picturebooks present a less apparent storyline, instead offering a series of connected images from which the reader must create their own story. This allows each reader to bring to the fore their own interests and interpretations meaning the reader response is truly individual and situational (Rosenblatt 1994).

Beyond the particular pathways of reading these visual texts, however, is the need for a literacy that enables us to unlock different elements of the visual code presented. Placement, color, size of image and composition, all give us clues to intended meaning, but just as 'decoding' words in verbal texts is just the start of reading for meaning, so 'noticing and naming' is only the surface level of being visually literate. As Arizpe and colleagues describe, visual literacy provides, "a way of deepening understanding and critical appreciation through the readers active engagement in the interpretative process" (2014, 31). The affordance of the wordless

[2]It should not be assumed that this means a movement from left to right. In the DIALLS project some picturebooks were produced in Arabic speaking countries, and whilst still wordless, their reading logic led from right to left, fitting with the conventions of the Arabic language, and verbal book traditions. See more at www.dialls2020.eu/library-en/.

picturebook is the opportunity to look spatially in addition to linearly to enrich the reading experience, to slow down the reading and experience the ensemble.

In their work exploring teacher mediations of what they call "picturebooks with sparse verbal text", Ghiso and McGuire (2007, 341) provide a useful framework of teacher utterances they found in readalouds, and these relate to the visual literacy and narrative interpretation layers. They describe "visual analysis strategies" (347), that include supporting children to develop denoting or noticing skills. Further categories include "probing for underlying relationships" between characters depicted and "building a cohesive whole" (361). As their work revolves around picturebooks which include sparse verbal text they also highlight the importance of mining any verbal text that is available.

5.4 Co-construction and Mediation

If the opportunities for discussion, open and imaginative interpretation and co-constructive meaning-making are afforded by the modes of wordless narrative, then this presents a powerful opportunity for teachers to enable this intersubjective enterprise. A dialogic classroom which embraces an ethos of collaboration, underpinned by collective, purposeful, reciprocal principles (Alexander 2020) serves as a rich environment for teachers and children to make the most of these visual reading experiences. However, this goal does not come without its challenges. Dombey (2010) highlights four dimensions to be considered when sharing a text together: who decides the stance of the discussion; who controls the turns taking; who has interpretive authority and who chooses the topics?

In their study of nine different reading contexts, Soter and colleagues (2008) found that authentic questioning and uptake by teachers played a significant part in effective discussions. The researchers also highlighted the role of modelling on the part of the teacher to support children's reasoning. Taking this further, Nystrand (2006) argues that successful approaches involve "elaborative interrogations" (397) where children are probed to make explicit the connections that they are making to their prior knowledge and experience. The research by these authors highlights the importance of the themes for discussion being led by the children and framed by teachers, calling for careful, considered mediation by teachers not leading children to the 'correct' interpretation, but honoring their own sense-making (Aukerman 2013).

We now turn to an exploration of this visual literacy in action, as we illustrate the processes of co-construction in two classes reading picturebooks offering different reading pathways.

The wider DIALLS project involved capturing video recorded data from a number of lessons where children and teachers explored wordless texts together. In this chapter we draw on video data from these two classes from lessons that were not part of the core DIALLS data. Classroom talk was transcribed verbatim, and significant gestures were noted. The researchers were present in the classes and made observational notes to support their analysis of the videoed data. In one case the teacher is a co-author of this chapter. Children's names have been changed to anonymize them, but with consent, the teachers retain their first names. In the transcript, emphasis on words is shown through capitalization.

5.5 Class 1: Reading *Mein Weg mit Vanessa* (Kerascoet 2018)

The first case explores Class 1 and their reading of *Mein Weg mit Vanessa* (Kerascoet 2018) hereafter *Vanessa*. This is a wordless picturebook with a linear narrative that presents a traditional reading pathway to lead the readers through their co-construction. In the story, a little girl, Vanessa, we assume, joins a new school where she is bullied by a classmate. Consequently, other children in her class have to make choices about their own actions and the book ends with the children realizing the strength of unity and teamwork as they join together to walk with Vanessa to school. The text uses space dynamically to sequence small but significant character reactions with some openings offering up to six vignettes showing development of plot over time.

In Class 1, Beci the teacher sets the scene by introducing the whole class of children to the book, inviting them to make observations about the cover and endpapers. She navigates a co-construction of the narrative, sharing, mediating and weaving the children's contributions to establish a shared interpretation of both the narrative and the complex themes it explores. The gaps of meaning (Iser 1978) afforded by the wordless nature of the text provide a rich opportunity for co-construction and the challenge for Beci is to skillfully build a cohesive whole (Ghiso and McGuire 2007). Although it could be argued that the traditional linear pathway of *Vanessa* provides increased correlation between the author's intended meaning and the reader's interpreted meaning, the situational nature of the co-construction (Rosenblatt 1994) and the specific affordances of the wordless text offer a unique and productive dialogic space of possibility (Maine 2015), and the children are able to respond to each image as they feel it to be important.

As part of their framework of conceptual categories for mediating wordless texts, Ghiso and McGuire (2007, 347) identify the need for readers to "attend to body positioning and facial expressions", as a key visual analysis strategy, and this important in *Vanessa*. Whilst the images in the picturebook are small, the faces of the characters depict subtle changes in emotion beyond simply showing sadness and happiness. In one opening, the images show the children leaving school and walking home. In the top verso (left-hand) image a scene is shown with a group of children walking ahead, Vanessa behind them and a boy behind her. All the figures are situated within a street scene showing trees and houses. The second two verso images (middle and bottom) show just Vanessa and the boy with no surrounding scenery, isolated from the other children. The boy is positioned leaning back, then forward with an angry face. The story progresses to the recto (right-hand) page where now, the figures are engulfed in a red 'haze' as the boy's anger spills out into the page. In the final recto image in the opening we see the full scene again, this time with the boy walking away left, Vanessa standing mournfully in the center, and the other group of children to the right with one of them looking back. Turning the page, the next verso image shows the same scene, but this time boy is smiling as he walks. The following interaction in the class, where the children are discussing the bully character and his interaction with Vanessa, shows that the children pay careful attention to body positioning and facial expressions and this allows a richer co-construction of the narrative, supporting them to reveal a deeper layer of meaning:

Noel: I don't really think he was mad. I just think he was a bully.
Beci: Do you? What made you think that then, Noel, because that's a bit different from what we thought before?
Noel: Because, look (*pointing to book*), he's looking quite proud of himself of what he's done to Vanessa.
Beci: Do you know, I HADN'T noticed that.
Jonny: I did.
Emily: I did.
Beci: Noel, you've changed my thinking. I thought he was just really, really angry, but you're right, he does look proud of himself, doesn't he?
Noel: (Nods).
Beci: So, you've got this little boy feeling proud of himself and Vanessa running away. Mmm…
Class: Sad.
Beci: I wonder if all the children at this school are horrible. I wonder if every single child at this school is just horrid. Lucy, what did you notice or what do you wonder?
Lucy: The little boy has a-, the angry smile on his face.

In this exchange, Beci models how she has been supported by Noel to 'look closer'. Positioning herself as a participant of the co-construction, she shows that readers can change their minds when presented with new evidence. To understand that the mean boy makes Vanessa sad is enough to carry the reader through the narrative of this book, but in noticing the pride and 'angry smile' on the boy's face, Lucy begins to use the richness of the visual text to more fully explore the complex concept and motivations of a bully. Noel is testing his narrative interpretation that the little boy is indeed a bully rather than simply a child reacting angrily to a stimulus and he does this by noticing illustrative detail. Beci supports this aspect of meaning-making by subsequently encouraging the young readers to regularly 'notice' the details on characters' faces.

A key feature of Beci's mediation of the text is that she makes the process of meaning-making explicit to the children by supporting them to understand the process of their own inference and the cultural references they engage. In the extract below Charlie has inferred that the bully is angry but struggles to identify what supported this inference:

Beci: …Charlie, what were you THINKing? What were you wondering? What were you noticing?
Charlie: I was thinking that he was saying, 'GO AWAY and go and play with someone else.'
Beci: OK. They're quite, they're quite nasty things. Why do you think they're nasty things that he's saying? What gave you a clue?
Charlie: Because he's shouting and putting his hand over there.
Beci: Hang on a minute, I can't HEAR him shouting. How did you know that he's shouting?
Charlie: Because he's angry.
Beci: How do you know? I agree with you. I think the same, but what gave you a clue?
Charlie: Because he's very cross.
Beci: Yeah, his face. Look, look at his eyeBROWS, look at his eyes.

This interaction begins as an "elaborative interrogation" (Nystrand 2006, 397) with Beci encouraging Charlie to make his connections and meaning-making explicit. Once it becomes apparent that Charlie does not yet have the ability to identify or articulate his meaning-making connections, Beci moves to guide and model these processes, helping him to notice details that enable him to see how his ideas are accountable to the text (Dombey 2010), to test his interpretation against the visual clues in the text.

This explicit identification of comprehension strategies is further developed in the following passage when Beci supports the children to identify a visual clue that they have used to infer the boy's anger, the red haze surrounding the character.

Beci: … What's special about THIS illustration here? It's quite different on the page, isn't it? What's special about it? Why is it different, Freddie?
Freddie: Probably, when someone gets angry, there, there's red all over the place.
Beci: Oh, I know what you MEAN… It's quite an angry color, isn't it? Red's quite an ANGRY color. So, you said probably he's FEELing quite red, a bit like our zones, when you're angry, we put it on the red zone, don't we?

Here, the co-construction draws on multiple cultural references; the use of red to represent anger, and a more local cultural reference to the children's classroom behavior management system where colors symbolize different emotions, the combination of which results in highly situational meaning-making (Rosenblatt 1994). This example also works to demonstrate the unique affordances of the wordless picture book in allowing different visual literacy tools to become central to the co-construction, in this case understanding the symbolic use of color. Without the use of verbal text, the author relies on the reader's interpretation of and ability to make links between different visual features and cultural references, and Beci makes Freddie's use of this strategy explicit.

In another example of engagement with *Vanessa*, the children explore a further visual feature that supports their deeper meaning making, this time moving beyond the tiny details into broader image design. The book's prominent use of pathetic fallacy across two openings symbolizes a significant turning point in the narrative: first after Vanessa has been bullied, and then where the outcome begins to look hopeful for her. In the story, a double-page spread in one opening shows a night scene of houses with two small lit windows, one in the verso page and one in the recto page. In one window we can see Vanessa, and in the other, the child who noticed her being bullied. Their separation is enhanced by their positions on opposite pages, but their unity is demonstrated through the light in their windows and how these draw the eyes of the reader. The night is dark, and the darkness is further emphasized through what we can see as rain streaks and a large dark cloud hanging over the houses.

Beci draws the children's attention to the imagery in the extract below:

Beci: Do you know what I notice? I know that even the sky is sad in this picture.
Class: Yeah.
Beci: Miserable, raining, stormy night.
George: It's all rainy.
Beci: Everything's making me feel quite sad. Natasha.
Natasha: I, I can see a tree that looks like it's fallen over.
Beci: Yeah. It's just a sad picture that one, isn't it? Let's see what's going to happen (*displays next page*). Oh, a brand-new day. Right, a BRAND new day.

Turning the page, the opening now shows a brand-new morning, with sunlight streaming through the 'friend's' window as she realizes the action she can take to support Vanessa. The children discuss this positive turn of events and how it is reflected in the image:

Beci: She's gone to VANESSA'S house, hasn't she? LOOK! Is it a sad, miserable day anymore?
Class: No…
Beci: Daniel, what kind of day is it now?
Daniel: Happy.
Beci: Happy. I'm hopeful. I'm hopeful, because I think something happy is going to happen in the story now. The colors are giving me a clue.

Scaffolding the discussion in this way supports the children in determining significance within the plot; noticing that something has changed. Daniel is able to make the visual link and although he clearly demonstrates the ability to infer the mood from the color tones of the illustrations, Beci scaffolds the links between this inference and co-construction of the narrative, to make the meaning-making explicit. As an experienced reader, she uses the phrase "I'm feeling hopeful" to support their co-construction by recognizing this pivotal change in the narrative and creates a sense of anticipation in their co-construction.

Modelling is a central feature in Beci's mediation of the text, but she also listens to the children's ideas and makes their reasoning explicit. In this way she steers the class towards a coherent co-construction. This pedagogical approach also works to include other children, as whilst they have to listen patiently as she engages with just one child, they are included by her explanation of the comprehension strategies that they can then employ for themselves.

5.6 Class 2: Reading Naar De Markt (Smit 2017)

In our second case, Class 2 were reading *Naar De Markt* (Smit 2017)[3] which offers a variation of the traditional linear narrative as a wordless picturebook with a looser, open-linear style. The openings consist of vibrant double-page spreads that follow a mother and daughter's trip to the market, alongside a number of simultaneous mini parallel stories. Goldstone (1999) argues that non-linear narratives can provide an alternative rhythm to reading and necessitate a higher degree of co-authoring and this is evident in the mediation of the text by the Class 2 teacher, Cecilia. We describe the pathway as 'open-linear' to reflect that whilst the pages show different market scenes with the central characters in each, their 'story' is not led by narrative causation, even if there are multiple smaller parallel stories shown in the background. Attention is not immediately drawn to the minor characters as the placement of an adult and child is central and recursive, leading the reader to see them as the key protagonists. That said, in the children's reading of the story, they are quickly drawn to these parallel stories and prioritize them over these central protagonists.

After exploring the title and reading the blurb in Dutch to the children (who are fascinated by the sound of the language), Cecilia turns to the first opening. The extract below shows how the children quickly seek to impose a traditional linear narrative upon the text. From the outset they show that they are searching for the story, to find a foothold for their journey through the text. Without prompting by Cecilia, the children begin:

Jay:	Once upon a time, there was, there was...
Charlotte:	A man...
Jay:	A big city full of people.
Cecilia:	Jay's sharing his version of the story. Once upon a time there was... what did you say Jay? A city?
Rose:	A big city.
Jay:	Full of lots of people.
Milly:	And there was a market.
Cecilia:	Milly said, and there was a market.
Christopher:	And people were all very busy and it was noisy and not very peaceful only at night.

The children seem to indicate a level of unease with the text and its lack of a single narrative pathway and they quickly collaborate to narrate a traditional story start.

[3]The affordance of *Naar de Markt* as a text is discussed in the next chapter in the book where Rodosthenous, Chatzianastasi, Stylianou discuss its themes of diversity.

Cecilia skillfully navigates this disquiet initially by mediating the dialogue to support the children to use simple visual literacy strategies to notice elements on the page:

Ffion: I've spotted them.
Cecilia: Tell me more -who have you spotted?
Ffion: The girl the dog and the mum.
Cecilia: You've spotted the girl the dog and the mum. Has anyone spotted, or noticed something else? Let's make sure we all have a turn (*whispers*); Josh what have you spotted?

Similar to Beci, Cecilia's technique of making the strategy of 'noticing' explicit in this way helps to children to determine the importance of key events that are happening, and Johnny moves to an interpretation:

Johnny: The people that are on the front cover must be the main people of the book.

With *Naar de Markt*, the children seem to struggle to identify the pattern or rhythm to use to track and determine significance through the text so Cecilia helps them by leading them to transactional strategies for comprehension (Pressley and Allington 2015): making connections to knowledge, determining importance, asking questions and making predictions to find out more. Once the children label the main characters on the cover, deciding they are a mother and daughter, they are provided with the hook they need to begin to explore the rich range of narratives and parallel stories on the pages as they occur around 'the mum', 'the girl' and 'the dog'. The children's determination to discover a traditional causation in the narrative, however, continues beyond identification of the main characters. The children search for a problem in need of resolution (Nodelman 1988), the evil that needs to be vanquished or the lost treasure that need to be found. Searching around the page they notice that in the foreground are oranges that appear to have fallen to the ground, and also that a previously apparent shopping bag is now missing.[4]

Cecilia: Logan said their doggy's there, but they have lost something I wonder what have they lost? Lauren thinks she knows (*Lauren waves hand*) What have they lost?
Lauren: The orange things.
Cecilia: The oranges. Harry?
Harry: That bag.
Cecilia: Which bag?
Harry: That one – the one that that man is holding.
Cecilia: So what's that man doing?
Ella: He's trying to steal it.
Cecilia: You think he's trying to steal it. You think that people are always trying to be mean and steal things. Just like the little girl was being mean and stealing the oranges.

[4]These parallel stories are considered more fully in Chapter 6.

This sense of anticipation, which results from children's experience of traditional story structures and patterns, supports them to determine significance (Mackey 2004) in the images that they see, though in this case the children overinterpret and their ideas are not completely supported by the visuals.

A key difference afforded by the reading logic of *Naar de Markt* is the opportunity to move backwards and forwards in the text to quickly check that interpretations made have validity. Cecilia supports the children to move back through the temporal space of the illustrations to discover the cause of the lost bag, "connecting and talking across pages toward synthesis" (Ghiso and McGuire 2007, 354). As the children's attention is drawn to different details in the scenes depicted, Cecilia supports their co-construction by regularly moving backwards and forwards in the book so that they can trace the origins of the parallel stories and test their theories. This enables a sophisticated resequencing of events:

Cecilia: Let's go back to this page (*turns pages*) Where were we.. on this page... She was being helpful wasn't she (*all children are engaged – many with mouths open*)

Craig: I see the man I see the man!

Cecilia's approach here is interesting as it highlights the challenge when mediating such an open text (Aukerman 2013; Dombey 2010). Keen to support the children's agency and to encourage their ideas, rather than correcting the children, she leads them back a few pages. For Craig this is the opportunity to find evidence in the text to support his theory about the thief, showing his idea to be accountable to the text, even if it presents a reading that might not be intended by the author.

The extracts from Class 2 show that scaffolding the navigation and co-construction of the open-style linear narrative encourages children to employ high-level comprehension strategies to synthesize logic of sequence and causation; to determine significance retrospectively and to hypothesize both forwards and backwards through the text. The children have to work harder to co-construct a narrative arc with causation, so they search for meanings beyond the literal level of the visual text and explore the detail to expose multiple threads of narrative that are further interpreted by moving backwards and forwards in the text. The responses from Class 2 represent the rich affordances for dialogic co-construction of the reading pathway of this open-linear narrative.

5.7 Conclusion

The extracts shown in the two cases begin to demonstrate the range of complexities facing teachers as they mediate visual texts in whole class teaching. Recent theory around dialogic education has moved the discussion away from analysis of individual interactions between teachers and children, instead considering dialogic stance and values (Aukerman and Boyd 2020; Alexander 2020). In addition to their teaching of visual literacy and text comprehension, these teachers are also facilitating a dialogic ethos in the class where children feel included and learn to be tolerant and empathetic to the ideas of each other, values situated at the heart of the DIALLS project. As such, the affordance of ambiguous, visually stimulating texts is clear. With no 'correct' answers, and an open dialogic space between reader and text, children are able to explore possibilities for interpretations alongside each other, and importantly, their teacher, who can genuinely co-construct meaning alongside the children.

It is important that visual narratives (not just picturebooks, but films and video games too) are not seen as homogenous, requiring the same simple technical skills of visual literacy to interpret. As shown in this chapter, even two seemingly similar cases demonstrate the flexibility afforded by reading pathways not limited by verbal temporal logic. Movements backwards and forwards through the text helps readers to quickly identify important details that may only become apparent at later stages of the story.

This means that teachers need to be prepared, as Cecilia and Beci were, to adopt alternative styles and pathways of mediation: simultaneously balancing the duality of their role as participants in the co-construction who *also* hold responsibility for supporting other participant's meaning-making skills and dialogic competency. This role is complicated and requires chains of responsive micro-decisions to realize the potential of the dialogic space between readers and text and between readers themselves (Maine 2015). These decisions happen in the moment and will not always capture the rich affordance of children's interpretations. With each child's contribution, teachers have to decide instantly whether to move the discussion forward with the whole class, or take an opportunity to engage extensively with one child to help them make their connections and meaning-making explicit, to add or respond personally to the co-construction or to act proactively in some way to promote inclusivity. The explorations above suggest that using a diverse range of texts, modes and reading pathways, and trusting in the dialogic space of possibility they provide will itself support practitioners to navigate and balance their multi-faceted role. Rich texts and dialogic spaces will produce naturally rich co-constructions and each reading pathway offers new structures for this co-construction.

References

Alexander, R. 2020. *A dialogic teaching companion.* London: Routledge.

Arizpe, E. 2014. Wordless picturebooks: Critical and educational perspectives on meaning-making. In *Picturebooks: Representation and narration*, ed. B. Kümmerling-Meibauer, 91–108. New York: Routledge.

Arizpe, E., T. Colomer, and C. Martínez-Roldán. 2014. *Visual journeys through wordless narratives: An international inquiry with immigrant children and* The Arrival. London: Bloomsbury.

Aukerman, M. 2013. Rereading comprehension pedagogies: Toward a dialogic teaching ethic that honors student sensemaking. *Dialogic Pedagogy: An International Online Journal* 1. https://doi.org/10.5195/dpj.2013.9.

Aukerman, M., and M.P. Boyd. 2020. Mapping the terrain of dialogic literacy pedagogies. In *International handbook of research on dialogic education*, ed. N. Mercer, R. Wegerif, and L. Major, 373–385. London: Routledge.

Bosch, E. 2014. Texts and peritexts in wordless and almost wordless picturebooks. In *Picturebooks: Representation and narration*, ed. B. Kümmerling-Meibauer, 71–90. New York: Routledge.

Buber, M. 1947. *Between man and man*, trans. R.G. Smith. London: Routledge.

Dombey, H. 2010. Interaction and learning to read: Towards a dialogic approach. In *The Routledge international handbook of English, language and literacy teaching*, ed. D. Wyse, R. Andrews, and J. Hoffman, 110–121. London: Routledge.

Ghiso, M., and C. McGuire. 2007. 'I talk them through it': Teacher mediation of picturebooks with sparse verbal text during whole-class readalouds. *Literacy Research and Instruction* 46 (4): 341–361.

Goldstone, B. 1999. Traveling in new directions: Teaching non-linear picture books. *The Dragon Lode* 18 (1): 26–29. https://citeseerx.ist.psu.edu/viewdoc/download?doi=10.1.1.520.1344&rep=rep1&type=pdf. Accessed 29 June 2020

Hardy, B. 1977. Narrative as a primary act of mind. In *The cool web: The pattern of children's reading*, ed. M. Meek, A. Warlow, and G. Barton. London: The Bodley Head.

Iser, W. 1978. *The act of reading: A theory of aesthetic response.* London: John Hopkins Press.

Kerascoët. 2018. *Mein Weg mit Vanessa.* Hamburg: Aladin.

Kress, G. 2003. *Literacy in the new media age.* London: Routledge.

Kress, G., and T. van Leeuwen. 2006. *Reading images: The grammar of visual design.* London: Routledge.

Mackey, M. 2004. Children reading and interpreting stories in print, film and computer games. In *Literacy moves on: Using popular culture, new technologies and critical literacy in the primary classroom*, ed. J. Evans, 48–58. London: David Fulton.

Maine, F. 2015. *Dialogic readers: Children talking and thinking together about visual texts.* London: Routledge.

Maine, F. 2020. Reading as a transaction of meaning-making: Exploring the dialogic space between texts and readers. In *International handbook of research on dialogic education*, ed. N. Mercer, R. Wegerif, and L. Major, 336–347. London: Routledge.

Maine, F., V. Cook, and T. Lähdesmäki. 2019. Reconceptualizing cultural literacy as a dialogic practice. *London Review of Education* 17 (3): 384–393.

Nodelman, P. 1988. *Words about pictures: The narrative art of children's picture books.* Athens: University of Georgia Press.

Nystrand, M. 2006. Research on the role of classroom discourse as it affects reading comprehension. *Research in the Teaching of English* 40 (4): 392–412.

Pressley, M., and R. Allington. 2015. *Reading instruction that works: The case for balanced reading.* New York: Guilford Press.

Rosenblatt, L.M. 1994. *The reader, the text, the poem: The transactional theory of the literary work.* Carbondale and Edwardsville: Southern Illinois University Press.

Serafini, F. 2014. *Reading the visual: An introduction to teaching multimodal literacy.* New York: Teachers College Press.

Smit, N. 2017. *Naar de Markt*. Amsterdam: Querido.
Snow, C., and A. Sweet. 2003. Reading for comprehension. In *Rethinking reading comprehension*, ed. A. Sweet and C. Snow, 1–11. London: The Guilford Press.
Soter, A.O., I.A. Wilkinson, P.K. Murphy, L. Rudge, K. Reninger, and M. Edwards. 2008. What the discourse tells us: Talk and indicators of high-level comprehension. *International Journal of Educational Research* 47 (6): 372–391.

Fiona Maine is a Senior Lecturer in literacy education at the University of Cambridge. Her research focusses on the responses of children as they read multimodal texts together. She is the principal Investigator of DIALLS.

Beci McCaughran is Co-Headteacher at Fulbourn Primary School and part-time Literacy Tutor at the University of Cambridge. She is a Lead Teacher on the DIALLS project.

Chapter 6
Creative Ways to Approach the Theme of Cultural Diversity in Wordless Picturebooks Through Visual Reading and Thinking

Marina Rodosthenous-Balafa, Maria Chatzianastasi, and Agni Stylianou-Georgiou

6.1 Introduction

Cultural diversity, as one of the most important characteristics of European community in the framework of the DIALLS project (see Chapter 1 for overview), is integral to notions of cultural identity and cultural literacy. The acknowledgement of identity formation as an ongoing, dynamic process through interaction rather than a preconceived characteristic arises as an imperative need, in order to encourage democracy to thrive through constructive confrontation and integration (Rapanta et al. 2020). According to Bland, picturebooks that authentically reflect cultural diversity can move even young readers towards "flexibility of perspective" (2016, 45). Bishop (1990) highlights the need for young readers to recognise themselves in books they read, learn about the lives of other people, and be able to cross between groups and worlds. However, reading wordless picturebooks can be a challenging task, because of the ambiguity and open nature of their visually rendered narratives. The affordances of wordless picturebooks and the challenges embedded in their reading are discussed by the authors in Chapter 5 of this volume. This chapter presents several creative ways to analyze and approach the theme of cultural diversity in class, through various disciplinary lenses and methodological approaches.

Our methodology combines elements from book and picturebook analysis drawing from the work of key theorists such as Gérard Genette, William Moebius, Emma Bosch, Perry Nodelman, Frank Serafini and Evelyn Arizpe. Specifically, it considers peritextual elements, characters and visual codes such as color, position, perspective, size, frames and line work together to represent cultural diversity. Focusing on the wordless picturebooks *Naar de Markt* (2017), by Noëlle Smit, and *Zaterdag* (2018), by Saskia Halfmouw, which reflect diversity through multiple layers

M. Rodosthenous-Balafa (✉) · M. Chatzianastasi · A. Stylianou-Georgiou
Department of Education, University of Nicosia, Nicosia, Cyprus
e-mail: rodosthenous.m@unic.ac.cy

F. Maine and M. Vrikki (eds.), *Dialogue for Intercultural Understanding*,
https://doi.org/10.1007/978-3-030-71778-0_6

and ways, our analysis addresses the complexity and plurality of a picturebook and of the various readings that emerge through the different disciplinary perspectives and experiences of readers. It is useful to mention that the particular books belong to a subgenre of wordless books called 'wimmelbooks' (Rémi 2011). Such books display a series of panoramas involving richness in detail and a large number of characters. This kind of book heightens the role of readers and allows them to find their own way through their rich material as they engage in manifold reading options (Rémi 2011). In order to highlight the significance of such layered readings in a classroom setting, this chapter suggests using "thinking routines" from Project Zero (Ritchhart et al. 2011) that encourage the exploration of multiple viewpoints as a way to enrich students' understanding of cultural diversity. Our choice of such techniques suits well the affordances of picturebooks, since they allow readers to acknowledge cultural diversity, arising from the visual narrative of each book, through zoom-in or zoom-out perspectives.

6.2 *Naar de Markt*

A substantial expression of cultural diversity as well as of the richness in the heritages comprising contemporary societies can be found in Noëlle Smit's *Naar de Markt* [*To the Market*], a thirty-two-page long picturebook depicting an outdoor market, published in the Netherlands in 2017 by Querido Publishers. On every double-page spread[1] of this book, readers are invited to follow a mother and her daughter around the market and explore its multisensory experiences. Vendors promoting local goods and diverse people walking and shopping around the market represent a diverse community. Each double-page spread features a different market stall and stages the dynamic encounter and interactions between people. "The effect of this is celebratory; the book demonstrates that European identity is by definition diverse and encourages readers to consider the role of food and shopping in their own life, local community, and European community" (DIALLS 2018, 56).

The book's covers work as the starting point of this visual narrative. On the front cover, a mother and a daughter—we assume—are walking among the trees, holding a shopping basket each while their dog stares at a bird on top of a white and yellow tent in the distance. As they turn their backs to the reader, the image invites readers to follow them and make hypotheses about the content of the book. A straight diagonal line—the dog's leash—also draws attention to the dog on the lower right quadrant of the image. The image of the dog, which repeats itself in the title page, elicits hypotheses about its role in the narrative. Just like the book's characters, the role of the dog seems significant since it is involved in the multiple parallel stories taking place in the book from a diverse point of view that enhances the richness and diversity

[1]Double-page spread is a term referring to an illustration spreading across two facing pages (opening). In the two picturebooks discussed in this chapter all the openings are double-page spreads (see Serafini 2014, 76–77).

of the market experience. On the back cover, the pair is seen riding their bikes, moving inwards to the right of the page, as if they are entering the scene. Their bikes are loaded with empty shopping baskets and the dog appears in the bicycle's basket.

The title helps to clarify the content of the two cover pictures for readers. Specifically, *Naar de Markt* is a thematic title, meaning that it suggests the subject matter of the book (Genette 2001). There is a direct link between the title and the content of the book. Paying attention to the title, readers can assume that the pair presented on the cover pictures might be heading towards a marketplace and this is the reason why they are carrying their shopping baskets with them. Beckett (2012) notes, "If the title is considered a paratextual element, it is certainly the most important one and the most intimately linked to the text itself" (117). Exploring the title can prepare readers for the market they are about to see. It orientates and contextualises the reading, providing readers with clues in order to interpret both the visual signs of covers, as well as those inside the book (Bosch 2014). Although it can answer some of the potential hypotheses inspired by the images regarding where mother and daughter are heading, this brief title also creates some space for readers to make their own interpretations (see the discussion in Chapter 5).

Opening the book, a bird's eye view of a number of colorful umbrellas features on the endpapers. The endpapers—"elements of the overall format and design of the book"—are deliberately chosen to suit the mood and tone of the book and can be essential in the storytelling process (Gamble 2013, 210). Here, the choice of this endpaper illustration has both literal and metaphorical connotations, as a coded marker of diversity. Recognizing signs like this is essential in reading what this visually rich book has to offer, especially because "picturebooks are artefacts that convey cultural ideas to help readers learn about their world" (Koss 2015, 32). Moving from what is noticed in the visual images towards its meaning is therefore an important aspect of the comprehension process (Serafini 2011). Important elements to be considered here in how they convey meaning are borders, line, and color. In the book, the absence of borders allows the illustrations to bleed into the edges of the page. The absence of borders can offer a more holistic reading experience, allowing readers to connect with the artistic elements of illustration and see things from within. Because of the richness of the visual experience offered by the illustrations of *Naar de Markt*, it is very important that the reader pauses and slows down in order to connect and engage with visual codes to make sense of both the artistic elements and the cultural connotations these have to offer. Lines, which define the objects on the page, are evidently absent, drawing readers attention to the use of color. Color can be considered "one of the most emotionally evocative artistic elements", meaning that it is particularly suitable for suggesting symbolic associations (Giorgis et al. 1999, 148; Gamble 2013). The wide range of colors used in this vibrant depiction of the market can help readers to recognize cultural diversity, through differences in the color or clothes, objects, or even skin and hair showing that diversity is everywhere.

These elements can be recognized in the first double-page spread of the book, which opens the story with a panoramic bird's eye view revealing the market, as well as in the next pages. The tents and umbrellas spread out under the trees between two lines of buildings. The focal point of the page is the market in the center of the picture, with people coming and going. On the lower right corner of the page, the mother and daughter are seen with their dog. The two function as a guide for readers to follow throughout the pages. Their white clothes let them stand out and be spotted easily in the otherwise full of color setting; the neutral white color creates an antithesis of the other bold colors used in each page.

Following the two protagonists, readers get the opportunity to visit first a Dutch fish market and a stall with seafood delicacies. Next is a butchers' stall with different types of sausages, and large pieces of meat hanging from the top, as well as a rich variety of meats. The shopping continues to a fruit market stall, with green and white patterns on its tent. There is also a cheese market stall, a market table with olives and other delicacies, a bakery stall, a book seller, a seller of dresses and hats, a flower market, and a corner stall with second-hand items. As mother and daughter continue their shopping from one stall to another, readers get the opportunity to explore the various cultural markers hidden in the illustration such as the color patterns possibly pointing to the flags of specific countries, the traditional costumes or products traditionally linked to specific cultures and heritages. The variety of goods and food sold in this market as well as the cultural markers that some readers can identify on the pages of the books point towards the richness of diversity in the heritages at the roots of many European societies. Crucially, however, reading this book in the class needs to be done with a sense of caution to avoid stereotyping diversity and reproducing a representation of cultures that can challenge the acceptance and celebration of such diversity.

While the shopping continues, diversity is also revealed as parallel stories and incidents unfold. A cat leaves its owner and steals smoked anchovies from a vendor, who angrily follows the cat. An old lady turns to look at what is happening, while another lady, who is later seen living with her cat in an apartment with a balcony above the market, keeps walking indifferently. The young girl stops to help a lady collect the oranges that have fallen on the ground, and leaves her basket behind, while she later tries some cheese with her mother. When she finally realizes she lost her basket, a man, who found it, approaches the girl to return it. People of different ages, gender, backgrounds, origins, national and cultural identities, color, and status equally coexist in this colorful and rich celebration of diversity and cultural heritages. Vendors and customers with traditional clothes or garments, people from next door with different personalities and styles, as well as people from minority groups, all have an active role in this book. They mix and mingle, communicate, and interact with each other, transforming the market into a place of social and cultural encounters and intercultural exchanges, visually helping readers to experience cultural diversity. This attests to Bland's argument that, by demonstrating the commonality of human experience and opening a space for the exploration of cultural identities and the ability to change perspective, picturebooks can potentially contribute to the acquisition of intercultural competence (2016). Each character in this visual narrative carries his/her own story, but at the same time, each is offered the opportunity to negotiate his/her identity and be influenced by others.

This identity formation in relation to others' cultural identity is finally celebrated in the last double-page spread of the book in which the mother prepares a party table with all the goods and food she bought. All the different heritages are evident through the items on the table. Previously dressed in white, the mother and daughter now wear the dresses they bought from the market; the change from neutral white may symbolically reflect the continuous process of one's construction of cultural identity in relation to the identities of others. Mother and daughter work as examples of an "individual's disposition and competence to encounter cultural differences and to elaborate one's own identity in respectful social interaction with other people", which is integral in the DIALLS' reconceptualization of cultural literacy (Maine et al. 2019, 387). This competence can also be recognized in the multiplicity of recurring characters, appearing in *Zaterdag*, the second Dutch wordless picturebook that is discussed next.

6.3 *Zaterdag*

Zaterdag is a wordless picturebook by Saskia Halfmouw published by Leopold Editions in Amsterdam in 2018. It is a book about various activities people selectively do throughout the year "on the best day of the week"; that is Saturday, which is also the translation of the book's title in English. The picturebook is a series of twelve facing pages (openings), representing one setting at a time and various characters who do different activities within that setting. Number twelve also echoes the twelve months of the year, showing how, in particular, countries' activities on Saturdays could vary from season to season.

Starting from the first opening, readers face several football fields, where mixed teams of children play; the second one is a central square, with open food markets, restaurants, and apartment buildings; the third one is a supermarket; an indoor swimming pool follows, then a library, a beach, several neighborhood playgrounds, a forest, an open market with a variety of goods, a dinosaur museum, a ski resort, and finally a Christmas decorated piazza. All illustrations of settings have a panoramic perspective, and they are unframed, "constituting", according to Moebius (1986), "a total experience, the view from 'within'" (50).

Before exploring the cultural dimensions of the content and the characters of the book, the reader might find it useful to focus on its peritextual elements (Genette 1997) such as the note on the back cover, the note by the illustrator or the publisher at the left-hand side (verso) of the title page, and the notes on the final endpapers of the picturebook. All these brief verbal texts provide clues about the content of the specific wordless book and help the reader decode certain dimensions of the visual narrative, since it has multiple meanings and perspectives.

The note on the back cover is in red typeface and functions as an alternative "summary" of the wordless picturebook to help readers decide whether the picturebook is interesting to them:

> Finally. It's Saturday. No school. What do you do on the best day of the week? Playing football, swimming, going to the supermarket or on an adventure in the dinosaur museum...

> Wander through this large viewing and search the book, which is full of Saturday fun. Can you find everyone?

Another note (in smaller, black characters) is added below, introducing the illustrator, who is well-known in her country for illustrating a famous book character by Paul van Loon called Foeksia, who is a little witch in a purple hat.

Although the above final note refers to the variety of activities in which the book's characters engage every Saturday, the initial note inside the book concentrates on the variety of the main characters themselves:

> Can you find everyone? Find the cowboy boy, the escaped dog, the boy with the ball, famous book characters, and many more children, dads, moms, grandfathers and grandmothers. Can you also recognize a fairy tale figure on every opening?
>
> You will find the solution on the endpaper in the back.

Both notes include the question "Can you find everyone?", which makes the whole procedure of reading the visual narrative a game. Bosch points out: "Some *wordless* and *almost wordless picturebooks* include games to encourage re-reading. These games are complementary given that, if the game were the essence of the book, it would be a *game book*" (2014, 86). This specific note reveals two important hints: (a) fairy tale figures to be found in each opening; and (b) guidelines that are provided at the back endpage of the picturebook. The reader, looking at the final endpapers, observes the same exact depictions of characters that are found on the initial endpapers, with an extra addition of a note at the back verso endpage, mentioning the setting of each opening, followed by a name of a fairy tale figure. In this way, the reader realizes that the particular figures appear in certain settings, waiting to be found, and turning reading playfully multidimensional, since the reader needs to follow the story of several realistic characters as they mingle with various fictional ones.

At this point, a reader might be prompted to consider how many kinds of characters appear in *Zaterdag* and what their possible interconnections are. This question helps readers understand how culture is illustrated in this picturebook and how cultural diversity encourages a peaceful and respectful environment. Therefore, our analysis focuses on a detailed description of the different type-characters appearing in the book.

As is shown on the endpapers of the picturebook, the characters of *Zaterdag* include a variety of dogs and realistic persons of everyday life. Although the majority of characters are young children, there are characters of all ages (babies, young people, middle-aged and third-aged people). In this way, not only does *Zaterdag* depict children's activities in each setting but it presents the activities of all ages. These realistic characters, who appeared on the endpapers, are recurrent in every double-page spread, where a particular setting is presented. They are kind of "stock" characters who have distinct characteristics or duties, and the reader can easily spot them in each opening. In particular, there is an elegant seventy-year-old lady accompanied by a small dog;·a middle-aged man;·a young woman in a style like that of a mermaid (green hair, a fish-shaped bag, and a mermaid swimsuit when it is applicable); children who are in groups or stand alone, playing with their favorite toys, gadgets, or sports equipment (balls, mobiles, ski equipment); a young cowboy who has several responsibilities and carries out tasks (delivers balls to the football fields, potatoes to the market, frozen pizzas to the supermarket, ice-creams at the beach, snowballs at the ski resort, etc.); babies in buggies; children who pretend to play roles, such as pirates and donut sellers; a girl in a wheelchair or a sleigh, according to where she is. Usually, children are accompanied by their mothers or fathers, or their friends who are the same age. A total of thirty-three characters appear on the endpapers. Nuclear families are rare.[2] Dogs, unlike cats, have protagonistic roles. Seven dogs appear as stock characters on the endpapers and they usually accompany children.

Apart from these repetitive characters, there are many more everyday, secondary characters in each opening. For example, coaches appear at the football fields, whereas outside the fields, two old men are walking and chatting. There are different dogs in each opening, various sellers in the markets, people of different nationalities, grandparents of the stock characters, beggars, and homeless people. At the museum, a punk is taking a selfie in front of a dinosaur, the famous Dutch children's writer Paul van Loon can be spotted in the library, and there is a huge diversity of other people experiencing Saturday activities in the book, as in real life.

The third category of characters are fictional ones, particularly the twelve fairy tale figures mentioned on the final endpaper. These are Tom Thumb, Rapunzel, Pinocchio, the Frog Prince, Puss in Boots, Aladdin and the Wonderful Lamp, the Girl in the Red Shoes, Little Red Riding Hood, Sleeping Beauty, Cinderella, Snow White, and the Little Match Girl. Interestingly, these figures are related to the depicted background in either a more symbolic or clearer way. For example, Snow White, as her name denotes, appears at the ski resort, and the heroine in Hans Christian Andersen's story, *The Little Match Girl*, appears in the Christmas opening, sitting alone outside a shop, holding a lit match, since Andersen's story takes place on a freezing New Year's Eve. Little Red Riding Hood appears with her basket in the forest where the Big Bad Wolf lurks in the trees. Aladdin is spotted sitting on his magic carpet at the beach, which is like the beach mats the other swimmers use. In an ironic way, the sneaky Puss in Boots is on the library's staircase reading a book as a witty man. The blending of different realistic characters with completely dissimilar fairy tale characters, who represent certain positive or negative attitudes of human beings, shows in a metaphoric, fascinating, and playful way that diversity is part of life and culture.

The fourth category of characters includes famous book characters, who appear in the settings, particularly in the library, where they come to life from the books. There, the reader can spot Harry Potter dressed in a robe and holding his magic wand. Foeksia, the little witch, is hiding behind the sofa and there is also Dolfje the Werewolf, who are both characters from Paul van Loon's stories and illustrated by Saskia Halfmouw (Van Loon 2014). More book characters can be spotted by a well-informed reader, who can see the intertextual game of the illustrator.

---

[2]There is a hint on the endpapers of a same gender parent family, but it is not clear throughout the book whether this is a nuclear family or two single parents, getting along with each other.

The fifth category of characters that take part are those drawn by children, and they "revive" while watching the kids playing. Between the paintings and real life, there is often confusion, and this is illustrated by a realistic dog that wants to get acquainted with a painted dog (see the opening of the neighborhood playgrounds). These imaginary characters can be found in the museum, where a girl is drawing a dinosaur on a floor; in the snow at the ski resort; on the street in the open market; and in the sand at the beach.

It is without a doubt that *Zaterdag* is a picturebook with many intertextual connotations in relation to Saturday activities of realistic, fictional, and imaginary characters. In this way, the cultural diversity element appears at multiple levels, first, through the appearance of folk characters and characters of eponymous literary history, and their interaction with realistic characters. The fictional characters, just like the realistic ones, come from different cultures and narratives, and share different mentalities and ways of living. Despite all that, their coexistence in the setting is harmonious and fully acceptable. The second aspect of cultural diversity in this picturebook is relevant to social interaction (either direct or indirect) and acceptance of the *other*, who is of different nationality, gender, age, style, abilities, needs, or tastes. All people live together in the same community, in different but peaceful and respectful ways. All twelve openings of this picturebook do not simply show the variety of activities one can do on the best day of the week but they comprise a significant tool to approach cultural diversity in and outside the class.

6.4 Creative Practices of Approaching Cultural Identity Wordless Picturebooks

Our analysis of *Naar de Markt* and *Zaterdag* has shown that picturebooks' visual richness offers various paths of interpretation—a point also made in Chapter 5—that may give rise to students' multiple points of view and encourage the expression of diverse ideas. Arizpe suggests that classroom practices involving wordless picturebooks do not take into account their "particular nature" and the "heightened role of the reader" (2013, 164). There is to date no systematic study of what Nodelman (1988, 191) refers to as the "communicative powers of visual codes" in wordless books.

The following approaches consider the two wordless books examined above as points of reference to start a visual reading journey towards a creative play of perspective-taking to unfold multi-layered meanings. We consider learning to read a wordless picturebook as an enculturation process (Brown et al. 1989). Participating in meaningful activities, readers can learn how to use thinking dispositions (Tishman et al. 1993) as tools to understand the "silent language of images" (Tan 2011, cited in Arizpe 2013, 174). Therefore, they are adopting the practice but also the set of beliefs and idiosyncrasies of the community in and out of a wordless book. Approaching wordlessness requires skillful facilitators of close reading who are willing to take the "beautiful risk" of welcoming uncertainty in the classroom (Beghetto 2017, 24), tolerating ambiguity, and communicating to readers that not everything may be answered or understood (Arizpe 2014). Readers should experience the polyphonic creative process of teaching which evolves "not in a single line of action or thought, but in several strands and directions at once, enabling the risk to be borne or not" (Burnard 2011, 58).

6.5 Using a Thinking Palette Metaphor as a Toolbox to Read Wordless Books

Using an artist's palette as a metaphor, where colors represent tools for participating in a creative process, readers can engage in visual reading by picking up the colors to create meaning. The "Artful Thinking Palette" framework has been introduced and used in the Artful Thinking Project by Project Zero at the Harvard Graduate School of Education (Tishman and Palmer 2006). According to this framework, students are encouraged to use six thinking dispositions each represented by a different color (Red: Reasoning; Blue: Questioning & Investigating; Yellow: Exploring Viewpoints; Green: Observing & Describing; Orange: Comparing & Connecting; Purple: Finding Complexity). The objective is to make thinking visible by strengthening forms of intellectual behaviors as an enculturation process (Tishman et al. 1993). Each thinking disposition has several "thinking routines" (Ritchhart et al. 2011, 43) which can be used flexibly to deepen students' thinking not only with visual art but with diverse topics in the school curriculum. This framework has been used in grades K-12 as well as in post-secondary education. We propose that the six thinking dispositions could be useful tools for guiding the reading of wordless picturebooks. In this chapter, we chose to focus on the yellow color, which involves thinking routines functioning as a zoom-in perspective to imagine things differently as well as routines for zooming-out to explore diverse perspectives.

6.5.1 Exploring Viewpoints While Reading: Diversity Through a Zoom-In Perspective

6.5.1.1 Thinking Routine "Stories"

The "Stories" thinking routine (Project Zero's Thinking Routine Toolbox, n.d.) aims to encourage rethinking the various angles of complex issues. Learners are prompted to answer three questions: "What is the story that is presented?", "What is the untold story?", and "What is your story?".

What is the story? In both wordless books, there are many stories presented. *Zaterdag*: the inhabitants of the town spend their Saturday doing diverse activities.

Naar de Markt: a mother and daughter visit an open market. Each character carries his/her/its own story.

What is the untold story? Readers are invited to observe what has been emphasized in the visuals of the two wordless picturebooks and what has been made less significant. For example, an untold story in both books is the complex issue of cultural diversity in many forms (gender, personality, objects, etc.). Educators can use questions such as: What might the characters not want us to know about? What do the characters not pay attention to or don't think about? How/Why do characters find themselves in specific settings? For example, How do fairy tale characters relate to the specific setting they appear in? (see *Zatertag)*, or How and why do vendors with various cultural heritages end up selling their products in that particular market in a Dutch town? (see *Naar de Markt)*.

What is your story? Readers are invited to bring their own perspective to the issue of cultural diversity and ask themselves: What would you do on a Saturday or what would you do at an open market? How would you rewrite the story if you were a main character? How would this story be like in your local context? How would you represent yourself in the book? How would this representation be similar/different from the existing characters?

Applying this thinking routine, reading zooms into the stories of the main characters, considering three different perspectives (told story, untold story, your own story) encouraging an intercultural understanding of diversity. Readers can think how visual symbols are used to present identity and cultural heritage in a Dutch context (i.e. of vendors and customers in *Naar de Markt* or inhabitants of a town in *Zaterdag*).

6.5.1.2 Thinking Routine "Pass the Parcel"

The "Pass the Parcel" thinking routine (Project Zero's Thinking Routine Toolbox, n.d.) is another way to encourage a zoom-in perspective through play. The well-known children's party game is used as a metaphor to foster deep learning and understanding. The layers are removed as learning and understanding deepen. With each layer unwrapped, students get closer to the prize: core knowledge, understanding. We claim that such a routine can be used with wordless picture books to provoke curiosity and introduce reading as a playful, dynamic, and interactive process. Teachers can invite students or groups to suggest what they would like to explore in a wordless picturebook. A list of key points discovered in their visual journey is created and wrapped up as a "treasure". Students continue wrapping up this treasure, placing on each layer a question that they had been asking themselves. Then, they invite other classmates in to play the game. In this way individuals or small groups could share views seen through different perspectives. For younger readers, the teacher can scaffold the process by posing students' questions for each layer.

Using this thinking routine when reading *Zaterdag* and *Naar de Markt*, readers can be prompted to choose any aspect of the book they would like to explore (i.e., characters, peoples' clothes, animal behavior, flags, products) and think how they are related to cultural diversity. For example, readers can choose a character and focus on visual symbols as expressions of their identity and how they interact with others in a multicultural context (e.g., *Zaterdag*: the girl on the wheelchair, or *Naar de Markt*: the party table with goods from various places). The treasure in this case could be a main idea arising from the books, like "diversity is everywhere." Questions for the visual journey could be: How are certain objects part of our identity? How do people coexist in a locale? Such questioning requires skillful facilitation of group or whole-class discussion so as not to lead children to stereotyping (i.e. make judgements or assumptions about people based on their visual representations).

6.5.2 Exploring Viewpoints While Reading: Diversity Through a Zoom-Out Perspective

6.5.2.1 Thinking Routine "Projecting Across Distance"

"Projecting Across Distance" thinking routine (Project Zero's Thinking Routine Toolbox, n.d.) encourages a broader, multi-perspective view of a topic, since students are invited to consider how it is viewed in (a) their community; (b) another city or town in their country; and (c) other countries. Therefore, they can compare and discuss what might be the reason behind the similarities and/or differences between and within the communities and countries. A zoom-out perspective when reading the book *Naar de Markt* allows readers to consider the role of food and shopping in their own life, the role of the market in their community and other contexts (countries), and how the marketplace is at the root of social European and other identities. Readers can be prompted to answer questions such as: Does an open market in my local community look like a market in The Netherlands/Europe/other countries in the world and why?

Projecting across distance while reading *Zaterdag*, children open up their thinking and look at cultural diversity in their own locale, considering the inhabitants of their own community and the activities they engage in on a Saturday. Questions like: What are the activities that people in your community/country/other countries do on a Saturday? Which fictional characters would appear from your literary local tradition/your country's tradition/neighboring country's tradition? As readers adopt a zoom-out perspective, they might consider and appreciate diverse social and cultural contexts, other than the ones appearing in *Zaterdag*. For example, in Israel Saturday is not reflected in *Zaterdag's* pages, since Jewish children would not be out playing on Sabbath.

Readers can benefit from close reading of the visual narrative of the two wordless picturebooks by adopting zoom-in or zoom-out perspectives that provide insight into cultural diversity. However, we acknowledge that teaching diversity to young children is a challenging and complex task. It requires skillful educators who guide visual reading journeys using tools that centralize critical thinking, thus making it visible to others and open to dialogue. In this way stereotypical assumptions can be challenged. The two wordless picturebooks should be used as springboards for celebrating difference, without reinforcing notions of "others" being different but rather reinforcing "we" are all different.

6.6 Conclusion

The two picturebooks are a clear reflection of how modern societies are characterized by plurality of cultures and heritages, as well as divergent, even competing, narratives and notions of cultural artifacts and traditions. The individual's identity-building process thus always occurs in relation to surrounding "super-diversity" (see the discussion in Chapter 4) and social interaction with other people. This interconnection between people's lives is key for constructing one's own cultural identity as well as for encountering other people and facing cultural differences (Maine et al. 2019, 386). As this chapter has shown, the close-reading of such books can offer a number of critical and creative ways of analyzing and understanding how visual narratives potentially help readers acknowledge and understand cultural diversity. Moreover, the chapter has suggested several thinking strategies that can contribute to the systematic implementation of various ways to consider multiple viewpoints in the classroom. Our methodology offers ideas for empirical implementation in future studies that can show how this approach can offer pathways for young readers to experience, accept, and celebrate early on their lives' cultural diversity. This can be an advantage for future citizens and the societies of the twenty-first century.

References

Arizpe, E. 2013. Meaning-making from wordless (or nearly wordless) picturebooks: What educational research expects and what readers have to say. *Cambridge Journal of Education* 43 (2): 163–176.

Arizpe, E. 2014. Wordless picturebooks: Critical and educational perspectives on meaning making. In *Picturebooks: Representation and narration*, ed. Bettina Kümmerling-Meibauer, 91–106. New York, NY: Routledge.

Beckett, S.L. 2012. *Crossover picturebooks: A genre for all ages*. London: Routledge.

Beghetto, R.A. 2017. Inviting uncertainty into the classroom: Five strategies to help students respond well to uncertainty and foster complex problem-solving skills. *Educational Leadership* 75 (2): 20–25.

Bishop, R.S. 1990. Mirrors, windows, and sliding glass doors. *Perspectives: Choosing and Using Books for the Classroom* 6 (3): ix–xi. https://www.psdschools.org/webfm/8559.

Bland, J. 2016. English language education and ideological issues: Picturebooks and diversity. *CLELE Journal* 4 (2): 41–64.

Bosch, E. 2014. Texts and peritexts in wordless and almost wordless picturebooks. In *Picturebooks: Representation and narration*, ed. Bettina Kümmerling-Meibauer, 71–90. New York: Routledge.

Brown, J.S., A. Collins, and P. Duguid. 1989. Situated cognition and the culture of learning. *Educational Researcher* 18 (1): 32–42.

Burnard, P. 2011. Creativity, pedagogic partnerships, and the improvisatory space of teaching. In *Structure and improvisation in creative teaching*, ed. R. Keith Sawyer, 51–72. New York: Cambridge University.
DIALLS (DIalogue and Argumentation for Cultural Literacy Learning in Schools). 2018. *Bibliography of cultural texts*. https://dialls2020.eu/wp-content/uploads/2019/09/Bibliography-of-Cultural-Texts.pdf. Accessed 27 June 2020.
Gamble, N. 2013. *Exploring children's literature. Reading with pleasure and purpose*. London: Sage.
Genette, G. 1997. *Thresholds of interpretation*, trans. J.E. Lewin. Cambridge: Cambridge University Press.
Genette, G. 2001. *Umbrales*. Mexico, DF and Buenos Aires: Siglo XX1.
Giorgis, C., N.J. Johnson, A. Bonomo, C. Colbert, A. Conner, Gloria Kauffman, and Dottie Kulesza. 1999. Children's books: Visual literacy. *The Reading Teacher* 53 (2): 146–153.
Halfmouw, S. 2018. *Zaterdag*. Amsterdam: Leopold.
Koss, M.D. 2015. Diversity in contemporary picturebooks: A content analysis. *Journal of Children's Literature* 41 (1): 32–42.
Maine, F., V. Cook, and T. Lähdesmäki. 2019. Reconceptualizing cultural literacy as a dialogic practice. *London Review of Education* 17 (3): 383–392. https://doi.org/10.18546/LRE.17.3.12.
Moebius, W. 1986. Introduction to picturebook codes. *Word and Image: A Journal of Verbal/Visual Enquiry* 2: 141–158. https://doi.org/10.1080/02666286.1986.10435598.
Nodelman, P. 1988. *Words about pictures: The narrative art of children's picture books*. Athens, GA: University of Georgia Press.
Project Zero's Thinking Routine Toolbox. n.d. Retrieved from Project Zero of Harvard Graduate School of Education website: https://www.pz.harvard.edu/thinking-routines. Accessed 1 September 2020.
Rapanta, C., M. Vrikki, and M. Evagorou. 2020. Preparing culturally literate citizens through dialogue and argumentation: rethinking citizenship education. *The Curriculum Journal*. https://doi.org/10.1002/curj.95. Accessed 17 January 2020.
Rémi, C. 2011. Reading as playing. The cognitive challenge of the wimmelbook. *Studies in Language and Literacy* 13: 115–140.
Ritchhart, R., M. Church, and K. Morrison. 2011. *Making thinking visible: How to promote engagement, understanding, and independence for all learners*. San Francisco, CA: Jossey-Bass.
Serafini, F. 2011. Expanding perspectives for comprehending visual images in multimodal texts. *Journal of Adolescent & Adult Literacy* 54 (5): 342–350.
Serafini, F. 2014. *Reading the visual: An introduction to teaching multimodal literacy*. New York: Teachers College Press.
Smit, N. 2017. *Naar de Markt*. Amsterdam: Querido.
Tishman, S., E. Jay, and D.N. Perkins. 1993. Thinking dispositions: From transmission to enculturation. *Theory into Practice* 32 (3): 147–153.
Tishman, S., and P. Palmer. 2006. *Artful thinking: Stronger thinking and learning through the power of art* (Final Report). Cambridge, MA: Project Zero, Harvard Graduate School of Education, November.
Van Loon, P. 2014. *Een miniheks in het Weerwolvenbos*, illust. S. Halfmouw and H. van Look. Amsterdam: Leopold.

Marina Rodosthenous-Balafa is an Associate Professor in Modern Greek Literature in the Education Department at University of Nicosia. She is the coordinator of the MA Programme: *Teaching of Language and Literature* (MEd).

Maria Chatzianastasi is a Postdoctoral Researcher at the University of Nicosia. Her research interests focus on the aesthetic and pedagogic aspects of children's literature, children's literature in education, contemporary trends and controversial themes in children's books.

Agni Stylianou-Georgiou is an Associate Professor of Educational Psychology at the University of Nicosia. Her current research is in the area of metacognition, creative curriculum design, and problem-solving.

Chapter 7
The DIALLS Platform: Supporting Cultural Literacy and Understanding of European Values Over the Internet

Lucas M. Bietti, Ben Zion Slakmon, Michael J. Baker, Françoise Détienne, Stéphane Safin, and Baruch B. Schwarz

7.1 Introduction

In this chapter we present the process of designing and developing a novel online platform for supporting cultural literacy learning, involving the elaboration and understanding of European values in collaborative dialogue between students, with teacher-led reflection on wordless texts. Wordless texts are books or videos that comprise sequences of pictures which stimulate student readers to reconstruct the attendant narratives (see Chapters 5 and 6, this volume). The narratives in question, available publicly, are designed to stimulate discussions relating to European values, notably tolerance, empathy and inclusion (Lähdesmäki et al. 2020). The main questions for platform design were therefore how to facilitate productive discussions involving European values, on or around such wordless texts, and to structure such discussions in a way that is closely anchored in the texts.

Computer Supported Collaborative Learning (CSCL) systems can support and guide productive dialogue and argumentation (Andriessen et al. 2003; Schwarz and Baker 2017), leading to deeper understanding in the sense of knowledge building (Bereiter and Scardamalia 2003), or in the sense of knowing the other across cultural

L. M. Bietti (✉)
Norwegian University of Science and Technology, Trondheim, Norway
e-mail: lucas.bietti@ntnu.no

L. M. Bietti · M. J. Baker · F. Détienne
Centre National de La Recherche Scientifique, Paris, France

B. Z. Slakmon
Tel Aviv University, Tel Aviv, Israel

M. J. Baker · F. Détienne · S. Safin
Télécom Paris, Paris, France

B. B. Schwarz
Hebrew University of Jerusalem, Jerusalem, Israel

F. Maine and M. Vrikki (eds.), *Dialogue for Intercultural Understanding*,
https://doi.org/10.1007/978-3-030-71778-0_7

differences (Wegerif et al. 2017). CSCL systems can play an important role in such learning to the extent that they enable task sequences and interpersonal communication media to be structured in ways that favour the co-elaboration of knowledge (e.g. Dillenbourg 1999).

The DIALLS Platform facilitates dialogue both within countries and across them, as well as the sharing, use and co-creation of cultural resources (such as multimodal texts, images, videos), thereby opening up various pedagogical opportunities for building a shared culture. The objective of the DIALLS Platform is to support the educational activities proposed by the project (see overview in Chapter 1), and to meet user needs. Three categories of users were defined: (1) *students* (at three age groups; 5–6, 8–9 and 14–15 years old), across the project participants' countries; (2) *teachers*, relating to 1; and (3) *researchers*, analyzing data from use of the DIALLS platform.

The design of the platform thus faced a number of specific challenges. The first related to the need to provide a platform that was usable across a broad age-range of students, from 5 to 15 years old. Depending on the age, language abilities and the roles of teachers in mediating discussions are quite varied. The second challenge was the need to focus and structure discussions on and around sequences of images, still or animated, comprising the wordless text. Thirdly, use of the platform across several EU countries (e.g. UK, Lithuanian, Portugal, Cyprus, Portugal, Spain, Germany), as well as Israel, of course raises the thorny 'language problem'. Given the broad age range, most students can not be expected to discuss in a language that is not their own native language; and yet, reliable automatic translation does not exist for all of the project languages, especially with respect to free input, on chat systems, that would bear many traces of everyday and SMS language.

Our general approach (Fig. 7.1) to the design and development of the DIALLS Platform was user centered (Sharp et al. 2019). Indeed, users of the platform -i.e. teachers, researchers and learners-, were involved in the design phase as well as in the evaluation phase. Following an analysis of the DIALLS educational concept as

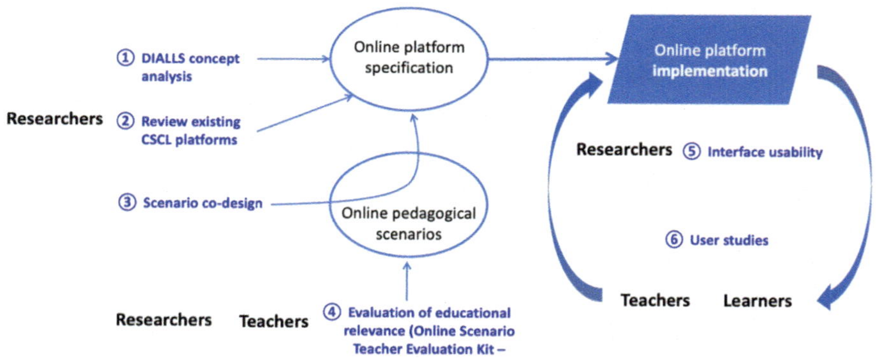

Fig. 7.1 General approach taken for the design and development of the DIALLS platform

well as a detailed literature review of relevant CSCL research, which provided a preliminary identification of the functions of the platform, a scenario-based design phase (Carroll 1997) was conducted in co-design workshops involving teachers and researchers. The objective was to further refine the functionalities of the platform in order to fit users' requirements. In the evaluation phase, two kinds of methods were mobilized: (1) user studies involving teachers and researchers aimed at evaluating the educational relevance and usability of the platform; (2) an expert inspection method (Scapin and Bastien 1997) aimed at evaluating the interface usability (this step is not detailed in this chapter). Finally, user studies with teachers and learners have been carried out in order to further adapt the platform to use in classrooms.

In this chapter, we first present a systematic review of existing computer tools that support the co-creation of multimedia teaching resources on the basis of the functionalities described in the DIALLS user requirements document (Sect. 7.2). The aim of such a systematic review was to identify the specific functions of existing CSCL systems that could be relevant for the development and design of the DIALLS Platform. The co-design workshops with expert users (researchers and teachers) of the DIALLS Platform are reported in Sect. 7.3. The aim of the co-design workshops was to further specify the functionalities of the platform, by envisioning the tools that would be required to support computer mediated DIALLS activities (i.e. online pedagogical scenarios). In Sect. 7.4, we introduce a description of the main functionalities of DIALLS platform and its interface that corresponds to the version of the platform tested by teachers in June and July 2019.

In Sect. 7.5, we present the user studies with teachers who were recruited to implement the DIALLS educational program in their classroom. User studies were conducted in Cyprus, Germany, Lithuania, Spain, and the United Kingdom and provided essential information for the incorporation of successive changes to the platform before its implementation in Europe and Israel in the second part of the DIALLS project. In Sect. 7.6 we present some general reflections on the entire design process and include some recommendations for the development of similar computer tools in large interdisciplinary research projects. In the last section (Sect. 7.7) we discuss the importance of applying a comprehensive socio-technical system approach to the design and development of new educational technology for innovative pedagogical and societal objectives.

7.2 Systematic Review

The aim of our systematic review of the literature and the CSCL systems supporting dialogue and argumentation was to provide initial insight into the computer tools (e.g. synchronous CHAT tools) that the DIALLS Platform should incorporate in order to support the educational activities that are part of the DIALLS project and its educational concept (see Chapter 1 in this book). Given that we aimed to reuse existing tools as far as possible in implementing the DIALLS platform, we also searched for CSCL tools that were still available for download and installation, including, if possible, publicly available source code. In May 2018 we searched for systematic reviews of CSCL systems supporting dialogue and argumentation published between 2010 and 2018. Two digital libraries were searched: the library of the University of Paris-Saclay and Scopus. Searches were facilitated using four sets of keywords covering "CSCL", "argumentation", "software", "program(me)", and "dialogue". We ended with 72 research articles that were published in academic journals and peer-reviewed conference proceedings. Research articles included empirical studies that evaluated 34 CSCL systems supporting dialogue and collaborative argumentation. We decided to exclude eight CSCL systems from our review because they were only tested with university students, whereas our own student users are in primary and secondary schools. We employed inductive and deductive methods for the analysis of the literature. Inductive methods were used for the identification of the basic characteristics shared by most the CSCL systems included in the corpus. Deductive methods were employed for the analysis of the CSCL tools that would support the required functionalities of the DIALLS Platform. We paid particular attention to the following five computer functionalities whose importance for the DIALLS Platform we considered to be essential, described below: (i) Session set-up; (ii) Text display; (iii) Online discussion; (iv) Document repository; and (v) Annotation. We applied these five thematic categories to each of 72 research articles reporting the use and assessment of CSCL systems included in the corpus.

Session set-up. Teachers have to initiate sessions and invite learners to join those sessions. Teachers and learners have to choose nicknames and passwords as an authentication mode and to create their user identities. Log-on management, session creation and document upload tools are the most frequent features reported in the literature. Limited studies have examined how users interact with log-on management functionalities in computer systems (Kim et al. 2007). Kim et al. have observed that primary school students experienced problems when using the log-on management function. Some children could not recall their identification numbers and passwords, which resulted in increasing feelings of frustration and blockage. For this reason (amongst others), primary school students are not required to log onto the DIALLS platform, their discussions being mediated by their teachers.

Text display. These are tools that learners use to have access to texts, video and multiple forms of media included in the activities. They also enable teachers to send talk prompts to learners whenever needed. Teachers' use of prompts (e.g., wordless texts) have positively affected students' discussions and engagement with the activities (Kim et al. 2007). These are CSCL functionalities that are generally taken for granted in the literature; therefore, there is limited information on teachers' and students' user experience in the corpus we selected for the review. However, CSCL systems such as ARGUNAUT (Schwarz and Asterhan 2011) and CoFFEE (Belgiorno et al. 2008) contain all or some of those functionalities (the video display tool can be found in more recent software only).

Online discussion. Online forums for asynchronous discussions and synchronous chat are the most common online dialogue and discussion tools found in CSCL systems. CSCL systems supporting asynchronous communication generally support an online forum only whereas those supporting synchronous and asynchronous communication (e.g. CoFFEE) support an online forum and a CHAT system (see *Talkwall*, Ludvigsen et al. 2020). Kim and colleagues found that primary school students experienced problems using online forums due to low proficiency in keyboarding or use of the computer systems, and some were concerned about spelling errors (Kim et al. 2007). This finding has been validated by studies that used other computer systems too (Prinsen et al. 2007). Low proficiency in keywording and writing skills required frequent interventions from research assistants that interfered with the progression of the task. With respect to secondary school students, research has focused on the benefits of using synchronous CHAT compared to face-to-face dialogue in collaborative argumentation situations (Baker et al. 2007).

Document repository. These tools allow users to store and share text and image files. Document repositories are tools largely supported by most of the 26 CSCL systems included in the review. However, its systematic assessment in the literature seems to be rather limited. With respect to primary school students, document repositories have been used to store teachers' comments and feedback on quality of arguments produced by children in online discussion forums. CSCL systems such as Digalo, and CoFFEE allow teachers to upload wordless texts and instructions onto the platform in order to stimulate and structure students' discussions. For example, the document upload tool has been used to present questions to students for later reflection and discussion on the online forum between primary (Kim et al. 2007), and secondary (Ding 2009) students. Prinsen et al. (see below) have shown that a record of teachers' feedback on children's arguments facilitated students' appropriation of positive behaviours and inhibited the use of ineffective behaviours in future collaborative argumentation tasks (Prinsen et al. 2009). Another functionality investigated in the literature was the possibility for gathering data from the Internet for storage and later use in the online forum, which has been shown to positively affect group discussions (Clark et al. 2009).

Annotation. These are basic features in CSCL systems that are in line with the key premises in CSCL research presented above—i.e. annotation tools provide external scaffolds for learners to produce high quality discussion. Together with online discussion tools (see above), annotation tools have been the most evaluated features of CSCL systems. Forty-eight empirical studies included in our corpus dealt with annotation tools. Research has shown that highlighting relevant portions of dialogues and arguments may help students easily identify parts of the solution they need to pay special attention to (Dragon et al. 2006).

After carefully reviewing the literature and the computer tools that each of the 26 CSCL systems included in the review encompass, it was found that there is no single existing system that satisfies all the requirements of the DIALLS Platform. CoFFEE and Talkwall were the currently available systems that came closest to satisfying design requirements of the DIALLS Platform. However, these computer systems meet these requirements almost exclusively for older children, with little or consideration of teacher-mediated discussions at primary school level. None of the CSCL systems included in the review contained a semi-automatic text translation option. This is a crucial feature for the DIALLS Platform to include considering its multi-cultural and multi-lingual perspective on computer-mediated cultural literacy learning in schools in Europe and Israel.

7.3 Co-Design Workshops

In September and November 2018, two co-design workshops with future users of the DIALLS Platform (researchers and teachers) were held in Paris and Cambridge, respectively. Co-design workshops were of crucial importance at the beginning of the design of the DIALLS platform, for anticipating future educational activities to be supported. Workshop participants were asked to collaboratively design educational activities for the classroom in order to provide a detailed contextualization of the CSCL system functionalities analyzed in the review and how they could be adapted to the DIALLS project.

The co-design workshop technique proposed for the development of the DIALLS platform was rooted in the concept of scenario-based design (Carroll 1997). The aim is to contextualize design proposals in a narrative form at the beginning of projects. This is important because, as the design of the DIALLS platform progressed, the possibilities for changes and modification decreased. Therefore, the co-design workshop technique provided a space where potential users of the DIALLS Platform could collaborate in the co-construction of design features of the platform and test out different ideas in a simulated environment. This occurred before designers and developers made irreversible technical choices.

The co-design workshops were developed to ensure that future users of the DIALLS Platform would be able to co-construct detailed educational scenarios that would resemble those included in the actual foreseen classroom activities. Co-design workshops were organized following the DIALLS core educational activities. These involve (1) observing and interpreting wordless texts (framed by the teacher) and (2) discussing interpretations in order to co-create meanings/interpretations.

The user-centered activity scenarios produced by DIALLS researchers during the co-design workshop had some general features depending on each of the specific age groups included in the DIALLS project. Researchers and teachers agreed on the fact that the DIALLS Platform should come with a user-friendly interface. Users would prefer to interact with a relatively easy-to-learn-and-use interface that would not require them to participate in an excessively long training program. They indicated that for pre-primary (5–6 years old) and primary school (8–9 years old) children, the DIALLS Platform was used as a tool to connect classrooms in different countries and display cultural artefacts produced by students in order to promote collective reflection and dialogue. However, in DIALLS teachers play a key role in the collaborative activities between classrooms, whilst most existing CSCL systems (e.g. synchronous CHAT) consider students to be the primary main users. This led to a further specification of the functionalities of the DIALLS Platform for supporting 5–6 and 8–9 years old. In the user-centered activity scenarios for older students, teachers play a limited role in the individual and collaborative activities, in the classroom and in between classrooms. Finally, workshop participants indicated that the DIALLS Platform should contain tools to support the semi-automatic translation of text when classrooms from different countries were participating in online discussions.

Co-design workshops provided a detailed contextualization of the CSCL system functionalities analyzed in the critical review and how they could be adapted and refined for the DIALLS Platform. Co-design workshops led to our functional recommendations of the list computer tools that the DIALLS Platform should contain. Both co-design workshops have served to validate the tools that we retained from existing CSCL systems and to propose new ones in order to support the specificities of the DIALLS project. The user-centered activity scenarios created by DIALLS researchers and teachers allowed us to further specific those tools and to adapt them to the particular age groups.

7.4 The DIALLS Platform

In this section we present the main functionalities of the DIALLS platform that teachers across the project consortium tested in June and July 2019 (Fig. 7.2). The general description of the platform is organized into the following categories: users; language support; resources; features; training; and data privacy and protection.

Users. The platform supports two types of users: teacher and student.

Language support. The system has been designed to support any language, including Semitic languages (right to left writing systems).

Resources. The platform supports three types of resources: images (PDF, JPG, PNG and TIFF files); texts (PDF and Word files); and films (MP4 and MOV files).

Fig. 7.2 DIALLS Platform interface: image discussed (middle); annotations/participants (left/right)

Features. The platform includes several features: discussion rooms; annotation tools; resource management tools; and separate box for notes. In *discussion rooms*, a teacher can create a new discussion based on resources and select the participants from the DIALLS list of users. A teacher may choose the discussion's age group, and thereby adjust the interface and font size accordingly. Users (teachers and students) can start a *discussion* on any part of the uploaded resources and comment on any discussion in which they are participating. Any discussion has a start time and may have an end date. Once the end date has passed the discussion state is set to be "closed" (a "closed discussion" becomes read-only). Then, the discussion that is relevant for a specific user can be seen on the users' dashboard. *Annotations* are posts in a threaded discussion. A user may choose to start a new discussion and annotate on a specific area of the discussion resource. She can pick the relevant point and start a new discussion from there or write the annotation and then link it to the relevant point on the uploaded resources. In addition, a user may decide to post a comment or start a discussion without being anchored in the resource being discussed in the discussion room—this is particularly important for the phase of discussion where the students move from reconstructing the narrative to a more general discussion on the ethical questions and concepts at stake. A teacher can use *resource management* tools to upload and manage resources on the platform. The actions that teachers can perform include: uploading a new resource; sharing a resource with the DIALLS platform for broader use; saving a link as resource; and utilizing the platform library of shared resources to create new discussion rooms. *Notes* are initially personal and are not seen by the other participants of the discussion. Any user can write her own notes, and these can be found on a "notes" widget in the specific page in which it was created. Notes can be related to a specific area in the uploaded resource for discussion and/or particular comments. This is not a requirement as notes can also be without any discussion context. Finally, notes may be published and become part of the discussion and thereby seen by the other participants in the discussion room.

Training. Online training workshops were offered to DIALLS researchers in 2019 and 2020 in the form of video tutorials addressing specific needs (e.g. adjusting contents to digital literacy skills of teachers and students across the consortium).

Data privacy and protection. The platform meets European GDPR (The General Data Protection Regulation) requirements, which include the anonymization of private users, users' data retrieval and users' data removal. The system contains an automatic anti-virus tool for newly uploaded resources.

7.5 User Studies with Teachers

7.5.1 Online Scenario Teacher Evaluation

In this section we present the user-study (hereafter, "Online Scenario Teacher Evaluation Kit"—OSTEAKIT) that we designed and coordinated to test (i) the functions of the DIALLS platform as described in Sect. 7.4 and (ii) a subset of blended online pedagogical scenarios with teachers involved in the DIALLS project. These blended online pedagogical scenarios were based on lesson plans as developed by project partners. The transformation of lesson plans into online scenarios followed the general guidelines set in the co-design workshops held in Paris and Cambridge.

Our goal with OSTEAKIT was to obtain as much feedback as possible on the DIALLS platform and the proposed blended online pedagogical scenarios. Pedagogical scenarios are teaching and learning models that present scripts of what students and teachers should do when they participate in educational activities (Andriessen and Sandberg 1999). Such scripts include a set of activities, methods and resources that are used to introduce students to concepts and processes in relation to specific learning objectives (Wichmann et al. 2010). Pedagogical scenarios provide meaningful and ecologically valid contexts for the achievement of those objectives. They are used to create learning situations with well-defined roles, activities, sequences of actions, resources and tools (Wichmann et al. 2010). Thus, pedagogical scenarios scaffold educational activities and enable students to accomplish learning objectives. Pedagogical scenarios can encompass different levels of detail which are determined by specific educational goals.

User studies were coordinated locally, by DIALLS researchers in Cyprus, Germany, Lithuania, Portugal and the United Kingdom between June and July 2019. OSTEAKIT included six blended online pedagogical scenarios, three for synchronous lessons (two classes in the same country/language) and another three for asynchronous lessons (two classes in different countries/languages). We added two online scenarios for each age group, that is one synchronous and asynchronous blended online pedagogical scenarios for students aged 5–6, 8–9 and 14–15 years old respectively. They combined and integrated face-to-face teaching and learning approaches with activities that may involve, to a greater and lesser extent the use of online information and communication technologies.

OSTEAKIT also contained a general System Usability Scale (SUS) questionnaire that we used to measure the usability of the DIALLS platform in relation to the teachers' general user experience with the platform (e.g. interface design, consistency and simplicity) and a questionnaire related to the blended online pedagogical online scenarios. SUS is a standardized 10-item Likert scale questionnaire that provides an at-a-glance look at the ease of use (or lack thereof) of the DIALLS platform. At the end of the questionnaire there was a section where teachers could add any comments they had on the DIALLS platform. The aim of the questionnaire specifically related to the blended online pedagogical scenarios was to obtain as much feedback as possible about their educational value within the framework of the DIALLS project. In addition, the questionnaire invited teachers to suggest changes to the online scenarios and propose alternative ways of using the DIALLS platform in the form of new scenarios or new functionalities to support.

Teachers ($n = 21$) were familiar with the general DIALLS concept as they were part of the pool of teachers who were recruited to use the platform in their classrooms. Thus, we ensured that teachers participating in the DIALLS project and project partners were actively involved in the design and development of the online tools supported by the DIALLS platform and the blended online pedagogical scenarios that the same teachers would use with the students. Such active involvement also enabled researchers and teachers to be introduced to the platform's functionalities.

Teachers' responses explained what functions should be added and how existing tools could be modified to improve the platform so it could support the pedagogical goals of the project.

They mentioned that they would want the platform to have new tools such as a separate chat tool, a tool that would allow them to upload multiple resources, not only PDF files. Some teachers' responses manifested a general concern about the necessity of receiving more specific training about how to use it properly to achieve the pedagogical goals contained in synchronous and asynchronous lessons. However, others reported not needing additional training in general IT skills and that they believed they could use the DIALLS platform without the support of technical personnel. Teachers' responses at the country level showed some of the diversity in teachers' experiences with information and communication technologies, and probably the impact of different cultural and institutional practices with regards to the use of technology in the classroom. Differences in teachers' responses at the country level were used for the design of highly targeted training materials, including more specific teachers' guides for the use of the platform, online training sessions and video tutorials.

Additionally, teachers referred to the different ways to improve the blended online pedagogical scenarios. Teachers expressed issues with time management in the sense that using the platform and completing the blended online scenarios was too time consuming. Hence, they suggested limiting the use of the platform to particular tasks (e.g. sharing and commenting on cultural artifacts) and that teachers/students should try to avoid creating several discussion rooms. Teachers also suggested that more time could be allocated to face-to-face class discussion and that the blended online pedagogical scenarios should promote increased physical manipulation of picture books and allocate more time for the students' selection of features in them that they consider to be relevant and worth exploring.

7.5.2 Addressing Cultural and Linguistic Diversity

One of the DIALLS project's strengths and innovative approaches is that it takes into consideration the cultural and linguistic diversity of Europe and beyond. This also creates important challenges, notably, the "language problem": how can teachers and students engage in cross-national discussions over Internet, who have different native languages (in the case of DIALLS: English, Lithuanian, Hebrew, Greek, German, Portuguese, Spanish and Catalan)? Teachers expressed that online automatic translation software only would not be a suitable option for translations in asynchronous and expressed the possibility of having teachers writing messages in English only in those lessons. In order to solve this issue, we developed four translation strategies that DIALLS partners may want to consider for translating dialogue traces as result of interactions between classes located in different countries, to be used partially or conjointly in a flexible way, depending on the situation (see Fig. 7.3).

1. Technical: This strategy involves the use of existing tools, such as Google Translate or similar tools available and free on the web include Microsoft Translator; Bing Translator; Yandex.Translate; Babylon; Apertium; and DeepL Translator. This strategy is highly dependent on the language and pairs of languages concerned.
2. Socio-technical: This strategy lies in the use of the linguistic expertise in the immediate environment of the partners, to do human translation and/or checking of automatic translation (see Strategy #1).
3. Multi-lingual: This strategy involves the use of an "interlanguage" between classes located in different countries. That is, depending on specific pairs of partner countries whose school children are discussing, it may be possible to consider discussions in: (i) L2/L2—e.g. schools in Portugal and Lithuania discussing in English, with foreign language classes/teachers; (ii) L1/L2 e.g. schools in England and in Cyprus discussing in English. The priority should be communication and mutual understanding rather than grammatical correctness.

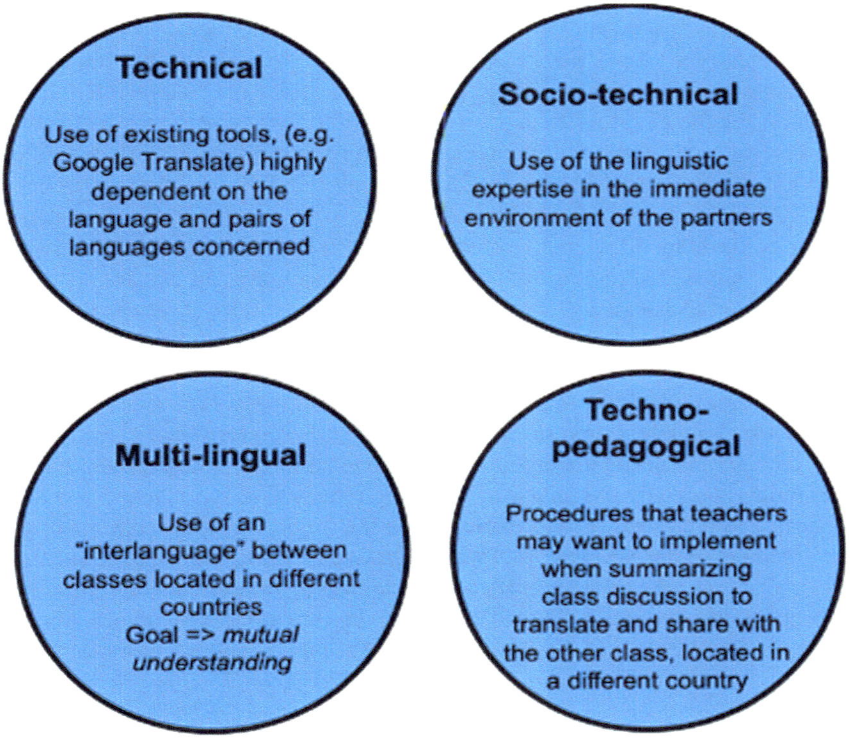

Fig. 7.3 Translation strategies for dialogue tracing

4. Techno-pedagogical: This strategy involves trying to reconcile technological limitations—for example, absence of automatic translation tools for a pair of languages—and pedagogical affordances. Thus, asking students in each country, or even their teachers, in the case of younger children, to write a short synthesis of their chat discussions can at the same time facilitate translation (e.g. via the socio-technical approach) and also be a pedagogically valuable activity, facilitating knowledge integration.

7.6 Reflections

The design of the DIALLS platform came with important challenges. One of the most important of them was the management of the expectations of members of a large interdisciplinary research group. The research partners responsible for the design and development of the computer tool (Hebrew University of Jerusalem and CNRS Paris) learned that it was essential to discuss with project partners who were not familiar with the field education technology what type of Internet-based platform could be developed considering multiple constraints. These constraints included technological constraints, budgetary constraints, and time constraints, amongst several others (e.g. GDPR data management and ethics regulations). Technological constraints determined what type of computer system we were able to realistically produce within the framework of the project. For example, the inclusion of an automatic translation function for the chat tool to support intercultural communication was far beyond the kind of technology and computational engineering knowledge we had at our disposal. Researchers who are not familiar with the field of education technology may assume that technological advancements such as the Google Translate tool might be developed for computer tools in education, or otherwise be easily integrated as embedded applications into system. Technological constraints are very much related to budgetary constraints. The design of most of the freely available Internet tools (e.g. video-chat tool) we use, without much effort, on a regular basis were developed by some of the largest corporations in the world. Such commonly used Internet tools shape researchers' expectations regarding what research partners working in CSCL in a scientific project could produce. Time constraints were also crucial; and despite being intrinsically related to technological and budgetary constraints, they are also given by the time schedule of the planned activities in large research projects. For example, in the DIALLS project the time spent on the development of the computer tool was determined by institutional agreements with hundreds of primary and secondary schools indicating the period when data could be collected in the classrooms. In order to better manage users expectations it is crucial to have open discussions about issues like these at the beginning of the endeavour.

7.7 Conclusion

In this chapter we presented a detailed description of the general approach we undertook to design a new Internet-based platform (DIALLS platform) for supporting cultural literacy and understanding of European values based on collaborative and teacher-led reflection on wordless texts (Fig. 7.1). The design and development of a novel online platform included a (i) systematic review of existing computer systems in CSCL, co-design workshop with researchers and teachers involved in the DIALLS project, (ii) the design and development of the platform and (iii) exhaustive user studies with teachers who were familiar with the DIALLS goals. Most research in CSCL focuses on the evaluation of usage of systems, giving few details of the initial, possibly collaborative system design process. We have shared general reflections on the processes of design and development of the DIALLS platform, designed for a specific and original educational purpose, within a large interdisciplinary research project. We included some recommendations based on our experience, namely being realistic about the types of functions the computer tool may afford and having open discussions about them from the beginning of the project.

Our challenge was to make sure that tools and structures provided by the DIALLS Platform would on one hand support and yet not limit the pedagogical diversity involved in the DIALLS project. The tools of the DIALLS Platform enabled its users to analyze the dynamic development of cultural values (e.g., tolerance and inclusion) in dialogue. Thus, the structures provided by the platform support such fluid dialogue that allows building on other students' responses, elaborating and justifying ideas and synthetizing group thinking processes.

We proposed that the most adequate way to address users' expectations with the DIALLS platform was to adopt a socio-technical system approach (Cooper and Foster 1971), involving a web of mutual dependencies between users, other technologies, and cultural and institutional practices. This has enabled meeting two challenges that, to our knowledge, have not been addressed by existing CSCL research, based on concurrent co-design of educational scenarios and tools: designing and developing a system that is adapted to achieving specific educational goals (cultural literacy learning) across very different age groups of students, and overcoming the language barrier in cross-country collaboration.

References

Andriessen, J., and J. Sandberg. 1999. Where is education heading and how about AI? *International Journal of Artificial Intelligence in Education* 10 (2): 130–150.

Andriessen, J., M.J. Baker, and D. Suthers, eds. 2003. *Arguing to learn: Confronting cognitions in computer-supported collaborative learning environments*. Dordrecht: Kluwer.

Baker, M.J., J. Andriessen, K. Lund, M. van Amelsvoort, and M. Quignard. 2007. Rainbow: A framework for analysing computer-mediated pedagogical debates. *International Journal of Computer Supported Collaborative Learning* 2 (2–3): 315–357.

Beaver, J.K., B. Hallar, and L. Westmass. 2014. *Blended learning: Defining models and examining conditions to support implementation.* PERC Research Brief. Philadelphia: Research for Action.
Belgiorno, F., R. De Chiara, I. Manno, and V. Scarano. 2008. A flexible and tailorable architecture for scripts in F2F collaboration. In *Times of convergence. Technologies across learning contexts. EC-TEL 2008.* Lecture Notes in Computer Science, vol. 5192, ed. P. Dillenbourg and M. Specht, 401–412. Berlin and Heidelberg: Springer.
Bereiter, C., and M. Scardamalia. 2003. Learning to work creatively with knowledge. In *Unravelling basic components and dimensions of powerful learning environments*, ed. E. Corte, L .Verschaffel, N. Entwistle, and J. van Merriënboer, 55–68. EARLI Advances in Learning and Instruction Series. Bingley, UK: Emerald.
Carroll, J.M. 1997. Scenario-based design. In *Handbook of human-computer interaction*, ed. M.G. Helander, T.K. Landauer, and P.V. Prabhu, 383–406. Amsterdam: North Holland/Elsevier.
Clark, D.B., C.M. D'Angelo, and M. Menekse. 2009. Initial structuring of online discussions to improve learning and argumentation: Incorporating students' own explanations as seed comments versus an augmented-preset approach to seeding discussions. *Journal of Science Education and Technology* 18 (4): 321–333.
Cooper, R., and M. Foster. 1971. Sociotechnical systems. *American Psychologist* 26: 467–474.
Dillenbourg, P. 1999. *Collaborative learning: Cognitive and computational approaches.* Amsterdam: Pergamon/Elsevier Science.
Ding, N. 2009. Visualizing the sequential process of knowledge elaboration in computer-supported collaborative problem solving. *Computers and Education* 52 (2): 509–519.
Dragon, T., B.P. Woolf, D. Marshall, and T. Murray. 2006. Coaching within a domain independent inquiry environment. In *Intelligent tutoring systems. ITS 2006.* Lecture Notes in Computer Science, vol. 4053, ed. M. Ikeda, K.D. Ashley, and T.-W. Chan, 144–153. Berlin and Heidelberg: Springer.
Kim, I.-H., R.C. Anderson, K. Nguyen-Jahiel, and A. Archodidou. 2007. Discourse patterns during children's collaborative online discussions. *Journal of the Learning Sciences* 16 (3): 333–370.
Lähdesmäki, T., A.-K. Koistinen, and S.C. Ylönen. 2020. *Intercultural dialogue in European education policies: A conceptual approach.* New York: Palgrave Macmillan.
Ludvigsen, S.R., P. Warwick, I. Rasmussen, K.A. Rødnes, O. Smørdal, and L. Major. 2020. Learning as gap-closing. Investigating digitalized dialogues. In *Designs for experimentation and Inquiry: Approaching learning and knowing in digital transformation*, ed. Å. Mäkitalo, T.E. Nicewonger, and M. Elam. London: Routledge.
Polson, P. G., C. Lewis, J. Rieman, and C. Wharton. 1992. Cognitive walkthroughs: A method for theory-based evaluation of user interfaces. *International Journal of Man-Machine Studies* 36 (5): 741–773.
Prinsen, F.R., M. Volman, and J. Terwel. 2007. The influence of learner characteristics on degree and type of participation in a CSCL environment. *British Journal of Educational Technology* 38 (6): 1037–1055.
Prinsen, F.R., M. Volman, J. Terwel, and P. Van den Eeden. 2009. Effects on participation of an experimental CSCL-programme to support elaboration: Do all students benefit? *Computers and Education* 52 (1): 113–125.
Scapin, D.L., and J.M. Bastien. 1997. Ergonomic criteria for evaluating the ergonomic quality of Interactive systems. *Behaviour & Information Technology* 16 (4–5): 220–231.
Schwarz, B.B., and C.S. Asterhan. 2011. E-moderation of synchronous discussions in educational settings: A nascent practice. *The Journal of the Learning Sciences* 20 (3): 395–442.
Schwarz, B.B., and M.J. Baker. 2017. *Dialogue, argumentation, and education.* New York: Cambridge University Press.
Schwarz, B.B., and R. De Groot. 2007. Argumentation in a changing world. *International Journal of Computer-Supported Collaborative Learning* 2 (2–3): 297–313.
Sharp, H., J. Preece, and Y. Rogers. 2019. *Interaction design: Beyond human-computer Interaction*, 5th ed. New York: John Wiley & Sons.

Suthers, D.D. 2003. Representational guidance for collaborative inquiry. In *Arguing to learn: Confronting cognitions in computer-supported collaborative learning environments*, ed. J. Andriessen, M.J. Baker, and D.D. Suthers, 27–46. Dordrecht: Kluwer.
Wegerif, R., J. Doney, A. Richards, N. Mansour, S. Larkin, and I. Jamison. 2017. Exploring the ontological dimension of dialogic education through an evaluation of the impact of internet mediated dialogue across cultural difference. *Learning, Culture and Social Interaction* 20: 80–89.
Wichmann, A., J. Engler, and U. Hoppe. 2010. Sharing educational scenario designs in practitioner communities. In *Learning in the disciplines: Proceedings of the 9th international conference of the learning sciences* (ICLS 2010), ed. K. Gomez, L.B. Lyons, and J. Radinsky, 750–757. Chicago IL: International Society of the Learning Sciences.

Lucas M. Bietti is an Associate Professor in psychology at the Norwegian University of Science and Technology. He holds an honorary affiliation with Centre National de la Recherche Scientifique at Télécom Paris.

Ben Zion Slakmon is an Assistant Professor of Education at Tel Aviv University.

Michael J. Baker is a tenured Research Professor in language sciences of the Centre National de la Recherche Scientifique at Télécom Paris. His research aims to understand the processes of collaborative learning and work, drawing on dialogue and argumentation analysis.

Françoise Détienne is a tenured Research Professor in cognitive ergonomics of the Centre National de la Recherche Scientifique at Télécom Paris. Her research focuses on technology-mediated collaboration, co-design and online epistemic communities.

Stéphane Safin is an Associate Professor in cognitive ergonomics, at Télécom Paris. His research is on the role of technology mediation in group design and creativity.

Baruch B. Schwarz is a Professor of Education at the Hebrew University of Jerusalem. His research focuses on learning in social interaction, especially within the context of collaborative learning and argumentation in various domains of knowledge.

Chapter 8
Dialogue on Ethics, Ethics of Dialogue: Microgenetic Analysis of Students' Moral Thinking

Talli Cedar, Michael J. Baker, Lucas M. Bietti, Françoise Détienne, Erez Nir, Gabriel Pallarès, and Baruch B. Schwarz

8.1 Introduction

In this chapter we propose a methodological approach: we intend to explore the relations between children's representations of moral issues as elaborated in dialogue (dialogue on ethics, DoE) and the ethical dimension of the children's moral conduct towards each other (ethics of dialogue, EoD), where we expect to find interesting relations to explore. For example, if a child expresses tolerance towards a character in a video, to what extent does that child express tolerance towards the ideas and utterances of other children present in the interactive situation? The values we intend to focus on are the three main values at the heart of DIALLS: tolerance, empathy, and inclusion. We will examine the possible reciprocity between talking and doing, form and content, meta-dialogue and dialogue.

The moral development of the child has been much researched, yet rarely considered in contexts of social interaction at a sequential microgenetic level of analysis (Lemke 2001). This situation is surprising since moral development involves cognition, emotion and conduct in a rich social context, and microgenetic analysis can help

T. Cedar (✉) · E. Nir · B. B. Schwarz
The Hebrew University of Jerusalem, Jerusalem, Israel
e-mail: talli.cedar@mail.huji.ac.il

B. B. Schwarz
e-mail: baruch.schwarz@mail.huji.ac.il

M. J. Baker · F. Détienne · G. Pallarès
Centre National de La Recherche Scientifique, Télécom Paris, Paris, France
e-mail: michael.baker@telecom-paris.fr

F. Détienne
e-mail: francoise.detienne@telecom-paris.fr

L. M. Bietti
The Norwegian University of Science and Technology, Trondheim, Norway
e-mail: lucas.bietti@ntnu.no

F. Maine and M. Vrikki (eds.), *Dialogue for Intercultural Understanding*,
https://doi.org/10.1007/978-3-030-71778-0_8

comprehend this complexity. Short and midterm time spans in particular settings, as well as during long-term time spans (Scribner 1985) fit the observation of moral development. However, much research on the child's moral development aims to understand the child's individual moral stance towards, for example, classical moral dilemmas (i.e. "my mummy does not see me and would not know I did it, then should I play with the prohibited toys?"), yet takes for granted the relevance for children of the question, pre-defined by adults, involved in understanding children's moral stances in their social interactions with their peers. Additionally, much of such research deals with observing young children with and without surveillance, in order to examine compliance with parent/adult "dos" vs. "don'ts", hardly considering the quality of the parent–child discourse, and not all considering any kind of peer-interaction (Grusec and Goodnow 1994; Konchanska and Aksan 1995).

Considering the moral development of the child over different timescales, through different age groups, and within both adult and child interactions, seems an advantageous perspective that can allow the researchers gain new insights regarding moral development, in the present case, within the DIALLS project (see Chapter 1). The project is based on the implementation of a *dialogic* perspective, an ethical stance deliberately adopted by pedagogues: children and young adolescents are invited to interact around wordless books and videos that invite the construction of a narrative, while being accountable to the other, to reasoning and to knowledge (see Chapter 5). The design of the activities in the program affords the emergence of emotions by skimming over the wordless stories, conducting discussions in which emotions felt are articulated, and internalizing these emotions in further discussions. The program opens an opportunity to explore the general hypothesis—largely grounded in research on moral development—that moral development depends on different kinds of interactions between children and adults, or among children. The DIALLS project aims at identifying phenomena that indicate this development in the context of dialogic teaching.

The design of this program offers three different levels of participation: whole-class teacher-mediated interaction; small-group teacher-mediated interaction; small-group unmediated interaction (for more details see Chapter 1). It is important to stress that in the framework of the DIALLS program the teacher does not play the role of a lecturer holding knowledge and correct answers, but rather that of a mediator conducting guided participation within a framework of adaptive intervention. The different interaction levels (whole-class, mediated group, unmediated group) are all performed within context, thus enabling the DoE/EoD analysis. This analysis is expected to bridge between aspects of moral conduct and moral judgement, both interwoven into the dialogue.

We first introduce a short review of research on moral development (Sect. 8.2), after which we outline an educational interventionist program on moral development, focusing on the DIALLS-EU project (Sect. 8.3), then present a proposed methodological approach to microgenetic analysis of DoE, EoD and the relations between them (Sect. 8.4). Finally, we conclude and discuss future work (Sect. 8.5).

8.2 Moral Development: A Succinct Review of Moral Education in the Light of Advancements in Moral Development

8.2.1 Foundational Theories of Moral Development

The first psychologists that studied moral development considered the needs of the individual vs. the needs of society. For Freud, these needs lead to tension, and moral development proceeds when the individual's desires are repressed by the values of significant socializing agents. The behavioral theory replaced the struggle between internal and external forces by the power of external forces (reinforcement contingencies) in shaping moral development. Using the Clinical Interview Method, Piaget (1965) found that young children were focused on authority mandates, and that with age children become autonomous, and evaluate action from a set of independent principles of morality.

Kohlberg and Hersh (1977), whose research was influenced by Piaget's approach, saw imitation of perceived models and seeking to validate them as the beginning of moral development. For Kohlberg, the common patterns of social life are *universal* since they occur in all cultures in social institutions (families, peer-groups, cooperative work for mutual defense and sustenance). The more one is prompted to imagine how others experience things and imaginatively to take their roles, the more quickly one learns to function well in cooperative human interactions. Kohlberg's stages of moral development correspond to a sequence of progressively more inclusive social circles (family, peers, community, etc.), within which humans seek to operate competently. When those groups function well, oriented by reciprocity and mutual care and respect, growing humans adapt to larger and larger circles of justice, care, and respect. Each stage of moral cognitive development is the realization in conscious thought of the relations of justice, care, and respect exhibited in a wider circle of social relations.

Kohlberg's theory has been criticized as emphasizing justice to the exclusion of other values and so may not adequately address the arguments of those who value other moral aspects of actions. For example, Gilligan (1977) attacked Kohlberg's theory, considering it to be excessively androcentric. She developed an alternative theory of moral reasoning based on the ethics of caring (cf. also Higham and De Vynck 2020). Kohlberg's theory is still vibrant, however, because he has greatly contributed to applied work on moral education in schools. Kohlberg's first method of moral education was to examine the lives of moral exemplars who practiced principled morals such as Socrates, Abraham Lincoln and Martin Luther King. His understanding that moral exemplars have an important place in moral education has growing support. He also initiated the introduction of discussions around moral dilemmas in schools. It was found that such discussions best increase moral reasoning when the individual's interlocutor is using reasoning that is one stage above their own.

In spite of the strong criticism of the alleged universality of Kohlberg's stage-theory of moral development, research on moral development has adopted a persistent universalist twist. Turiel's *Social Domain Theory* (1983) shows how individuals from many cultures differentiate moral (fairness, equality, justice), societal (conventions, traditions), and psychological concepts from early in development throughout life.

8.2.2 Emotions, Values and Moral Development

A major research trend has focused on how emotions motivate individuals to engage in moral acts and influence moral development. These emotions are said to be linked to moral development because they are evidence to, and reflective of, an individual's set of moral values; moral values which must have undergone beforehand a process of internalization. The values we focus on are the three main values at the heart of DIALLS: tolerance, empathy, and inclusion (Lähdesmäki et al. 2020; Chapter 4—this volume). Empathy, inclusion and tolerance are not emotions, but are studied especially within the Social Domain Theory perspective, according to which children pay attention to different variables when judging or evaluating exclusion. These variables include social categories, the stereotypes associated with them, or children's qualifications as defined by prior experience. This prior experience has to do with an activity, personality and behavioral traits that might be disruptive for group functioning and conformity to conventions as defined by group identity or social consensus. Research has documented the presence of a transition occurring at the reasoning level behind the criteria of inclusion and exclusion from childhood to adolescence (Horn 2003). As children get older, they become more attuned to issues of group functioning and conventions and weigh them up in congruence with issues of fairness and morality (Killen and Stangor 2001).

8.2.3 The Role of Social Interactions in Moral Development

Children's interactions with caregivers and peers have been shown to influence development of moral understanding and behavior. Researchers have addressed the influence of interpersonal interactions on children's moral development from two primary perspectives: socialization/internalization (Grusec and Goodnow 1994; Kochanska and Askan 1995) and social domain theory.

Research from the social domain theory perspective focuses on how children actively distinguish moral from conventional behavior, as they learn what is expected from them through responses of their parents, teachers, and peers. Social domain theory suggests that there are different areas of reasoning co-existing in development that include societal, moral, and psychological perspectives. Adults tend to respond to children's moral transgressions (e.g., hitting or stealing) by drawing the child's attention to the effect of his or her action on others, and doing so consistently across various contexts. In contrast, adults are more likely to respond to children's conventional misdeeds (e.g., eating with their hands) by reminding children about specific rules and doing so only in certain contexts (e.g., at school but not at home). Peers respond mainly to moral but not to conventional transgressions and demonstrate emotional distress (e.g., crying or yelling) when they are the victim of (or bystanders with respect to) moral transgressions.

8.2.4 The Relevance of Advances in Research on Moral Development in Moral Education

This short review on research on moral development stresses the importance of discussion and dialogue/argumentation, of value-education and of rich social settings. Experiences during which emotions can be discussed, reflected and internalized towards the identification of moral values susceptible to lead to advancement in moral judgment. Educational research in this domain is badly missing although some effort has been invested in this direction (c.f. Patry et al. 2008). To this end, a relatively long-term intervention, enabling reflection and internalization, is needed.

8.3 Moral Education, Moral Development and Dialogicity

8.3.1 The Ethical Justification of Programs in Moral Education: The Dialogical Ethics Approach

Moral education and the development of values imply a prior philosophical notion of morality and understanding what "good" means, a notion which is not obvious at all and in fact is highly contested in contemporary thought. Plato (2013) based the validation of ethical notions on the objective knowing of ideal goodness that is given in ideal knowledge coming from high-level philosophical reflection. Naturally, this is an aristocratic understanding of moral judgment, which accordingly justifies an aristocratic *polis* ruled by a philosopher-king. In modern thinking, Kant (2015) replaces Plato's objective knowledge with a transcendental rationality which is the condition of all experience. Kantian ethics draws on a 'categorical imperative' for morality which is based on generalization and abstraction: judging my actions whether they are ethical and moral when generalized to all situations. This Kantian morality of rationality is criticized by Nietzsche (1966) as a disguise for actual power-relations between people. Nietzsche sees values as human acts of power and creation in which we create ourselves, making the only possible ethical education, one that empowers pupils' ability to create their own values.

In the twentieth century these Nietzschian critiques were developed in the post-modern school, emphasizing the highly constituted nature of what we understand as knowledge and morality (Bauman 1988; Foucault 1972). Universal ethical notions are specifically criticized from the standpoint of modern anthropology, which reveals the highly contingent nature of ethical norms (Marcus and Fisher 1986). Many anthropologists argue that moral values cannot be separated from their cultural sources and background, making universal morality non-existent and implying moral relativism. This line of thought sees ethical universality as a western justification for colonial and imperial actions, giving priority to western values as universal over different moral-cultural values.

Despite the apparent contradiction, values can be regarded as both universal and culture-specific, such as in the case of Politeness theory (Brown and Levinson 1987), introduced as a universal, as is evident by the mere title of this seminal work: *Politeness: Some universals in language usage.* The notion of *politeness*, researched from a variety of perspectives (interactionist linguistics, anthropology and developmental psychology, to name just a few) refers to interactants' efforts to facilitate/enable communication by mitigating affronts to each other's *face* (Goffman 1967). The theory has been critiqued for its claim to universality, and yet *politeness* still constitutes a universal value (Scollon and Scollon 1995; Morand 1996), crucial to human interaction, and particularly cross-culturally, despite—or rather precisely because of—the fact that specific norms and values of politeness differ between cultures (Armaşu 2012). Although the expression of a certain value might vary from culture to culture, the value itself might still be upheld as unitary.

In our research we suggest following a different kind of moral thinking in response to the challenges of moral relativism, a conception which is also inherent to the pedagogic practice we use—dialogical ethics. The ethics of dialogue, viewing dialogue as a primary ethical moment, represent a principle of morality enabling humans to co-create meaning. Dialogical ethics are not weakened by the constituted nature of truth and values, nor by the cultural relativism of morality. This notion of deep *différance* (Derrida 1973) is the starting point for dialogical ethics, which embraces this meaning-making and meaning-constituting nature of man as not denying ethical views, but rather commanding them. Lévinas (1969) argues that the unexhausted 'otherness of the other' is the basis of all morality, which has 'priority' over any ontology or knowledge we have of the world. This view does not see morality as a result of any kind of understanding or knowledge, cultural or universal, it is a basic intention which is a kind of 'borderline' to our own knowing. A human is a meaning-making being and a valuing creature. However, this act is not only personal, rather it is always shared and intertwined with others who disagree, approve, acknowledge or not this personal valuing. Dialogical ethics could be understood as the actual term that makes this dialectic of personal/collective meaning-making and valuing, which we call 'dialogue', at its best. Dialogical ethical values are therefore intentions and norms that increase the inclusiveness, fertility and 'meeting of otherness' in the intersubjective, transcultural human process of meaning-making.

In the framework of DIALLS there are certain values we wish to instill. This approach creates a mini-culture within a classroom meant to construct something new. Mutual respect, indeed, is not a universal principle: it depends on what you do, and on what you are habituated to.

8.3.2 An Interventional Educational Program on Moral Development

The CLLP (cultural literacy learning programme—see Chapter 1) is a mid-term program that spreads over a sequence of activities during several months through 15 lessons designed for 3 age-groups. It enables us to examine temporal development which we intend to analyze according to the microgenetic sequential approach.

Similar projects dealing with education and values have been conducted. To mention two such projects: REACH Beyond Tolerance (Hollingsworth et al. 2003) and VaKE—Values and Knowledge Education (Patry et al. 2008). REACH is a long-term wide scope USA-based program that promotes cultural-pluralism and tolerance. This program relies on long-term overall influence, and it uses a great variety of activities, not only dialogue/argumentation. VaKE is closer in nature to DIALLS. It follows a constructive approach via dilemma discussions, following Kohlberg's claim the values should be implemented not through content-instruction but rather through *arguing about* those values. The instructors present moral dilemma stories and ask the children to decide *what* to do and *why*. The influence on children's moral thinking, it is claimed, is certain though it will take weeks and months to be discerned. VaKE's declared uniqueness is in its focus on the *why* aspect: the knowledge accompanying the children's choices and arguments. The program takes the students through a repeating process of reflection and decision and sends them to get the information needed to justify or refute their decisions. The DIALLS program, on the other hand, uses wordless works (videos and picture-books) stimuli for the discussion (see Chapter 5). There is no dilemma *handed* to the children, but rather it is supposed to emerge from their discussion. Though the teacher can operate as a guide, s/he does not play the role of an instructor leading the children to the "right" discussion topic or answer. DIALLS is based on minimal guidance, and nurtures open dialogue between children. The interaction itself is the *goal*, rather than the *means*.

Hence, our work will focus on moral development via an interventional program intended to boost dialogic dimensions both in peer interactions and in teacher-students interactions.

The DIALLS program, adapted to different ages and cultures, was implemented in seven countries (cf. Chapter 1—Introduction to this volume). It focuses on certain values seen as universal—or at least, European—values (tolerance, empathy, inclusion). As discussed above (2.1; 3.1) perceiving certain values as universal might present a problem as values, in many cases, are culture-bound (i.e. justice, rights). We would like to maintain that in speaking of universality we do not mean universality of the nature of the values. We see the core values of DIALLS as universal; nonetheless, we do not expect their expression/interpretation to be identical within different cultures. The participating countries (UK, Germany, Lithuania, Spain, Portugal, Cyprus and Israel) are not geographically far apart, and could be defined as 'western', yet they are quite dissimilar from each other culture-wise. This aspect of the program will enable us to discuss and analyze the question of the universality of values, though admittedly in a somewhat limited way.

The program was designed as a three-tier project of expanding peer-circles: starting in the inner-circle of face-to-face interaction with classmates (LP1-5); moving on to the wider circle of synchronous computer-mediated interaction with intra-country peers (LP6-10); ending with asynchronous computer mediated interaction with inter-country peers (LP11-15) (for more details regarding the DIALLS online platform see Chapter 7). This design would have enabled us to compare value-learning both intra-culturally and inter-culturally. Due to COVID19 the third tier was not implemented as schools worldwide closed down. Nevertheless, we will be able to analyze EoD/DoE both within different countries, and to compare the results through an inter-cultural comparable corpus. We hope this comparison will allow us to gain some insights regarding the question of morality and universality.

8.4 A Microgenetic Approach to Analysis

8.4.1 DIALLS Key Values in Interaction

As was discussed above, research on the psychology of moral development has elaborated categories of students' understanding of moral questions or dilemmas, largely on the basis of interview and questionnaire data. There also exists a relatively restricted research literature on the evolution of children's moral reasoning in peer-interactions, inspired by the work of Baldwin (1906) and within a Vygotskian perspective. For example, Damon and Killen (1982) studied small group interactions with respect to a distributive justice problem, relating students' progress to 'patterns' in their discourse. Children who engaged in rejecting, conflictual discourse tended not to progress; higher levels of progress were associated with more varied types of discourse. We also discussed philosophical theories of dialogue, that insist on the ethical dimension of shared meaning-making. However, although such theories are the foundations of a prescriptive "dialogic pedagogy" (Wegerif 2020), they have not yet given rise to precise methods for analyzing ethical relations between children engaged in small-group interactions. With this in mind, we have two main aims here: firstly, to outline an approach analyzing the "ethics of dialogue" between children engaged in school tasks, and secondly, to study how this relates to children's ethical judgements and conceptions (Sect. 8.4.2).

The detailed analysis of the *hic et nunc* processes of co-elaboration of students' ideas on moral issues in specific dialogues can provide situated accounts of their moral thinking and pave the way for the study of its development across longer timescales. Within the framework of the DIALLS project, we take as reference points students' understandings ("conceptions") of three ethical concepts: tolerance, empathy and inclusion (Lähdesmäki et al. 2020). However, given that their definitions are largely stipulative, in official EU texts, understanding how they are in play in real interactions requires significant work in order to render them operational.

These research aims—understanding the relations between ethics *in* and *of* dialogue—need to be situated within the framework of the specific task that students are engaged in, within DIALLS teaching/learning situations, given that its structure is a major determinant of the structure of (epistemic) dialogue (Grosz and Sidner 1986). Here, the task involves elaborating a narrative on the basis of 'wordless texts' under teacher guidance, in a way that is oriented towards the emergence of ethical questions and constructive discussion in relation to them. In the next section we will delineate our proposed methodology for operationalizing this analysis.

8.4.2 DoE/EoD Dimensions and Indicators

Our proposed methodological framework comprises the main dimensions and indicators detailed in the following sub-sections and illustrated in Fig. 8.1. Each dimension and indicator presented will be followed by a brief transcript excerpt demonstrating our analysis methodology. All excerpts were taken from a group discussion carried out in Israel, involving a group of primary-school students discussing a wordless text. Examples were translated from Hebrew to English by the first author. The wordless text, *Papa's Boy*, is an animated short video (3:03 min) about a young boy-mouse who wants to become a ballet dancer as illustrated by his ballet costume. This goes against his father's expectations: he wanted his son to follow his footsteps and become

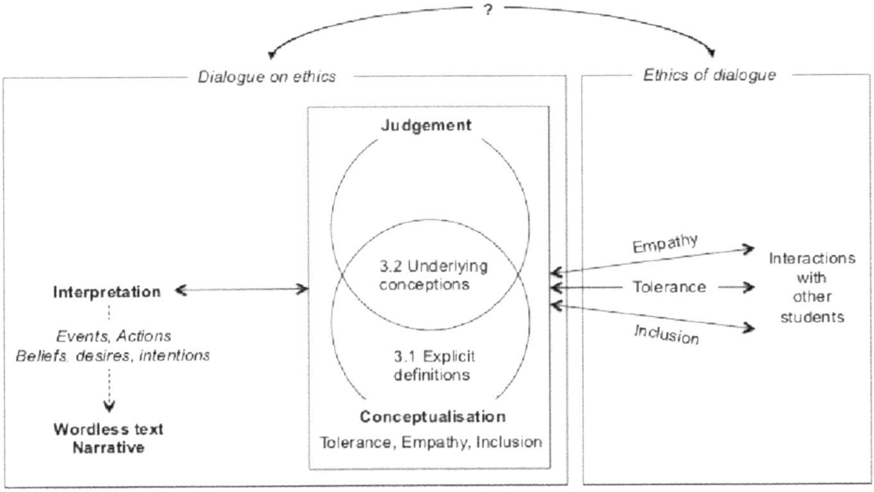

Fig. 8.1 Analysis approach: ethics in/of dialogue

a boxer. The father is disappointed with his son's decision until an unexpected event: a cat tried to attack their family. The boy-mouse saves his family by dancing and distracting the cat.

8.4.2.1 Dialogue on Ethics (DoE)

The first dimension is *interpretation*: reconstructing causality between events and attributing beliefs, desires and intentions to characters:

S4: "[…] in the beginning of the movie, the dad of the, boy mouse he didn't want him to dance, in the second part of the movie there was a cat who came to eat up his dad, and then eh the mouse saved him and then he thought it was really good that the mouse will dance".

S4 reconstructs the events and actions of the story and assigns attributes and intentions to the characters.

The second dimension involves a move from focusing on the narrative towards personal positioning and moral *judgement*:

S1: "Yes, I know but I think you've got, like, a whole world ahead of you. You can't just do girly stuff."

S1 makes a moral judgement about the young mouse's decision to become a ballerina.

The third dimension, *conceptualization*, underlies the two others. This can take two forms: (1) conceptualization underlying judgement (and interpretation), not expressed explicitly; (2) explicit discussion of moral concepts:

S32: "I wanna say it but there are colors that I really really, but really love, that are girls' colors like pink, violet".

S32 shares his personal preference implicitly conceptualizing his view on being tolerant, establishing an analogy between color preferences and gender.

In dialogue, students are likely to move freely between interpreting the story, making personal judgements and engaging in conceptual thinking. To summarize, students can reveal their concepts of moral issues in the judgements they make, in their explicit discussion of these concepts and also in the manner in which they interpret the story in the first place.

8.4.2.2 Ethics of dialogue (EoD)

Turning to the ethics of how students relate to each other, we study this through the prism of the DIALLS key moral concepts (tolerance, empathy, inclusion). In order to operationalize these concepts in interaction analysis, we restrict their definitions to particular intersubjective 'planes'—the different planes are not exclusive but may combine—and define sets of indicators for both the positive and negative facet of each moral value:

We operationalize *(in)tolerance* on the plane of *ideas*. Accordingly, example indicators are acceptance of others' diverging ideas (tolerance), or else rejecting them out of hand (intolerance).

S3: "I think that I differ in opinion from S1, because I think that, the father saw that the mouse-boy's ballet is like, it's like eh, it's like, kind of boxing […]"

S3 manifests tolerant behavior towards what another student said, though the things said go against his beliefs.

S113: "did you write an example too?"
S114: "no"
S115: "I'm not supposed to write an example, leave me alone!"

S113 asks a question, S114 gives a negative answer to S113; S115 reacts in an intolerant manner.

We operationalize *empathy/antipathy* on the plane of *emotions*. Accordingly, indicators might be regulating negative group emotions or rather showing positive support (we prefer to categorize "cognitive empathy" as a form of inclusion of the other in dialogue).

S1: "[…] you are not so right because at the end you said ehm, eh, that- never mind. It's just ehm I think that, that the dad's right".

S1 disagrees with another student's opinion but introduces her disagreement in an empathetic way.

S122: I have no place to write
S121: Do I care?

S122 informs S121 that he does not have enough space to write the assignment. S121 shows lack of empathy in her reaction.

We operationalize *inclusion/exclusion* in terms of interactive *participation*. Accordingly, indicators might be including/excluding others' interventions, transactivity in building on others' ideas.

S8: "I think that what you say is wrong because, any boy can do whatever a girl can do and any girl can play whatever a boy does".

S8 includes what another student has just said, despite her disagreement with the student's statement.

S6: "So, wait! And then at the end, the son showed him that he can dance ballet".

S6 blocks another student's willingness to participate in the discussion who seems to want to take the floor.

The main elements of our analytic approach are summarized in Fig. 8.1.

8.4.3 DoE/EoD Interrelation and Prospect

The example excerpts presented in Sect. 8.4.2, taken from a single classroom interaction, illustrate our general analytical approach. However, they provide slender information for deepening our research question regarding the *interrelation* between DoE/EoD (represented in Fig. 8.1 by the question mark at the top), with the exception of student S1.

Student S1 had made the moral judgement that the boy mouse could not do only "girly stuff", which could be considered as intolerant. Note that she does not say that he should not do that at all, but rather, "not *only*", which could be considered a type of hybrid or partial (in)tolerance. However, in her relations to another student, S1 expresses disagreement, but in an empathetic way. It is interesting to speculate on this example: how can we reconcile both (partial) intolerance towards a fictional character, yet empathy towards other students? Might not someone who shows intolerance in a fictional case try to attenuate possible negative judgement from others, by being empathetic with them? This is an example of the types of questions that we hope our methodology will enable us to raise and, following analysis, solve.

Finally, it may be of interest to shift the notion of ethics of dialogue from the inter-individual level to that of the group per se. In that case, we could study the relations between shared moral judgements and the overall 'ethical climate' of the group.

8.5 Discussion and Conclusions

This chapter explores moral development amongst children and the ways it has been conceptualized, studies and analyzed over time. Moral development through social interaction has been given little attention in research, and when it has been addressed, it focused mostly on parent–child interaction, to the detriment of the quality of peer-interactions. Our work involves new interventional settings that trace moral development in dialogue. Additionally, the DIALLS program addresses three levels of interaction: whole-class teacher-mediated; small-group teacher-mediated; small-group unmediated. This scaling produces very rich and diverse interaction data. So far, we have analyzed three lesson transcripts and drawn initial conclusions. For example, the data analyzed indicates that the mediator's role bears great influence on the students' behavior, revealing their understanding of what is *expected* of them. In future work we expect to present deeper and more diverse data analysis.

DIALLS also includes adaptation of the materials to three age-groups: young children, pre-adolescents and adolescents. A wider analysis of the data will allow us to examine differences in understanding, execution and application of EoD/DoE at different ages.

Our methodological approach concerns both aspects DoE/EoD and relates to conduct reflected in dialogue. Whereas in past research actual behavior and development of conceptions of morals were considered separately, our methodology studies relations between them. We focus on interaction in the context of moral development, this being an aspect which was not extensively discussed within the dialogic education approach. We hope that our theoretical approach and methodology will provide us with a way to see and understand the way development occurs, what kinds of values and ethics are discussed and performed by speakers.

In the framework of past research children were presented with a moral dilemma and asked to solve it. Researchers strived to understand children's morality through their answers to questions defined by adults rather than children themselves. This methodology was not process-oriented: how could they understand development by examining its result? Following a microgenetic approach to analysis and applying it to the DIALLS data, we are looking for the ethical dimension within a dialogue. This analysis approach might enable us to deal with another bias than the androcentric one pointed out by Gilligan (1977, see §2). Gilligan critiqued Kohlberg for asking females the same questions as males and expecting the same manner and character of morality in their answers: similarly biased is the adult-centered approach, seeing children's answers and results through the lens of those that an adult might come up with. Presenting a child with a problem that an adult sees as moral and having a certain solution is a problematic approach. There is a qualitative difference between a child's solution and that of an adult. In DIALLS the children are not presented with a moral dilemma, they carve it out of the texts themselves, albeit under teacher guidance in many cases, defining what is a moral dilemma themselves, which they are not asked to solve, but rather to engage in a rich discussion with respect to it. Thus, we do not judge children's answers because there is no pre-defined question. Rather, we analyze the way they interact around the narrative (interpreting it, judging it and conceptualizing it—DoE) and amongst themselves (EoD). The DIALLS settings and the methodology we promulgate opens the door for research on moral development as the development of dialogue among children on ethics, and of the ethics of dialogue.

References

Armaşu, V.D. 2012. Modern approaches to politeness theory. A cultural context. *Lingua. Language and Culture* 1: 9–19.

Baldwin, J.M. 1906. *Mental development in the child and the race*. New York: Macmillan & Co.

Bauman, Z. 1988. Strangers: The social construction of universality and particularity. *Telos* 28: 7–42.

Brown, P., and S.C. Levinson. 1987. *Politeness: Some universals in language usage*. Cambridge: Cambridge University Press.

Damon, W., and M. Killen. 1982. Peer interaction and the process of change in children's moral reasoning. *Merrill-Palmer Quarterly* 28 (3): 347–367.

Derrida, J. 1973. Différance. In *Speech and phenomena: And other essays on Husserl's theory of signs*, ed. J. Derrida. Evanston: Northwestern University Press.

Foucault, M. 1972. *Power/knowledge: Selected interviews and other writings*. New York: Patheon Books.
Gilligan, C. 1977. In a different voice: Women's conceptions of self and morality. *Harvard Educational Review* 47 (4): 481–517.
Goffman, E. 1967. On face-work. In *Interaction ritual: Essays on face-to-face behaviour*, 5–45. Harmondsworth: Penguin [Originally appeared 1955. *Psychiatry: Journal of Interpersonal Relations* 18 (3): 213–231].
Grosz, B.J., and C. Sidner. 1986. Attention, intentions and the structure of discourse. *Computational Linguistics* 12 (3): 175–204.
Grusec, J.E., and J.J. Goodnow. 1994. Impact of parental discipline methods on the child's internalization of values: A reconceptualization of current points of view. *Developmental Psychology* 30: 4–19.
Higham, R., and H. De Vynck. 2020. Creating and 'ethic of care' in a vertical tutor group. In *The Routledge international handbook of research on dialogic education*, ed. N. Mercer, R. Wegerif, and L. Major, 622–633. Routledge.
Hollingsworth, L.A., M.J. Didelot, and J.O. Smith. 2003. REACH beyond tolerance: A framework for teaching children empathy and responsibility. *Journal of Humanistic Counseling, Education and Development* 42: 139–151.
Horn, S.S. 2003. Adolescents' reasoning about exclusion from social groups. *Developmental Psychology* 39 (1): 71–84.
Kant, I. 2015. *Critique of practical reason*. Translated and Edited by M.J. Gregor. Cambridge: Cambridge University Press.
Killen, M., and C. Stangor. 2001. Children's social reasoning about Inclusion and exclusion in gender and race peer group contexts. *Child Development* 72 (1): 174–186.
Kochanska, G., and N. Aksan. 1995. Mother-child mutually positive affect, the quality of child compliance to requests and prohibitions, and maternal control as correlates of early internalization. *Child Development* 66: 236–254.
Kohlberg, L., and R.H. Hersh. 1977. Moral development: A review of the theory. *Theory into Practice* 16 (2): 53–59.
Lähdesmäki, T., A.K. Koistinen, and S. Ylönen. 2020. *Intercultural dialogue in the European education policies: A conceptual approach*. Cham: Palgrave Macmillan.
Lemke, J.L. 2001. The long and the short of it: Comments on multiple timescale studies of human activity. *The Journal of the Learning Sciences* 10 (1 & 2): 17–26.
Lévinas, E. 1969. *Totality and infinity: An essay on exteriority*, trans. A. Lingis. Pittsburgh: Duquesne University Press.
Marcus, G., and M.M.J. Fischer. 1986. *Anthropology as cultural critique: The experimental moment in the human sciences*. Chicago: University of Chicago Press.
Morand, D.A. 1996. Politeness as a universal variable in cross-cultural managerial communication. *The International Journal of Organizational Analysis* 4 (1): 52–74.
Nietzsche, F.W. 1966. *Beyond good and evil: Prelude to a philosophy of the future*, translated with commentary by W. Kaufmann. New York: Vintage.
Patry, J.L., S. Weyringer, and A. Weinberger. 2008. Interaction of science and values in schools: VaKE—A method to nurture moral sensibilities. In *Educating moral sensibilities in urban schools*, ed. K. Tirri, 157–170. Sense publishers.
Piaget, J. 1965. *The moral judgment of the child*. London: Kegan Paul [*Le jugement moral chez l'enfant*. Trench, Trubner and Co., 1932].
Plato. 2013. *Republic*. Edited and Translated by C. Emlyn-Jones and W. Preddy. Cambridge, MA: Harvard University Press.
Scollon, R., and S. Scollon. 1995. *Intercultural communication: A discourse approach*. Oxford: Bazil Blackwell.
Scribner, S. 1985. Vygotsky's uses of history. In *Culture, communication and cognition: Vygotskian perspectives*, ed. J.V. Wertsch, 119–145. Cambridge University Press.

Turiel, E. 1983. *The development of social knowledge: Morality and convention*. Cambridge, UK: Cambridge University Press.
Wegerif, R. 2020. Towards a dialogic theory of education for the internet age. In *The Routledge international handbook of research on dialogic education*, ed. N. Mercer, R. Wegerif, and L. Major, 14–26. Routledge.

Talli Cedar is a Postdoctoral Researcher at The Hebrew University of Jerusalem's school of education. Her research focuses on pragmatics, discourse analysis, positioning and translation studies.

Michael J. Baker is a tenured Research Professor in language sciences of the Centre National de la Recherche Scientifique at Télécom Paris. His research aims to understand the processes of collaborative learning and work, drawing on dialogue and argumentation analysis.

Lucas M. Bietti is an Associate Professor in psychology at the Norwegian University of Science and Technology. He holds an honorary affiliation with Centre National de la Recherche Scientifique at Télécom Paris.

Françoise Détienne is a tenured Research Professor in cognitive ergonomics of the Centre National de la Recherche Scientifique at Télécom Paris. Her research focuses on technology-mediated collaboration, co-design and online epistemic communities.

Erez Nir is a Postdoctoral Researcher at The Hebrew University of Jerusalem's school of education. His fields of research are philosophy of imagination, ontological and educational dialogue and the epistemology of 'torah' and revelation.

Gabriel Pallarès is a Postdoctoral Researcher in educational science at Centre National de la Recherche Scientifique at Télécom Paris. His research activities are mainly focused on understanding the teaching and learning of argumentation and critical thinking.

Baruch B. Schwarz is a Professor of Education at the Hebrew University of Jerusalem. His research focuses on learning in social interaction, especially within the context of collaborative learning and argumentation in various domains of knowledge.

Chapter 9
Being (Un)safe Together: Student Group Dynamics, Facework and Argumentation

Benjamin Brummernhenrich, Michael J. Baker, Lucas M. Bietti, Françoise Détienne, and Regina Jucks

9.1 Introduction

Small group work offers the opportunity for students to engage in many-sided discussions. Students can learn how to argue standpoints and develop argumentative competence (i.e. *learning to argue*: Kuhn and Crowell 2011) but may also, by using argumentative structures, learn about and tease apart relevant facets of the topic at hand (i.e. *arguing to learn*: Andriessen et al. 2003; Andriessen and Baker 2014). In the DIALLS project (see Chapter 1 in this volume) for example, student groups discussed what the concept of "home" could mean. On the one hand, this brought about multiple conceptualizations of the term, especially in diverse classrooms, because students brought very different personal histories regarding living spaces and migration to the table. On the other hand, from the teacher's insistence that the students find a common definition that would encompass all those different experiences, they found out what it meant to argue a point and make sure all sides were represented in the final product.

B. Brummernhenrich (✉) · R. Jucks
University of Münster, Münster, Germany
e-mail: brummernhenrich@uni-muenster.de

R. Jucks
e-mail: jucks@uni-muenster.de

M. J. Baker · F. Détienne
Centre National de la Recherche Scientifique at Télécom Paris, Paris, France
e-mail: michael.baker@telecom-paris.fr

F. Détienne
e-mail: francoise.detienne@telecom-paris.fr

L. M. Bietti
The Norwegian University of Science and Technology, Trondheim, Norway
e-mail: lucas.bietti@ntnu.no

F. Maine and M. Vrikki (eds.), *Dialogue for Intercultural Understanding*,
https://doi.org/10.1007/978-3-030-71778-0_9

Although these processes can be beneficial for both arguing to learn as well as learning to argue, their success is predicated on the characteristics of the group enacting them. Discussions happen in a social, interpersonal context. Especially in small group collaborative learning, the social relationships between students should have a stronger and more direct impact on the form and content of their contributions than in more direct, teacher-led instruction. In this chapter, we will seek to specify the relations between cognitive and social aspects of collaborative argumentation and illustrate them with an example from the DIALLS lesson recordings. These considerations will lead to a testable hypothesis: argumentation that thoroughly considers multiple perspectives thrives in social contexts in which students feel psychologically *safe* to provide novel viewpoints and critically engage with each other. We will also delineate methodological approaches to analyzing these different aspects empirically.

9.2 Interpersonal Tension, Face-Threatening Acts and Politeness Strategies

Argumentative interaction can be considered as an important test case for understanding the relations between social and cognitive dimensions of group work, given that the mutual recognition of disagreement creates interpersonal tensions (Andriessen et al. 2011), a 'problem to be solved', with respect to the task, the interaction and the interpersonal relationship. Critique of the other's proposals, expressed in a more or less aggressive manner, will usually be experienced as a critique of the person who expressed them (Muntigl and Turnbull 1998) and thereby as a threat to the recipient's *face*.

Politeness theory (Brown and Levinson 1987) defines face as "the positive social value a person effectively claims for himself" (Goffman 1967, p. 5), referring to a claim to certain interpersonal needs: appreciation and belonging (implying closeness to others), and autonomy (implying distance). These aspects of personal value can be threatened but also enhanced in interaction with others. This offers a useful perspective on the role of social considerations in small group discussions: students threaten their peers' face—and open themselves up to being threatened—when they are critical of what other group members do or say, face mistakes they have made themselves, tell or ask other students to show a certain behavior, or are asked to do so by others. Speech acts such as these, that represent an imposition on the recipient, are examples of *face-threatening acts* (for a more detailed definition see Brummernhenrich and Jucks 2013).

The relevance of face considerations in learning was first recognized from an instructor–learner relationship perspective (e.g., Kerssen-Griep 2001) but was soon extended to group learning (e.g., Chiu and Khoo 2003). In argumentative discourse, openly criticizing another student's argument, but also extending it and thus pointing out aspects that were previously lacking should be the most salient instances of face threats. Students can also risk threatening their own face by offering unusual perspectives that may invite ridicule.

Because all individuals endeavor to maintain their face, and because communication is by its nature cooperative (Grice 1975), people will generally try to mitigate the effect of face threats. Of course, one way to do this is to avoid face threats altogether, a phenomenon observed in one-to-one tutoring (Person et al. 1995). From this perspective, it is easy to see how face considerations can impede productive group discussions. However, it is also possible to mitigate face threats by using *politeness strategies* (Brown and Levinson 1987), such as hedging one's contribution ("maybe", "in a way", "if I understand correctly", etc.) and using indirect speech ("I would rather", "It would also be possible"). Another possibility is to include others ("Shouldn't we maybe", "Let's rather focus on") or to use solidarity markers.

Brown and Levinson (1987) suggested that the strategy that speakers would use depended on the "weight" of the imposition, the social distance between the interlocutors, and hierarchical differences. In a learning context, the nature and history of interpersonal relationships within the group thus plays an influential role: students who have not worked together for long will be more hesitant to be face-threatening. In groups that know each other well, this can reverse into "playful rudeness" (Ogan et al. 2012). In groups with a confrontational style, in which face threats are made routinely and bluntly, interpersonal relationships may suffer, leading to a deterioration of group members' goodwill and to less successful group work (Chiu and Khoo 2003). But whether this is so also depends on cultural discourse practices. For example, a particular culturally inscribed form of discourse in Israel known as "dugri" speech (approximately: "straight talk") welcomes open disagreement without necessarily seeking harmony or consensus (Matusov 1996). Such discourse contrasts markedly with the almost complete avoidance of overt disagreement and conflict in Japanese culture, in order to preserve group harmony, or *wa* (Détienne et al. 2017).

Thus, in argumentative interactions there is a fundamental paradox: the more an argumentative conflict is 'deepened', the greater will be the threat to maintaining a positive interpersonal relationship; therefore, the interaction would tend towards remaining on a more superficial level (cf. Isohätälä et al. 2017). However, such an educative interaction would risk losing its very point (i.e., deepening shared understanding of a problem). Thus, conflicts would tend to be deepened only to the extent that the interpersonal relationship would allow, which in turn implies that the best collaborative working relationship from the point of view of arguing to *learn* (Andriessen and Baker 2014) would be one that is sufficiently strong and 'safe' such that it allows students to take the necessary interactional risks.

9.3 Risk Taking and Psychosocial Safety

The concepts of *team psychosocial safety*, *conflict norms*, and *group climate* have been developed as group-level constructs in different fields of management, in particular organizational learning and group creativity (Paulus and Nijstad 2003). These constructs aim to explain or predict why some teams are more efficient than others, in particular for non-routine tasks that require knowledge elaboration, such as debates about new solutions or re-elaboration of procedures.

Team psychosocial safety is defined as a shared belief that the team is safe for interpersonal risk taking (Edmondson 1999; also compare this to the notion of a safe space, as laid out in Chapter 4 of this book). As a group-level construct, it assumes that team members share the same perception. It has to be distinguished from group cohesiveness, which can reduce willingness to disagree and challenge others' views as in the phenomenon of groupthink (Janis 1982), implying a lack of interpersonal risk taking. According to Edmondson (ibid., p. 354) "The term is meant to suggest neither a careless sense of permissiveness, nor an unrelentingly positive affect but, rather, a sense of confidence that the team will not embarrass, reject, or punish someone for speaking up. This confidence stems from mutual respect and trust among team members."

Team psychosocial safety is assumed to benefit an ongoing process of reflection and action, characterized by asking questions, seeking feedback, experimenting, reflecting on results, and discussing errors or unexpected outcomes of action (see e.g. Schön 1983, and the educational philosophy of Dewey). Edmondson's (op. cit.) analyses of work teams supported the idea that team psychosocial safety is positively associated with learning behavior in organizational work teams and that team learning behavior mediates between team psychosocial safety and team performance.

Jehn (1995) introduced the concept of *conflict norms*, which refers to group norms encouraging an openness to conflict and acceptance of disagreement. Related to team management and leadership style, this concept refers to elaborated norms within groups rather than shared perceptions, which are not necessarily reified as explicit rules (such as in the case of team psychosocial safety). Whereas conflicts can be detrimental for routine tasks, they tend to be beneficial for non-routine tasks, in particular when group norms promote open discussion of task issues, critical evaluation of problems and decision options (Jehn 1995).

Finally, research on group creativity has focused on the relationship between *group climate* and the creative process (Paulus and Nijstad 2003). Creativity involves both divergent (idea generation as broad as possible) and convergent (selection and deepening of ideas) processes. While openness of thought without overly critical debate is necessary while diverging, critical and constructive debates are necessary in converging moves. Whereas this approach has inspired methods for creativity and experimental studies testing them, other approaches based on surveys and field studies have advanced the concept of group climate, closely related to cultures of collaboration (Détienne et al. 2017), to account for better creativity and innovation in groups. West (2003) argues that group innovation requires high levels of trust between team members and a group climate characterized by participative safety.

To conclude, the concepts of team psychosocial safety, conflict norms, and group climate aim to explain differences in group performance, learning and creativity in non-routine tasks. In relation to the findings about interpersonal tension and face threats in collaborative argumentation, students' beliefs about the nature of the interpersonal relations within the group should determine how they deal with critiques, rebuttals, novel perspectives and other challenging situations. Empirical findings bear this out: peer acceptance seems to drive student engagement (Wentzel et al. 2020), and perceiving psychological safety is key for people to feel ready to take interactional risks (Edmondson 2003).

9.4 Supportive and Defensive Behavior

The novelty of our approach is to link these group-level constructs to concrete communication behaviors, as observed in task-oriented collective activities, on both the social level (i.e., face-threatening acts and supportive behaviors) but also the cognitive level (i.e., deepening and co-elaboration of knowledge). In other words, our question is: To what extent is students' willingness to engage in face-threatening communication determined by perceptions of psychosocial safety, and linked to the quality of argumentation within the group?

Communicative behaviors in the classroom can be either defensive or supportive (Gibb 1961; Garvin-Doxas and Barker 2004). Face-threatening acts from one student can lead to defensive communication in the addressee. Gibb developed a typology of behaviors that can help provide a comprehensive description of the communication 'climate' in the group. The typology consists of six categories each constituting a continuum, from defensive to supportive communication. Categories (Gibb 1961) are classified as either defensive or supportive with regards to how communicative behaviors are perceived and understood by interacting partners in dialogue.

Evaluation and description. Evaluation is a case of defensive communication because it relies on the (moral) judgment of students' ideas and opinions. It puts into question other students' performance in relation to the group activity. Description is an instance of supportive communication. It does not rely on judging students' performance but rather on the inclusion of additional information. This may involve requests to share students' feelings and more general experiences that may be relevant for the group activity.

Control and problem orientation. Control is an example of defensive communication aiming at changing students' attitudes and behaviors, based on the assumption that their performance is not appropriate. Problem orientation is supportive because it does not attempt to produce a sudden change in attitudes and behavior but rather to foster cooperation, in order to find more adequate solutions in a collaborative manner.

Strategic and spontaneous. Strategic communication is driven by the intention to manœuver students' attitudes and behaviors towards other students' and teachers' preferences. Hence, it represents a clear case of manipulative behavior in the classroom. On the other hand, spontaneous communication is not perceived to be prompted by hidden motives or selfish interests.

Neutrality and empathy. Neutrality as a communicative behavior in students and teachers may lead to the impression that other students' attitudes, behaviors and ideas are not valued or worth telling. Empathy is about understanding other students' beliefs, feelings and opinions and may lead to the identification with other students' experiences. Explicit understanding and identification increase trust among students and between students and teachers.

Superiority and equality. Superiority occurs when students or teachers include messages in their classroom communication that imply real or perceived higher status (e.g., power, wealth, intellectual ability and physical characteristics) compared to other students. Equality, on the other hand, appears when such differences are blurred and more horizontal forms of collaboration are perceived among students and between them and teachers.

Certainty and provisionalism. Certainty is associated with feelings of superiority. Students' and teachers' dogmatism about their attitudes, beliefs, behaviors and opinions blocks constructive dialogue and provokes a defensive reaction in other students. Provisionalism transmits openness and willingness to engage in collaborative activities, and it is essential for successful cooperation in group work.

Whether a group communicates in a predominantly supportive or defensive manner can be an additional indicator of the social climate of the group. Where face-threatening acts are unavoidable if an argument is to make progress and can only be mitigated when they become necessary, with supportive behavior there is a real choice: A disagreement can be communicated in an empathetic, provisional, problem-oriented manner, or in a seemingly neutral, but certain and controlling one. A group that shows supportive communication should be one in which the members feel psychosocially safe enough to tolerate the inevitable tension that is part and parcel of competent argumentation.

One step remains before we can fully operationalize our hypothesis, and that is to define what we mean by constructive argumentation in the sense of 'arguing to learn' and to specify which concrete argumentative strategies, visible in the group's argumentation, could be linked to interpersonal characteristics of the group as well as social aspects of their communication.

9.5 What Is a Good Argument to Learn From?

A main goal of dialogic classrooms is to engender high-quality argumentation. By 'high quality' here we refer primarily to argumentation that enables deepening of understanding of a problem, rather than to formal or quasi-logical validity. Students should consider multiple perspectives on a problem but also analyze each perspective critically by adding needed information and pointing out problems and suggestions for solving them.

This can be understood in terms of processes by which students "broaden and deepen" their understanding of a "space of debate" (Baker et al. 2007). The space of debate can be considered to be the set of theses that are maintained, with (counter-)arguments and systems of concepts and values underlying them as represented by a set of texts, circulating in society, studied by students as preparation for debate on socio-scientific questions. Broadening and deepening processes have

Table 9.1 Broadening and deepening understanding of a space of debate along conceptual and argumentative dimensions

	Broadening	*Deepening*
Solutions/concepts	[1] Multiplying alternative solutions, ideas, theses	[2] Discussing the meaning of key underlying concepts in the domain of discourse
Argumentation	[3] Multiplying alternative (counter-)arguments for a given thesis	[4] Chaining (counter-)arguments on (counter-)arguments, descending in the argumentative structure

two dimensions: (1) problem-solving solutions and concepts, and (2) argumentative. Usually the two go hand in hand, as argumentative interaction stimulates processes of meaning-making. The first dimension can also be understood in terms of the above-mentioned group creativity processes of divergence—proposing alternative ideas or solutions—and convergence (Paulus and Yang 2000)—further elaborating a given solution. Table 9.1 shows the way in which the two dimensions interact with broadening and deepening (the four cases are numbered for further reference).

A "good" argument is thus one that has sufficient deepening in the space of debate, meaning that students are considering the meanings of the key concepts and chaining arguments together, after having engaged in sufficient broadening by having considered multiple viewpoints and their arguments.

9.6 Bringing Back the Social Context

How do the interlocking dimensions defining the space of debate relate to social relations? It would be tempting to posit that argumentative broadening ([3], in Table 9.1) would be associated with an irenic interaction, making little threat to the interpersonal relation, and the opposite for deepening the argument ([4]). Similarly, on the level of concepts, broadening would pose no interpersonal threat, neither would deepening along this dimension ([2]).

Argumentative deepening ([4]) seems the best candidate for such a clear relation between cognition in interaction, social relations and emotions: the deeper the argument chain, the longer the conflict is pursued, the greater the threat to the interpersonal relation and the greater would be the problem of regulation of negative emotions.

However, the other cases are arguably more complex and contextual, depending on the argumentative *strategies* involved. Thus, multiplying alternative ideas ([1]) or discussing meanings could occur as attempts to explore, to find the best solution. They could also occur as strategic attempts to avoid losing an argument, to cloud the issue at hand, or as means to differentiate concepts from each other so that each can be 'right' (if x is understood as y, then you're right; if it's z, then I'm right), effectively 'diffusing' a potentially face-threatening situation. These strategies are likely in groups in which students are either not familiar enough to feel safe enough to get into the thick of disputative argumentation or in groups that know each other well but are too concerned with maintaining their positive relationships.

Other specific aspects of argumentation are also relevant to social–cognitive relations. For example, use of strategic manœuvering, trying to shift the burden of proof ("It's not for me to prove the existence of God, it's for you to prove he does not exist!") could be experienced as exasperating time-wasting, claiming the other is self-contradictory could be experienced as aggressive, insisting that the other admit defeat prevents the saving of face, and of course, the use of fallacies such as certain forms of *ad hominem* argument shift the debate onto a negative interpersonal plane. This should only happen in groups in which students are unconcerned about the potential interpersonal fallout.

Figure 9.1 visualizes the hypothesized relationships between the social and cognitive dimensions constructs that have been discussed and a real-life example will serve to illustrate them further.

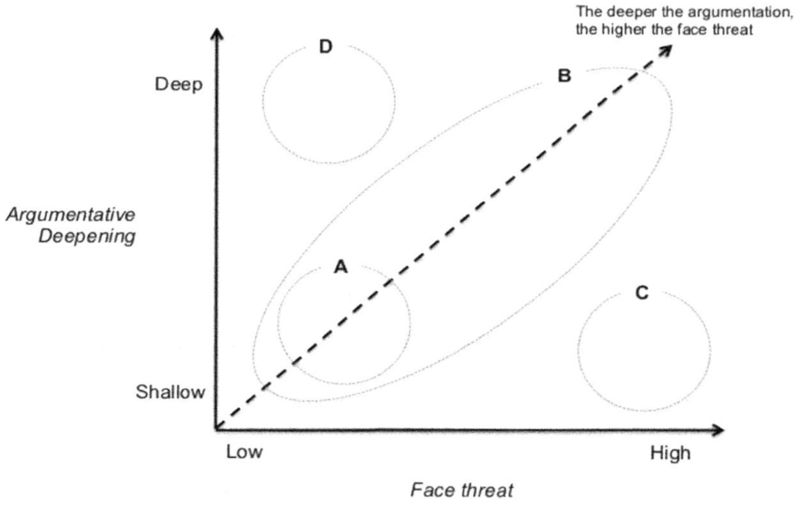

Legend: A: Group with weak interpersonal relationship and low psychosocial safety: remains in zone of shallow argumentation and low face threat

B: Group with strong interpersonal relationship: high psychosocial safety enables group to deepen argument yet bear and regulate higher face threat, moving flexibly between high/low, deep/shallow

C: Group with shallow argument yet high face threat: this corresponds to an interpersonal quarrel

D: Group that deepens argument yet manages to keep face-threatening low – e.g. with extensive use of polite redress ('it could possibly be said that …'), solidarity markers, supportive behaviour, etc.

Fig. 9.1 Visualization of the model: Relations between social and cognitive dimensions of small group argumentation

9.7 An Example

The following example illustrates the methods that would enable an analysis of the kinds of relationships that our model proposes. We try to highlight instances of broadening and deepening of arguments as a content-related, cognitive aspect as well as markers of social aspects of the interaction: politeness strategies and face threats, as well as supportive and strategic interaction.

The following excerpt comes from a group of four students in a German ninth grade classroom. The students are working in small groups and discussing the wordless cut-paper leporello book "Excentric City", depicting several city scenes with people engaged in diverse, sometimes fantastical, sometimes commonplace activities, such as sitting at a desk writing something or sitting on the back of a large bird-like animal. The aim of the lesson is for students to grasp the meaning of the concept of diversity.

In the excerpt shown below, the four 14–15 year old girls have been discussing the question "How are people different?" S3 has been tasked with writing down the results of the discussion for later presentation to the class. S4 is currently absent. The excerpt starts with S2 stating the question again:

S2 What other differences can there be between people?
S3 Appearance.
S2 That's not at all important though is it, actually.
S3 Yeah, or rather skin color {can be} different.
S2 NO.
S3 Yes, in the past they differentiated based on that.
S2 Yeah, in the past, but we're not in the past.
S3 But still, anyway. I'll write in brackets.
S2 That's racist, S3. It's not as if they're different people.
S3 Yes, now I have already put a bracket there. Then tell me something else that I can write.
S2 Although it's not actually racist. It's just-
S3 Yeah, that's why, yeah.
S2 Yeah, but you shouldn't DIFFERENTIATE between people based on their skin color.
S3 Yes, but some people differentiate them like that anyhow.
S2 Yes, but if we don't write it down, then perhaps it's not like that (laughs), you know?
S3 No, it's still like that. I don't know how to say it.
S2 That makes no sense.
(S4 returns to the table prompting some off-task discussion)
S2 Yes, what are the differences?
S4 What have you written?
S2 Yes, but they're not simply other people just because they have a different skin color.
S4 Look, a dark egg, a white egg, but inside they all look the same.
S2 YES. (S2 and S4 high five and laugh)

S3 Ah, okay. That wasn't even funny.
S2 I wouldn't write that about the skin color (points to the piece of paper), are you different to me just because we have different skin? Skin color doesn't matter one bit. When you've been to Majorca, you're brown too.
S3 Yeah. Then I'll say hair color.
S2 NO.
S4 No, don't do that.
S2 (pushes S3's pencil from the paper and takes out some tipp-ex to remove what she's written)

On the content level, the students are debating whether appearance is a meaningful category for distinguishing people. After S3's initial proposal S2 disagrees immediately. This prompts S3 to suggest skin color as a specific instance of appearance. They then go back and forth, basically repeating arguments without going much deeper on them: some people do differentiate based on skin color (S3's point) but they should not (S2). S4 seems to add the clinching detail to S2's side by providing the "egg analogy". In summary, we see some slight deepening of arguments and counterarguments [4], possibly constrained by the students' (in)ability to express their thoughts.

On the interpersonal side this development is paralleled by heightening social tension: The discussion already starts off as a confrontation between S2 and S3 but the disagreements are nearly always mitigated by politeness strategies, especially "Yeah, but …" (i.e., agreeing but disagreeing). As the discussion progresses, there are increasing instances of very direct, unmitigated face threats: "That makes no sense," "That wasn't even funny," "No, don't do that." and the fact that S2 prevents S3 from writing on the paper. This type of controlling communication from S2 will reoccur in the course of the discussion. Especially S2 and S3 are continuously engaging in socially risky behavior by insisting on their own standpoints and contradicting the other's.

It is telling, then, that after this episode the students move away from the topic for a while and talk about their mutual dislike for another student in the class instead. This can be seen as an attempt to "get back into the green" and ease the tension that has arisen (Baker et al. 2013). It is also important to know that the group has been joking together before and will do so again in the next part. This could be an indicator that the possibility of tenaciously arguing out contentious points is afforded by a secure interpersonal relationship, whose 'signature' corresponds to the specific way in which facework and argumentative deepening 'play out' in the interaction.

After the short off-topic intermission, the group returns to the topic with S2, again, restating the question:

S2 So, what are the differences between different people?
S4 Character.
S2 What?
S3 Exactly.
S2 Different ways of thinking (points to the piece of paper for S3 to write it down).
S4 Hear, hear.

S2 Different opinions.
S1 Haha, like you and {S3}.
S2 Oh, now it's getting personal here. We don't want that [...] Uh. Do we have different interests, we do, don't we? Hm and, um, what makes YOU different from S14 (to S1)?
S1 Girl, boy.
S2 Yes, yes.
S1 [Guys, hey, I'll tell you something. So, actually] we're not all that different, all his marks are as bad as mine, we're both dumb.
S2 Brain cells (laughs).
S3 Stupidity (laughs).
S4 And cleverness.
S2 What else? Age.
S3 Yes (writes).
S2 Don't always make a new dash straight away (to S3), otherwise we won't have any more ideas later on and there'll be a line there.
S3 Then don't write anything.
S1 Yeah, but S2 always has to have everything neat.
S2 And you're crumpling the paper at the bottom (takes the piece of paper).
S3 It's already crumpled now.
S2 No.
S3 It is.
S4 Oh he he he. Hey, hey, hey. Fingerprint as a thingy, there are different ones.
S3 Ah, right (wants to write).
S2 Nope (holds the pen tightly).
S3 DNA.
S4 IDENTITY.

Content-wise, this is clearly on the side of broadening concepts [1]: The group simply enumerates concepts that could fit the question. They are thus offering diverging views on the subject matter but there is no arguing about their validity, only about S3's handling of the paper and writing.

Accordingly, this part of the discussion starts off in a much calmer manner than the last. There is no confrontation and there are no face threats to speak of until shortly before the end, and quite a bit of joking and laughing together (including former opponents S2 and S3). However, tensions return when S2 makes it clear, in a face-threatening manner, that she is unhappy with S3's writing, showing a controlling stance. She is in turn mocked for it ("S2 always has to have everything neat"). S2 again prevents S3 from writing, but the mood is generally more joking than before, and most face threats are mitigated, however the discussion is also on a much shallower level. This changes again in the last part of the example when the concept of identity is elaborated:

S2 What is identity exactly?
S3 It's exactly the same as DNA.
S4 It's what makes you who you are.

S2 NO (to S3).
S4 It's what makes you who you are. TRUE.
S2 Identity?
S4 Name and that kind of thing.
S2 Crazy that we still don't even know what an identity is.
S3 Identity is when a person, um- You have an identity, everyone alive has an identity, when you-
S2 Yes, I know.
S4 Here people-
S2 S1. What is the difference between you and Mrs XY?
S1 Mrs XY is a teacher and I'm not.
S2 EDUCATION.
S4 No, no, roles, roles. Everyone has different roles.
S3 (To S4) Shh, be quiet.
S4 Everyone has different roles, we learned that in German class.
S3 Lol.
S4 Put it together now.
S3 That's what I'm doing.
S2 NO.
S3 Yes, I am (wants to write).
S2 She has to explain it first (holds the pen tightly).
S4 Roles. Everyone has different roles. At home you're the child that comes home. At school you're the pupil.
S1 Okay, I'll write.

This looks like a case of conceptual deepening [2]: The group argues the meaning of the concept "identity" by identifying subordinate concepts, such as names and roles. There is an interesting bit of metacognitive awareness, and thus problem orientation, when S2 realizes that it is "crazy that we still don't even know what an identity is." S4's suggestion of the concept of roles is not acknowledged immediately so she has to elaborate it until S1 finally takes it up.

S2 seems to be in a confrontational state of mind by now, uttering direct face threats ("NO") and holding onto S3's pen again. Her asking S1 about the difference between her and a teacher seems like strategic instead of spontaneous, supportive communication. But her insistence also induces S4 to make the concept of role clearer by adding another example: The socially risky behavior leads to (some) more deepening.

In summary, the excerpt shows a diverse range of argumentative as well as interpersonal behaviors. Our analysis also suggested ways in which the two may be intertwined: Phases of confrontational, face-threatening communication co-occur with progress in deepening arguments and concepts. However, this is only possible because the group seems to share a sense of psychosocial safety which rises to the surface in episodes of joking and supportive, but also less argumentatively progressive communication.

9.8 Concluding Discussion

How do interpersonal characteristics of a student group impact the epistemic quality of their argumentation? We propose that broadening and deepening the space of debate entails interpersonal risks. The willingness to take these risks and threaten one's own or other's faces depends on perceived psychosocial safety. If students feel valued and evaluate their interpersonal relationship with other group members as stable and positive, it will be easier for them to "go out on a limb" and present novel perspectives or critiques. As explained in Chapter 4 of this book, a group that is a (psychosocially) safe space is also a necessary prerequisite for successful and empathic intercultural dialogue. The examples illustrate some of these processes.

How can these relations be operationalized? When analyzing transcripts of small-group discourse, positive relationships within the group should be evident in the way students interact with each other, through supportive behaviors between the group members. Perceived psychosocial safety cannot be observed directly from the interaction alone. However, how the group deals with potential face threats, how willing they are to take interactional risks can be a proxy for how students feel about working in the group: how many face threats are made, relative to the number of total turns? If face-threatening acts appear, how many are mitigated by politeness strategies or uttered without redress? And finally, broadening and deepening can be analyzed by enumerating the different viewpoints that the group considers, whether terms are defined and argued, and the way in which arguments relate to each other, accumulating in a linear way, or else in a 'descending' structure of arguments on arguments. In our example, we took a qualitative methodological approach that allows in-depth insights into single interactions. However, quantitative approaches would also be viable, such as calculating the ratio of unmitigated face threats in an interaction and comparing this between discussions of differing argument quality.

However, it is unreasonable to assume a linear relationship between the three variables (supportive behavior in the group, risk-taking or face-threatening acts, and the quality of the students' argumentation). Certainly, negative relationships will lead to distrust and the unwillingness to make oneself vulnerable by offering a personal view, or alternatively to overly confrontational interactions where no empathetic perspective-taking occurs. However, a certain degree of tension and its regulation is needed for productive discussion.

A high ratio of positive affect and supportive behavior and few face threats might indicate a group focusing too strongly on relationship management, rather than working on a deep and multifaceted argument. In contrast, very frequent occurrences of blunt, direct face-threatening acts should be a sign of negative relationships, but the absence of face-threatening acts is also a bad sign as it signals that students are not comfortable to expose themselves. In a well-working group, we should see a rather high amount of face-threatening acts, but most of which should be mitigated by politeness strategies, excluding maybe some cases of "playful rudeness", going along with both broadening and deepening of the argument.

The DIALLS data offer a view into the discussions of student groups in very diverse classrooms and age groups all over Europe and Israel. The amount of variation that is likely to be seen in these discussions, along with the theoretical considerations and operationalizations of this chapter, will allow the testing of the hypotheses regarding the relationship between social and cognitive aspects of argumentation.

This will open up exciting possibilities for educational and learning research, such as analyzing the specific impact of online environments for argumentation (see Chapter 7, this book), a context that grows only more pertinent in a post-COVID-19 world. But it will also provide fuel for practical considerations: how can teachers and instructors engender contexts in which stable, safe relationships afford high-quality argumentation? We argue that fostering deep learning necessitates providing for one of the most basic human needs, the desire for positive social contact.

References

Andriessen, J., and M. Baker. 2014. Arguing to learn. In *The Cambridge handbook of the learning sciences*, ed. R. K. Sawyer, 439–460. Cambridge: Cambridge University Press. https://doi.org/10.1017/CBO9781139519526.027.

Andriessen, J., M.J. Baker, and D. Suthers. 2003. *Arguing to learn: Confronting cognitions in computer-supported collaborative learning environments*. Dordrecht: Kluwer Academic Publishers. https://doi.org/10.1007/978-94-017-0781-7.

Andriessen, J., M. Baker, and C. van der Puil. 2011. Socio-cognitive tension in collaborative working relations. In *Learning across sites: New tools, infrastructures and practices*, ed. S. Ludvigsen, A. Lund, I. Rasmussen, and R. Säljö, 222–242. New York: Routledge.

Baker, M., J. Andriessen, and S. Järvelä. 2013. *Affective learning together: Social and emotional dimensions of collaborative learning*. New York: Routledge.

Baker, M., J. Andriessen, K. Lund, M. van Amelsvoort, and M. Quignard. 2007. Rainbow: A framework for analysing computer-mediated pedagogical debates. *International Journal of Computer-Supported Collaborative Learning*. https://doi.org/10.1007/s11412-007-9022-4.

Brown, P., and S.C. Levinson. 1987. *Politeness: Some universals in language usage*. Cambridge: Cambridge University Press.

Brummernhenrich, B., and R. Jucks. 2013. Managing face threats and instructions in online tutoring. *Journal of Educational Psychology*. https://doi.org/10.1037/a0031928.

Chiu, M.M., and L. Khoo. 2003. Rudeness and status effects during group problem solving: Do they bias evaluations and reduce the likelihood of correct solutions? *Journal of Educational Psychology*. https://doi.org/10.1037/0022-0663.95.3.506.

Détienne, F., M. Baker, M. Vanhille, and C. Mougenot. 2017. Cultures of collaboration in engineering design education: A contrastive case study in France and Japan. *International Journal of Design Creativity and Innovation* 5: 104–128.

Edmondson, A. 1999. Psychological safety and learning behavior in work teams. *Administrative Science Quarterly*. https://doi.org/10.2307/2666999.

Edmondson, A.C. 2003. Managing the risk of learning: Psychological safety in work teams. In *International handbook of organizational teamwork and cooperative working*, ed. M.A. West, D. Tjosvold, and K.G. Smith, 255–275. Chichester, UK: Wiley.

Garvin-Doxas, K. and L.J. Barker. 2004. Communication in computer science classrooms: Understanding defensive climates as a means of creating supportive behaviors. *Journal of Educational Research in Computing*. https://doi.org/10.1145/1060071.1060073.

Gibb, J. R. 1961. Defensive communication. *Journal of Communication*. https://doi.org/10.1111/j.1460-2466.1961.tb00344.x.
Goffman, E. 1967. *Interaction ritual: Essays on face-to-face interaction*. Oxford: Aldine.
Grice, H.P. 1975. Logic and conversation. In *Syntax and semantics*, vol. 3, ed. P. Cole and J. Morgan, 41–58. New York: Academic Press.
Isohätälä, J., P. Näykki, S. Järvelä, and M. J. Baker. 2017. Striking a balance: Socio-emotional processes during argumentation in collaborative learning interaction. *Learning, Culture and Social Interaction*. https://doi.org/10.1016/j.lcsi.2017.09.003.
Janis, I.L. 1982. *Groupthink: Psychological studies of policy decisions and fiascoes*, 2nd ed. Boston: Houghton Mifflin.
Jehn, K.A. 1995. A multimethod examination of the benefits and detriments of intragroup conflict. *Administrative Science Quarterly*. https://doi.org/10.2307/2393638.
Kerssen-Griep, J. 2001. Teacher communication activities relevant to student motivation: Classroom facework and instructional communication competence. *Communication Education*. https://doi.org/10.1080/03634520109379252.
Kuhn, D., and A. Crowell. 2011. Dialogic argumentation as a vehicle for developing young adolescents' thinking. *Psychological Science*. https://doi.org/10.1177/0956797611402512.
Matusov, E. 1996. Intersubjectivity without Agreement. *Mind, Culture and Activity*. https://doi.org/10.1207/s15327884mca0301_4.
Muntigl, P., and W. Turnbull. 1998. Conversational structure and facework in arguing. *Journal of Pragmatics*. https://doi.org/10.1016/S0378-2166(97)00048-9.
Ogan, A., S. Finkelstein, E. Walker, R. Carlson, and J. Cassell. 2012. Rudeness and rapport: Insults and learning gains in peer tutoring. In *Intelligent tutoring systems*, vol. 7315, ed. S. Cerri, W. Clancey, G. Papadourakis, and K. Panourgia, 11–21. Berlin: Springer. https://doi.org/10.1007/978-3-642-30950-2_2.
Paulus, P.B., and B.A. Nijstad. 2003. *Group creativity: Innovation through collaboration*. New York: Oxford University Press.
Paulus, P. B., and H.-C. Yang. 2000. Idea generation in groups: A basis for creativity in organizations. *Organizational Behavior and Human Decision Processes*. https://doi.org/10.1006/obhd.2000.2888.
Person, N.K., R.J. Kreuz, R.A. Zwaan, and A.C. Graesser. 1995. Pragmatics and pedagogy: Conversational rules and politeness strategies may inhibit effective tutoring. *Cognition and Instruction*. https://doi.org/10.1207/s1532690xci1302_1.
Schön, D.A. 1983. *The reflective practitioner: How professionals think in action*. New York: Basic Books.
Wentzel, K. R., S. Jablansky, and N. R. Scalise. 2020. Peer social acceptance and academic achievement: A meta-analytic study. *Journal of Educational Psychology*. https://doi.org/10.1037/edu0000468.
West, M.A. 2003. Innovation implementation in work teams. In *Group creativity: Innovation through collaboration*, ed. P.B. Paulus and B.A. Nijstad, 245–276. New York: Oxford University Press.

Benjamin Brummernhenrich is a Senior Faculty Member at the Institute of Psychology for Education at the University of Münster in Germany. He researches the interplay of social processes and content in the communication between learners and instructors in diverse educational contexts.

Michael J. Baker is a tenured Research Professor in language sciences of the Centre National de la Recherche Scientifique at Télécom Paris. His research aims to understand the processes of collaborative learning and work, drawing on dialogue and argumentation analysis.

Lucas M. Bietti is an Associate Professor in psychology at the Norwegian University of Science and Technology. He holds an honorary affiliation with Centre National de la Recherche Scientifique at Télécom Paris.

Françoise Détienne is a tenured Research Professor in cognitive ergonomics of the Centre National de la Recherche Scientifique at Télécom Paris. Her research focuses on technology-mediated collaboration, co-design and online epistemic communities.

Regina Jucks is a Full Professor at the Institute of Psychology for Education at the University of Münster. Her research fields address various settings of instructional communication ranging from doctor–patient interaction to higher education.

Chapter 10
Engaging Teachers in Dialogic Teaching as a Way to Promote Cultural Literacy Learning: A Reflection on Teacher Professional Development

Riikka Hofmann, Maria Vrikki, and Maria Evagorou

10.1 Introduction

Effective teacher professional development (PD) is an important part of successfully implementing educational innovations (Bakkenes et al. 2010). However, research has shown that not all PD is effective, largely because it has not been developed based on theoretical understandings around teacher professional learning, such as reflective practice, teacher collaboration and teacher agency and inquiry (e.g. Borko et al. 2010; Hofmann 2019; Darling-Hammond et al. 2017). This chapter concerns the PD program developed as part of the DIALLS project. The chapter places particular emphasis on the ways in which the PD program was informed by the literature on teacher professional learning and effective features of PD, as well as the literature on promoting dialogic pedagogy. The literature on PD promoting dialogic pedagogy reports varied success (Hennessy and Davies 2019). Examining how PD programs can be informed more closely by the theory on teacher professional learning can contribute to this issue.

As mentioned in Chapter 1, a 15-lesson Cultural Literacy Learning Programme (CLLP) was created in order to promote the cultural literacy of students of three age groups, namely pre-primary, primary and secondary education. Each lesson introduced students to a cultural theme (e.g. tolerance, empathy, social responsibility) via a wordless text (short film or picturebook) as stimuli for dialogue and argumentation. The majority of teachers were novice to the use of wordless films or books and the

R. Hofmann (✉)
Faculty of Education, University of Cambridge, Cambridge, UK
e-mail: rjph2@cam.ac.uk

M. Vrikki · M. Evagorou
Department of Education, University of Nicosia, Nicosia, Cyprus
e-mail: vrikki.m@unic.ac.cy

M. Evagorou
e-mail: evagorou.m@unic.ac.cy

F. Maine and M. Vrikki (eds.), *Dialogue for Intercultural Understanding*,
https://doi.org/10.1007/978-3-030-71778-0_10

promotion of students' dialogue and argumentation skills. To address these innovations, a DIALLS PD program was developed in each of the seven countries where the CLLP was to be implemented.

The chapter starts by reviewing theories of professional learning and effective PD programs with a view to explain how these were incorporated in our PD program. It also describes the challenges often faced in supporting teacher reflection and collaborative learning and the ways in which these were addressed in our effort. It then discusses how the PD promoted dialogic pedagogy and argumentation as means to discuss cultural texts. It presents tool-mediated practices that were introduced in order to support teachers in promoting dialogue and argumentation in their teaching. We end by presenting the results emerging from a content analysis of qualitative comments made by teachers in the UK and Cyprus, reflecting on their experience with the PD and its benefits.

10.2 Theories of Teacher Professional Learning Incorporated in the DIALLS Professional Development

The development of the DIALLS professional development (PD) program built on literature on general features of effective teacher PD, and research on professional learning and change specifically related to developing productive classroom conversations. In a recent synthesis, we reviewed research on professional learning interventions for teachers (Hofmann 2019). The findings from across these reviews, alongside further research, suggest a number of key features for professional development to support teacher learning and change in classroom practice.

Firstly, professional development should focus on learning and teaching. This involves linking broad theoretical ideas about teaching to concrete examples of classroom practice, and critically examining those in light of new theories (see also Hennessy et al. 2016; Horn and Kane 2015). Secondly, PD should integrate opportunities for teachers to learn in communities of practitioners. Research suggests that collaborative conversations with colleagues are a key site for professional learning (Evagorou and Mauriz 2017; Bannister 2015; Rainio and Hofmann 2015, 2018; Vrikki et al. 2017). Thirdly, professional learning conversations should make salient challenging discourses and allow for opportunities to discuss those (Rainio and Hofmann 2015, 2018; Hofmann 2019). Based on this research, the professional learning principles of *reflection* and *collaborative learning* in *communities of practice* were identified (see also Chapter 11).

However, professional learning research has also identified a number of challenges in supporting teacher reflection and collaborative learning in communities of professionals. Research shows that learning is not an automatic outcome of conversations within communities of teachers (Horn and Kane 2015; Bannister 2015; Louie 2016). Discussing and reflecting on classroom evidence does not automatically lead to re-interpretation of practice (Rainio and Hofmann 2015, 2018; Vrikki et al. 2017). Instead, teaching and learning conversations often shy away from discussing challenges, or can be characterized by rushing into quick solutions. Research finds that this is due to unproductive discursive tools guiding professional conversations in teacher communities and professional development meetings (Vedder-Weiss et al. 2018), as well as teachers locating themselves as un-agentic vis-a-vis the desired change (Horn and Kane 2015; Rainio and Hofmann 2015, 2018). Finally, research on change towards integrating more pupils' ideas and dialogue into classroom practice shows the often under-appreciated importance of the underlying normative dimension as a hindrance to change (Hofmann and Ruthven 2018; Michaels and O'Connor 2015). Unspoken norms guide what teachers hold themselves and others accountable to in classroom practice (such as 'right answers' or 'offering immediate help'). If not explicitly addressed, the well-established classroom interaction norms can lead to dialogic interventions being implemented in a superficial way.

To support genuine professional learning and change in classroom practice, professional development therefore needs to focus on three key mechanisms of learning: the tool-mediated nature of professional change, fostering teachers' self-efficacy and understanding of their students' capabilities, and addressing the role of norms in changing sociocultural practice. We will discuss these in turn.

A sustained focus on learning and teaching in professional development conversations requires conceptual and discursive tools that enable practitioners to systematically address and re-interpret classroom practice and local challenges from the perspective of student learning (Hofmann 2016, 2019, 2020). An example of such tools was used by Dudley and Vrikki (2019) in their work with mathematics teachers who formed Lesson Study groups in order to collaboratively plan, teach and reflect on lessons. During these meetings, teachers followed a Lesson Study workbook,[1] which guided their discussions towards deeper reflection and evaluation of their teaching in relation to student learning. The tool had space for teachers to write their predictions about how specific students would respond to certain parts of the lesson and then compare those to how the students were observed responding. It also asked teachers to consider what they have discovered about how their students learn and how that would inform their future practice (Warwick et al. 2016). Another example is the 'People, Talk, Ideas' tool discussed below.

Professional learning research suggests that self-efficacy—professionals' belief in their ability to effectively handle challenges related to leadership, including self-motivational beliefs—is a key dimension in professional change (Endedijk et al. 2014), with greater self-efficacy linked to greater commitment and perseverance. We suggest that self-efficacy is central to counteract teachers' perceived lack of agency—participants' "possibility and willingness to impact (and eventually transform) the activity in the realisation of which they are engaged" (Hofmann and Rainio 2007, 309). A consistent finding from research on teaching and learning interventions in schools is that teachers often feel that dialogic and other reform interventions are going to be difficult to implement in their classrooms; an equally consistent finding

[1] Available at: https://lessonstudy.co.uk/new-lesson-study-workbook-free-to-download/.

is that they are commonly surprised at their students' learning and engagement once they do implement those interventions (Hofmann 2020).

Finally, our research has demonstrated the key role classroom norms play in shaping classroom practice (Hofmann and Ruthven 2018). Classroom cultures and practices are not simply attributable to individual teachers. Sociocultural norms of classroom interaction and practice affect those interactions and practice in ways that are often invisible to participants, unless broken. Unless explicitly addressed, established norms can hinder teachers' intentions to change their classroom practice. Key to developing more dialogic classroom practice is understanding the nature of the norms shaping dialogic interactions in schools. Our research has revealed the multi-dimensional nature of classroom norms which guide practice: surface level norms of classroom discussion, such as 'Respecting others' ideas', are not singular, but instead can be enunciated in terms of multiple underlying rationales which we have termed operational, interpersonal, discussional and ideational (Hofmann and Ruthven 2018). Professional development needs to make explicit the different dimensions in which rules for talk can be enacted in classrooms to avoid superficial adoption of new discursive practices. A tool developed based on this work, the People, Talk, Ideas tool (Hofmann and Ilie 2019), was employed in this project to support teachers in deepening their classroom dialogues. This tool makes salient the challenge that while many classroom discussions attend to the 'People' and the 'Talk' dimensions, they do not always attend equally to the important dimension of 'Ideas' (see Fig. 10.1). In making these dimensions of classroom dialogue visible to teachers and students

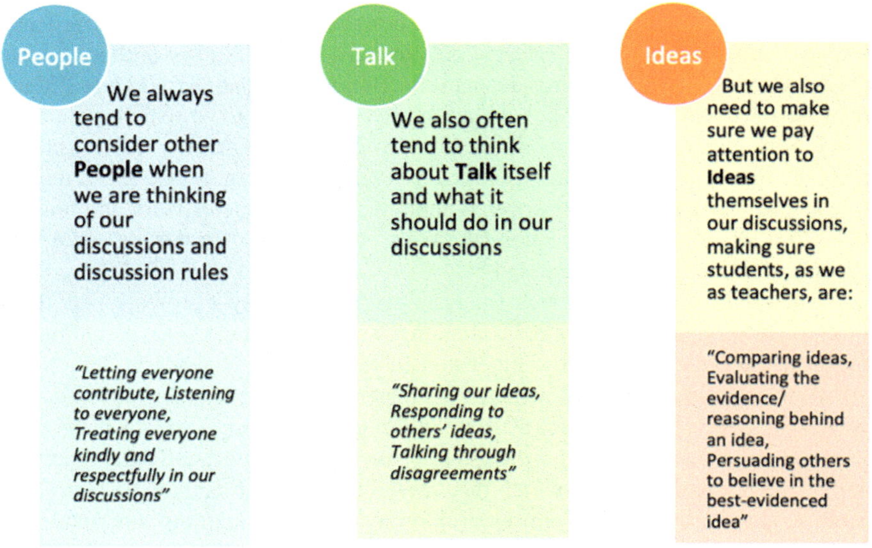

Fig. 10.1 People, Talk, Ideas tool (Hofmann and Ruthven 2018) (*Source* Hofmann and Ilie 2019; edtoolkit.educ.cam.ac.uk/toolkit/step2/)

alike, the tool helps them develop new forms of accountability to all of these three dimensions in classroom discussions.

10.3 Development and Implementation of the DIALLS Professional Development Programs

The described theoretical principles constituted the basis for the DIALLS professional development (PD) program. Specifically, we aimed to develop a PD that would enable reflective practices both on the part of the teacher participants and us as researchers, enhance teachers' sense of a community, and promote teachers' agency and inquiry. Teachers in the same school level (early years/primary/secondary) were involved in small-group and whole cohort discussions concerning key issues around dialogic teaching and learning, cultural literacy and using wordless texts. They were supported by a range of thinking and planning tools, and members of the DIALLS teams with significant expertise on facilitating teachers' professional learning.

Although each country locally adapted their own PD, the foundations were common. This section delves into PD development in two contexts, namely Cyprus and the UK, and the ways teachers were supported in their effort to implement the program in their practice. The researchers in both countries have a special interest in dialogue, argumentation and professional learning. In Cyprus, the PD was offered by the research team as a course of the Cyprus Pedagogical Institute, which is part of the Ministry of Education and Culture and it is the official body offering in-service training for teachers. The PD consisted of five two-hour sessions offered within a four-month period and it took place in three different cities covering the south and east part of Cyprus. In the UK, the PD was offered by the research team as three full days spread from October to June; the final one had to be offered as a part-day online due to COVID-19 lockdown.

A primary focus of the PDs was the promotion of dialogic pedagogy and argumentation as means to discuss the cultural texts and, thus, enhance students' cultural literacy over time. Literature has shown that transforming classroom practices to integrate dialogue and argumentation is challenging (Evagorou and Dillon 2011; Ruthven et al. 2017; Hofmann and Ruthven 2018; Maine and Hofmann 2016). Our PDs promoted dialogic pedagogy by incorporating the following four features:

- development of Ground Rules for Talk
- increasing teachers' awareness of different strategies supporting productive talk,
- highlighting features of productive student-student talk during collaborative group work
- introducing dialogue and argumentation within the context of cultural literacy learning, using wordless texts

These will be reviewed in turn.

10.3.1 Ground Rules for Talk

It was important to help teachers understand that a dialogic classroom ethos was crucial. During the implementation of the DIALLS lessons, students were expected to have opportunities to express their opinions freely in a safe place, without concerns of being judged or criticized. Similarly, they were expected to listen to others' views, consider them as alternatives to their own views and understand why they support one idea and not another. To this end, the PD introduced to the teachers a distinction between a dialogic classroom *ethos* (cf. Alexander 2008) and features of dialogic classroom *talk*. For the latter, 'ground rules for talk' were introduced as a strategy to the teachers to set social norms for talk both for teacher-student and student-student settings (Mercer et al. 2009; Littleton and Mercer 2013). According to Wegerif (2020), teaching ground rules 'is a form of culture change [because] any culture has implicit assumptions or expectations that shape explicit behaviour. These assumptions tend to be unconscious because you only become aware of them when they are challenged' (37).

Teachers were encouraged to negotiate such rules with their students at the beginning of the program and keep reminding them of the rules when necessary during the DIALLS lessons. Ground rules could vary from actions that create a collaborative and friendly environment to actions that encourage the critical evaluation of ideas. Decisions on which ground rules to agree on depends on the level of dialogicality a classroom already maintains and the maturity of the students. The teachers were encouraged to begin with ground rules that create a supportive environment for talk, such as "Everyone should contribute to the conversation", "Everyone listens to all ideas". Once embedded, teachers should revise the rules with their students in order to increase the level of dialogicality, supported by the People-Talk-Ideas tool described in Sect. 10.2. Examples of this could be "We build on each others' ideas", "We identify links between ideas".

10.3.2 Strategies Supporting Productive Talk

The PD concerned teacher strategies for supporting productive classroom discussions, such as questioning techniques and ways of responding to students' ideas during whole-class and small-group discussions. Literature has shown that classroom interactions typically follow the so-called Initiation-Response-Feedback/Evaluation pattern (Sinclain and Coulthard 1975; Howe et al. 2019). This consists of the following three parts: the teacher initiating an interaction with a closed question of low cognitive demand (Sedova et al. 2016); students responding with a short answer; and the teacher evaluating the answer based on correctness. As this interactional pattern does not allow for students to express 'half-baked' thinking which can be refined based on others' ideas and critical evaluations, PD on dialogic teaching has often focused on promoting teachers' use of open questions (e.g. Sedova et al. 2016;

Table 10.1 Examples of prompt questions to scaffold productive classroom discussions

	How to ask	How to respond
Exchanging ideas	What do you think ….?	I think that ……
Building on each other's ideas	What do you think about the idea proposed by X? Can someone continue on the idea proposed by X?	I agree with the idea proposed by X and I want to add that … I agree and also …….
Justifying argument	Why do you think that? What is your evidence?	I think that …. Because … If ……, then……
Discussing alternatives	What else could this mean? How did this make you feel?	I felt …… I was confused by …. I am not sure why…… This probably means……
Challenging ideas	Can someone challenge this idea?	Are you sure about this? I disagree with you because…… I do not agree with your idea because …

Wells and Arauz 2006; Lefstein and Snell 2014; Pehmer et al. 2015; Evagorou and Dillon 2020). These included authentic questions of high cognitive demand and with many possible answers. Examples are probe questions, such as asking a student for further explanation, clarification or reasoning. Similarly, uptake questions are follow up questions which incorporate a students' answer into a subsequent question. Particular attention was given to fostering *contingent* teacher responses to support students' group discussions (Hofmann and Mercer 2016). These are responses that link with students' current discussion without closing down student thinking or discussion. Examples of probe questions that were shared with the teachers during the PD, with prompts that can be used by the students to support productive talk are shown in Table 10.1.

10.3.3 Student-Student Talk

Collaborative learning is an important element of dialogic and argumentative teaching because it allows more students to express and discuss their views in the safe environment of their peers (Howe and Abedin 2013; Maine et al. 2020). Collaborative talk and argumentation, when appropriately scaffolded, lead to better learning outcomes (i.e. Evagorou and Osborne 2013) and the more the peers talk in the groups about conceptual issues, the higher the reasoning levels they achieve. This suggests that the ability to elaborate each other's ideas is associated with more sophisticated reasoning (Chin and Osborne 2010; Evagorou and Osborne 2013; Resnick et al. 2010).

Literature has shown that student-student interactions can vary in quality (Maine et al. 2020). Mercer and colleagues (e.g. Littleton and Mercer 2013) have identified three types of student-student talk: disputational, cumulative and exploratory. Disputational talk is characterized by disagreements and individual decisions; cumulative talk is characterized by general acceptance of all ideas and lack of critical evaluation; while exploratory talk is characterized by critical engagement with ideas, exploration of alternatives and attempts to reach consensus. Studies of students working collaboratively have identified that when students engage in exploratory talk, explicitly discussing each others' ideas, negotiating a shared understanding of what they are discussing and asking each other clarifying questions, this leads to better learning (i.e. Evagorou and Osborne 2013).

As group activities were central to our lessons, teachers were made aware of these three types of student talk with the help of two made-up examples of student-student talk around a text from the CLLP; one was characterized mostly by cumulative and disputational talk, while the other was characterized mostly by cumulative and exploratory talk. Teachers were asked to identify the one with more productive talk and explain why they chose it. Subsequently, teachers were asked to identify key words and phrases from their chosen example that supported their decision. We also discussed with them contingent but non-evaluative ways of supporting student discussions during group work (Hofmann and Mercer 2016; for practical examples see Hofmann and Ilie 2019, the ED:TALK Toolkit http://edtoolkit.educ.cam.ac.uk/).

10.3.4 The Context of Cultural Literacy Learning

Fourth, it was important to highlight how to facilitate dialogue and argumentation as a tool to develop cultural literacy using wordless texts. In order to discuss the themes that are included in the DIALLS Cultural Literacy Analysis Framework (DIALLS 2019), and therefore develop their cultural literacy skills, students should be able to participate in discussions that trigger the emergence of different, multiple perspectives (Rapanta et al. 2020). Dealing with multiple perspectives involves the ability to reflect on them, evaluate them and challenge them (Barrue and Albe 2013). Teachers can either approach cultural literacy through direct approaches—which aim to transmit and encourage the application of values defined by the teacher, or indirect approaches—also known as immersion approaches (Cavagnetto 2010)—which involve the implementation of dialogue. In DIALLS we applied the immersion approach and teachers were made aware during the PD that when engaging in the discussion of issues with multiple perspectives, their role is key, demanding and complex (Evagorou and Dillon 2011) and they should be prepared to allow different viewpoints, moral and ethical aspects to be discussed (Evagorou et al. 2014). During the PD in Cyprus, teachers reflected on their reluctance to discuss sensitive issues such as being different, or the issue of belonging, especially in classes with migrant students. Reflecting on teachers' needs, an external collaborator specializing on the discussion of sensitive topics (e.g. migration) in classes with young students was invited in order to help teachers introduce these topics, while maintaining a safe environment for everyone.

10.4 Teachers' Views of the PD

The professional development sessions in the UK and Cyprus were offered for pre-primary, primary and secondary school teachers. Throughout the PD the teachers were asked to reflect on the different aspects of the training and their experience from the implementation of the DIALLS lessons with their classes. Furthermore, at the end of the PD the teachers were asked to complete a reflection questionnaire, which contained questions about: (a) their experience with the PD, (b) their experience with the implementation of the program and (c) the impact of the program on their students. The questionnaire contained both closed and open-ended questions on these three topics.

This chapter focuses on the open-ended responses of 29 pre-primary ($n = 19$) and primary ($n = 10$) school teachers from Cyprus, and 6 secondary school teachers from the UK on their experience with the PD. A content analysis revealed themes that emerged from this data. This section is organised around these themes, citing some representative quotes.

10.4.1 Reflection About Teaching and Learning

The teachers reported that they really benefited from the opportunity "to reflect and react to the material we were going to teach" [UK_secondary] and to share "experiences teaching children the same types of lessons" [UK_secondary]. Teachers' enjoyed the focus of the professional development on "Strategies on how to deliver the lessons" and "Exploring new texts, and how these could be used analytically" which "added depth to analysis" [UK_secondary]. The use of wordless texts and videos (see Chapter 6 for more information) was also emphasized by pre-primary teachers in Cyprus "as they are important especially in supporting dialogue and argumentation skills for younger students". Teachers reported that they "enjoyed chatting and listening to other teachers' strategies and struggles when implementing the program in their classes" [UK_secondary] and would even "discuss the lessons both before and after the implementation with colleagues over the phone" [Cyprus_primary].

Teachers in Cyprus referred extensively to the fact that dialogue and argumentation were not part of their teaching practices, and initially they could not understand how to implement dialogue with younger students: "I did not know that it was possible to use dialogue and argumentation with younger students and during the PD I had the opportunity to acquire the skills of facilitating dialogue in a way that was easy, and provoked interest for my 5-year-old students" [Cyprus_pre-primary]. During the implementation of the DIALLS lessons the teachers reported a change in their practices, especially in relation to dialogue and argumentation: "I provide more time to listen to students' voices and now I invite my students to listen to each others' ideas and build on them when possible" [Cyprus_primary]. Teachers also reported on challenges that were related to the multiple perspectives of the issues that were discussed, and their difficulty facilitating a discussion "when I did not know what the correct response is" [Cyprus_primary]. These challenges were explicitly discussed during the PD sessions in Cyprus, and teachers engaged in exchange of practices and ideas as a way to support each other.

Teachers in both countries suggest that there was a change in their students as well, especially in terms of their dialogue and argumentation skills: "After the implementation of the DIALLS lessons the students in my class learned how to take turns during a discussion and offer their points of view. I am simply standing at the side of the class now watching students that would never offer their ideas before, turn into great speakers" [Cyprus_primary].

10.4.2 Collaborative Learning in Communities of Practice

The opportunity to discuss teaching and learning within the project together with other teachers, all implementing the same project, was repeatedly described by the teachers as one of the highlights of the professional development and teacher learning opportunities, and is also discussed in Chapter 11. Teachers in the UK reported that they benefited from "[b]eing able to work with others and meet teachers from different schools. Having the opportunity to reflect with other teachers and compare experiences" [UK_secondary]. Teachers in Cyprus said that "one of the most important aspects of the sessions was that we were able to share experiences, adaptations of the lessons and difficulties that we faced with colleagues from other schools" [Cyprus_pre-primary] but also with colleagues from other parts of Cyprus that were participating in PD sessions in other cities and they had never met in person. Furthermore, teachers highlighted the need for more PD sessions spread throughout the year as a way to "reflect on each of the lessons collaboratively before implementing another one" [Cyprus_pre-primary].

10.4.3 Indicators of Change in Self-Efficacy

We discussed above how teachers often experience themselves as un-agentic vis-à-vis school and student-related challenges, when asked to implement significant new teaching or curricular approaches in classrooms. Being able to see change in their students is a significant factor related to teachers' self-efficacy. Our teachers were initially sceptical about introducing dialogue and argumentation in their classes, mainly because they believed that their students lacked the ability to engage in dialogues. After participating in the PD and implementing the DIALLS lessons teachers report that "Implementing the lessons helped me and my students evolve. I can identify changes in my teaching, but also in my students' talk that can be attributed to DIALLS" [Cyprus_pre-primary]. Furthermore, teachers talked about how the changes in their classes further supported their own development: "Initially the PD helped me to change how I see my class as a whole. Now I focus on listening to everyone, I build on my students' ideas. My persistence in listening to each other also helped me with discipline issues that I had before the PD. I think it had to do with my students accepting everyone, a part of the cultural literacy theme of the PD" [Cyprus_pre-primary].

We also discussed theoretically how providing teachers with the tools to examine classroom norms and work together with students to change those to become more dialogic is central to professional change. An example of a key tool, the People, Talk, Ideas tool is illustrated above. The teachers responded very positively to this tool: they identified how hearing the ideas "on the rules of behaviour of group work and how this is different to the rules of dialogue" [UK_secondary] offered real new insights into developing classroom dialogic practice.

10.5 Conclusion

Effective professional development, according to Darling-Hammond and colleagues (2017), not only results in changes in teaching and teaching practices, but also in considerable changes in student learning. Teachers' views of the PD and the implementation of the DIALLS materials provide evidence of change in both directions, namely teaching practice and student learning. Teachers highlighted a change in their practices linked to introducing and facilitating dialogue and argumentation in their classes, but also reported improvements of the dialogic and argumentative ethos of their classrooms. Implementing innovations in education is never without challenges, and during the PD in the UK and Cyprus the researchers often reflected on the process and adapted their materials to support the needs of the teachers. The teachers' responses to the PD illustrate the benefits of the theoretical principles behind the PD design: reflection on learning and collaboration in communities of practitioners and supporting teachers' agency. In-depth reflection and productive collaborative dialogues among the teachers were made possible through the use of research-based tools supporting the teachers in re-thinking their practice and classroom dialogues. Beyond DIALLS, our case highlights the importance of building professional development interventions of solid theory of teacher learning and change.

References

Alexander, R.J. 2008. *Towards dialogic teaching: Rethinking classroom talk*, 4th ed. London: Dialogos.

Bakkenes, I., J.D. Vermunt, and T. Wubbels. 2010. Teacher learning in the context of educational innovation: Learning activities and learning outcomes of experienced teachers. *Learning and Instruction* 20 (6): 533–548.

Bannister, N.A. 2015. Reframing practice: Teacher learning through interactions in a collaborative group. *Journal of the Learning Sciences* 24 (3): 347–372.

Barrue, C., and V. Albe. 2013. Citizenship education and socioscientific issues: Implicit concept of citizenship in the curriculum. *Views of French Middle School Teachers, Science & Education* 22 (5): 1089–1114.

Borko, H., K. Koellner, and J.K. Jacobs. 2010. Contemporary approaches to teacher professional development. *International Encyclopedia of Education* 7: 548–556.

Cavagnetto, A. 2010. Argument to foster scientific literacy: A review of argument interventions in K-12 science contexts. *Review of Educational Research* 80 (3): 336–371.

Chin, C., and J. Osborne. 2010. Supporting argumentation through students' questions: Case studies in science classrooms. *Journal of the Learning Sciences* 19 (2): 230–284.

Darling-Hammond, L., M.E. Hyler, and M. Gardner. 2017. *Effective teacher professional development*. Palo Alto, CA: Learning Policy Institute.

Dudley, P. and M. Vrikki. 2019. Teachers' collaborative dialogues in contexts of lesson study. In *The Routledge International Handbook of Research on Dialogue Education*, ed. N. Mercer, R. Wegerif and L. Major, 217–226. Routledge.

Endedijk, M.D., M. Brekelmans, N. Verloop, P.J.C. Sleegers, and J.D. Vermunt. 2014. Individual differences in student teachers' self-regulated learning: An examination of regulation configurations in relation to conceptions of learning to teach. *Learning and individual differences* 30: 155–162.

Evagorou, M., and J. Dillon. 2011. Teachers' instructional practices and argumentation. In *Recognizing and judging quality science teaching*, ed. D. Corrigan, J. Dillon, and R. Gunstone, 189–204. Springer.

Evagorou, M. & Dillon, J. 2020. Socio-scientific issues as promoting responsible citizenship and innovation. In *Science Teacher Education for Responsible Citizenship*, ed. M. Evagorou, J. Nielsen and J. Dillon, 1–11. Springer. ISBN 978-3-030-40228-0.

Evagorou, M., and B.P. Mauriz. 2017. Engaging elementary school pre-service teachers in modeling a socioscientific issue as a way to help them appreciate the social aspects of science. *International Journal of Education in Mathematics, Science and Technology* 5 (2): 113–123.

Evagorou, M., and J. Osborne. 2013. Exploring young students' collaborative argumentation within a socio-scientific issue. *Journal of Research in Science Teaching* 50 (2): 209–237.

Evagorou, M., V. Albe, P. Angelides, C. Couso, G. Chirlesan, R. Evans, J. Dillon, A. Garrido, D. Guven, E. Mugaloglu, and J.A. Nielsen. 2014. Preparing pre-service science teachers to teach socio-scientific (SSI) argumentation. *Science Teacher Education* 69: 39–48.

Hennessy, S., and M. Davies. 2019. Teacher professional development to support classroom dialogue. In *The Routledge international handbook of research on dialogue education*, ed. N. Mercer, R. Wegerif, and L. Major, 238–253. Routledge.

Hennessy, S., B. Hassler, and R. Hofmann. 2016. Pedagogic change by Zambian primary school teachers participating in the OER4Schools professional development programme for one year. *Research Papers in Education* 31 (4): 399–427.

Hofmann, R., and A.P. Rainio. 2007. 'It doesn't matter what part you play, it just matters that you're there': Shared agency in narrative play activity in school. In *Language in action: Vygotsky and Leontievian legacy today*, ed. R. Alanen and S. Pöyhönen, 308–328. Newastle-upon-Tyne: Cambridge Scholars Publishing.

Hofmann, R. 2016. Leading professional change through research(ing): Conceptual tools for professional practice. In *Transformative professional doctoral research practice*, ed. P. Burnard, T. Dragovic, J. Flutter, and J. Alderton, 141–154. Rotterdam: Sense Publishers.

Hofmann, R. 2019. Dialogue, teachers and professional development. In *The Routledge international handbook of research on dialogue education*, ed. N. Mercer, R. Wegerif, and L. Major, 213–216. Routledge.

Hofmann, R., and S. Ilie. 2019. ED:TALK Toolkit: An evidence and dialogue toolkit. edtoolkit.educ.cam.ac.uk/. Accessed 29 June 2020.

Hofmann, R. 2020. *Reconceptualizing the mechanisms of change in professional learning and practice* [Paper Session]. AERA Annual Meeting San Francisco, CA, April 17–21. http://tinyurl.com/s2sokhv (Conference Canceled).

Hofmann, R., and N. Mercer. 2016. Teacher interventions in small group work in secondary mathematics and science lessons. *Language and Education* 30 (5): 400–416.

Hofmann, R., and K. Ruthven. 2018. Operational, interpersonal, discussional and ideational dimensions of classroom norms for dialogic practice in school mathematics. *British Educational Research Journal* 44 (3): 496–514.

Horn, I.S., and B.D. Kane. 2015. Opportunities for professional learning in mathematics teacher workgroup conversations: Relationships to instructional expertise. *Journal of the Learning Sciences* 24 (3): 373–418.

Howe, C., S. Hennessy, N. Mercer, M. Vrikki, and L. Wheatley. 2019. Teacher-student dialogue during classroom teaching: Does it really impact upon student outcomes? *Journal of the Learning Sciences*, 1–51.

Howe, C., and M. Abedin. 2013. Classroom dialogue: A systematic review across four decades of research. *Cambridge journal of education* 43 (3): 325–356.

Lefstein, A., and J. Snell. 2014. *Better than best practice: Developing teaching and learning through dialogue*. London: Routledge.

Littleton, K., and N. Mercer. 2013. *Interthinking: Putting talk to work*. Routledge.

Louie, N.L. 2016. Tensions in equity-and reform-oriented learning in teachers' collaborative conversations. *Teaching and Teacher Education* 53: 10–19.

Maine, F., S. Rojas-Drummond, R. Hofmann, and M. J. Barrera. 2020. Symmetries and asymmetries in children's peer group reading discussions. *Australian Journal of Language and Literacy* 43 (1): 17–32, Special Issue: Talk and Interaction.

Maine, F., and R. Hofmann. 2016. Talking for meaning: The dialogic engagement of teachers and children in a small group reading contexts. *International Journal of Educational Research* 75: 45–56.

Mercer, N., L. Dawes, and J. Kleine-Staarman. 2009. Dialogic teaching in the primary science classroom. *Language and Education* 23 (4): 353–369.

Michaels, S., and C. O'Connor. 2015. Conceptualizing talk moves as tools: Professional development approaches for academically productive discussion. In *Socializing intelligence through talk and dialogue*, ed. L.B. Resnick, C.S.C. Asterhan, and S.N. Clarke, 347–362. Washington, DC: American Educational Research Association.

Pehmer, A.K., A. Gröschner, and T. Seidel. 2015. Fostering and scaffolding student engagement in productive classroom discourse: Teachers' practice changes and reflections in light of teachers professional development. *Learning, Culture and Social Interaction* 7: 12–27.

Rainio, A.P., and R. Hofmann. 2015. Transformations in teachers' discourse about their students during a school-led pedagogic intervention. *The European Journal of Social and Behavioural Sciences* XIII (2): 1815–1829.

Rainio, A.P., and R. Hofmann. 2018. *Teachers' collaborative conversations during a pedagogic intervention: Dialogic shifts as professional change*. Paper presented at the American Educational Research Association Conference (AERA) in New York, United States.

Rapanta, C., M. Vrikki, and M. Evagorou (2020). Preparing culturally literate students through dialogue and argumentation: Rethinking citizenship education. *The Curriculum Journal*. https://doi.org/10.1002/curj.95.

Resnick, L., S. Michaels, and C. O'Connor. 2010. How (well-structured) talk builds the mind. In *From genes to context: New discoveries about learning from educational research and their applications*, ed. R. Sternberg and D. Preiss, 163–195. New York: Springer.
Ruthven, K., N. Mercer, K.S. Taber, P. Guardia, R. Hofmann, S. Ilie, S. Luthman, and F. Riga. 2017. A research-informed dialogic-teaching approach to early secondary school mathematics and science: The pedagogical design and field trial of the epiSTEMe intervention. *Research Papers in Education* 32 (1): 18–40.
Sedova, K., M. Sedlacek, and R. Svaricek. 2016. Teacher professional development as a means of transforming student classroom talk. *Teaching and Teacher Education* 57: 14–25.
Sinclair, JMcH, and M. Coulthard. 1975. *Towards an analysis of discourse: The English used by pupils and teachers*. Oxford: Oxford University Press.
Vedder-Weiss, D., N. Ehrenfeld, M. Ram-Menashe, and I. Pollak. 2018. Productive framing of pedagogical failure: How teacher framings can facilitate or impede learning from problems of practice. *Thinking Skills and Creativity* 30: 31–41.
Vrikki, M., P. Warwick, J.D. Vermunt, N. Mercer, and N. Van Halem. 2017. Teacher learning in the context of Lesson Study: A video-based analysis of teacher discussions. *Teaching and Teacher Education* 61C: 211–224.
Warwick, P., M. Vrikki, J.D. Vermunt, N. Mercer, and N. Van Halem. 2016. Connecting observations of student and teacher learning: An examination of dialogic processes in Lesson Study discussions in mathematics. *ZDM Mathematics Education* 48 (4): 555–569.
Wegerif, R. 2020. Orientations and ground rules: A framework for researching educational dialogue. In *Research methods for educational dialogue*, ed. R. Kershner, S. Hennessy, R. Wegerif, and A. Ahmed, 27–46. London: Bloomsbury Academic.
Wells, G., and R.M. Arauz. 2006. Dialogue in the classroom. *The Journal of the Learning Sciences* 15 (3): 379–428.

Riikka Hofmann is a Senior Lecturer at the Faculty of Education, Cambridge University, where she leads the 'Dialogue, Professional Change and Leadership' strand within the Cambridge Educational Dialogue Research Group (CEDiR).

Maria Vrikki is a Postdoctoral Researcher at the University of Nicosia. Her research interests focus on educational dialogue, teacher professional learning and professional development.

Maria Evagorou is an Associate Professor at the Department of Education, University of Nicosia. Her research interests focus on argumentation, socioscientific issues and teacher training.

Chapter 11
Educating Cultural Literacy with Open Educational Resources: Opportunities and Obstacles of Digital Teacher Collaborations

Elisabeth Mayweg-Paus and Maria Zimmermann

In this chapter, we set the context for how teachers can use the CLLP (see Chapter 1) and its resources sustainably by introducing why it is important for teachers to engage in long-term collaboration to implement the core aims and themes of DIALLS in a meaningful way. In the following chapter, we will introduce research on the opportunities and obstacles of online collaboration among teachers. Considering that the goals of DIALLS deal with issues of living together, social responsibility, and sustainable development, we will emphasize how effective online collaboration not only among students but also among teachers can help make DIALLS have a long-lasting impact that shapes the educational future of Europe. Thus, we will emphasize how to promote a long-lasting *community of practice* for DIALLS teachers and how this community may enable them to become professional DIALLS teachers.

The DIALLS project provides open educational resources (OER) (i.e., the project website's educational materials are open access for teachers) that can be used by teachers who are willing to integrate the DIALLS learning program into their teaching. While the open access status of educational resources per se is likely to increase teachers' willingness to use them, teachers still emphasize the need for technical and pedagogical support in using these OERs (Baas et al. 2019). So, how can we ensure that future teachers feel comfortable and competent in using the DIALLS resources, especially because professional trainings for DIALLS educators will be limited in the future (see Chapter 10 for a description of the professional trainings that were offered during the second year of the DIALLS project)? Here, we encourage teachers to support each other when using the DIALLS resources, as collaborations among teachers who use DIALLS may support each other's self-determined professional development. With respect to achieving the intended benefits of OERs,

E. Mayweg-Paus · M. Zimmermann (✉)
Faculty of Humanities and Social Sciences, Department of Education Studies, Digital Knowledge Management, Humboldt University of Berlin, Berlin, Germany
e-mail: maria.zimmermann@hu-berlin.de

F. Maine and M. Vrikki (eds.), *Dialogue for Intercultural Understanding*,
https://doi.org/10.1007/978-3-030-71778-0_11

UNESCO considers that OERs need to be embedded "by information and communication technologies, for consultation, use and adaptation by a community of users for non-commercial purposes" (UNESCO 2002, 24) (e.g., within communities in organizational or academic contexts). Similarly, teaching per se is a skill that is best developed within a supportive network (Cox 2004). In order to understand more precisely why such communities could be beneficial for helping teachers educate children on cultural literacy, we would like to describe the patterns of an online community of practice for DIALLS.

11.1 Communities of Practice—a Teacher Community of Practice for DIALLS

Considerable research states that learning is highly social (Bandura 1977) and, according to *social capital* approaches (Lin 1999), an individual's willingness to voluntarily help, share, and collaborate in groups can foster prosocial actions toward achieving shared objectives—such as achieving learning goals of a common learning program. Lave and Wenger (1991) were the first to coin the term *community of practice* (CoP), which describes how professional development can occur through participating in a group of practitioners that pool a broad base of knowledge and perform practices centered around three structural key features: *domain*, *community*, and *practice* (Wenger 1998). For example, for a CoP that aims to achieve the learning goals of DIALLS, the *domain* might be established as a result of teachers' shared interest in using the Cultural Literacy Learning Programme (CLLP) to foster their students' cultural literacy by instructing them to discuss about cultural (sub-)themes (e.g., tolerance, cultural heritage, climate change, solidarity). Furthermore, the feeling of belonging to a *community* would be the essential feature to "make mutual engagement possible" (Wenger 1998, 74). Wenger (2002) further stresses that, although members of a CoP would need to connect regularly, they wouldn't necessarily have to meet every day nor in person, as interactions can be promoted by the use of technologies which would then allow for online discussions and reflection. This is of particular importance, as teachers from all over Europe shall be able to use the CLLP. Thus, a CoP that is connected online would help to connect teachers remotely from several cities and even countries. However, to overcome language barriers of participating teachers who may not speak the same language, technical support by, for instance, automatic translation software would be needed.

However, the traditional understanding of a CoP may be not completely comparable to existing online learning communities, since CoPs often only come together in a purpose-oriented and unique way. Thus, to overcome a situation where members are only "searching for and sharing decontextualized ideas, resources, information, and knowledge without reference to authentic classroom learning settings" (Trust 2015, 78), especially in an online learning community, the sense of being part of a *community* needs to be strengthened.

Moreover, in a CoP for DIALLS, teachers would not only use the provided resources but would additionally develop and share their experiences with using the resources, including their successes and failures. Thus, the members of a DIALLS CoP would share *practices* and develop “a shared repertoire of resources: experiences, stories, tools, ways of addressing recurring problems” (Wenger 2012, 2). In this sense, they may share experiences about how students reacted to sensitive themes (e.g., homosexuality or migration) and may collaboratively discuss how to handle situations in which they may have experienced uncertainty in how to react toward students’ behaviors.

By considering the time that is needed to build a meaningful CoP and the challenges of directly assessing such a CoP’s success, the value creation framework (VCF) describes five dynamic interrelated cycles of value creation (Wenger et al. 2011). Each of these cycles is assumed to produce certain indicators that allow for monitoring a CoP’s success over time. The framework is particularly useful for describing the value created for individual members of a CoP regarding the CoP’s personal impacts on teachers themselves, its impacts on their teaching, and also its impacts on the school environment (McKellar et al. 2014). The first cycle refers to the *immediate value* of a DIALLS CoP by emphasizing the immediate value of teachers’ activities and interactions (e.g., one teacher may get help from another on how to deal with a challenging teaching situation). The second cycle would rely on the *potential value* of increasing knowledge capital (e.g., a teacher may improve skills in perspective taking or gain knowledge on how to teach DIALLS lessons). The third cycle expands these values to *applied value*, which refers to any changes in teaching practices (e.g., a teacher reuses and adapts DIALLS lesson plans to different classes). In the fourth cycle, *realized value* refers to any improvement in performance (e.g., a teacher changes practices but also reflects on how the application of her skills affects the students’ achievement of cultural literacy). In the last cycle, a CoP’s *reframing value* may be observed whenever the teachers in a DIALLS CoP redefine the success of the CoP (e.g., when teachers redefine what the CoP could be helpful for in the future).

Besides these intended values of a DIALLS CoP, the exchange of experiences—considered an immediate value—may be one of the main motivators for teachers to engage in a CoP (Macià and García 2016). Teachers’ actual reasons for engaging in online CoPs in particular are manifold and include (1) exchanging knowledge and materials, (2) developing common projects and didactical methods, (3) sharing and experiencing psychological support after emotional exchanges, and (4) overcoming loneliness and experiencing a sense of community (De Laat and Schreurs 2013; Hur and Brush 2009; Lantz-Andersson et al. 2018).

In addition, the observed benefits and values of online CoPs may go beyond teachers’ expectations and motivations for joining a CoP, as research indicates that pre-service teachers who participated in online CoPs had more pronounced self-efficacy beliefs regarding their teaching (Inel Ekici 2018). Furthermore, online CoPs were found to help teachers in developing self-efficacy regarding the use of technology and collaborating with other colleagues on the development of interclass-related curriculum units (Vavasseur and MacGregor 2008); the latter could be particularly important for DIALLS when students engage in dialogic exchange about cultural themes in other classes. In such instances, it is important for teachers to collaborate with the teacher of the other class so that both classes discuss the topic in a meaningful way. Furthermore, with respect to the benefits of informal teacher learning settings, a meta-analysis by Kyndt et al. (2016) reviewed 74 journal articles and found that engaging in such informal activities, such as being part of an informal learning community, led to improved subject knowledge, enhanced pedagogical skills and knowledge, as well as changed professional attitudes and identities.

Importantly, whether a CoP is organized formally or informally does result in different opportunities and obstacles that need to be considered in terms of the success of the CoP (Lantz-Andersson et al. 2018). While the learning and teaching materials from DIALLS have been created according to European educational policies as well as national curricula, the use of DIALLS resources is not a mandatory part of any European countries' curricula. Thus, teachers and school principals can voluntarily decide whether they want to use the resources to educate their students' cultural literacies with argumentation and dialogue. Accordingly, teachers' participation in a DIALLS CoP would also be voluntary, which again emphasizes not only the importance of a CoP but also the CoP's informal character, since a non-structurally anchored use of DIALLS materials makes it unlikely that a learning community would be formally organized by schools. In contrast to formally developed CoPs, the teacher members of an informally developed DIALLS CoP would not necessarily collaborate with colleagues from the same school but instead would contribute to a community with members from all over Europe.

11.1.1 Opportunities and Obstacles of a Community of Practice for DIALLS

Harnessing the perceived values of online communities of practice across educational contexts requires well-designed conditions and settings to achieve a sustainable level of functionality, communality, collaboration and knowledge sharing, which would allow the CoP to overcome challenges often observed in online teacher communities: For instance, informally developed online teacher communities often consist of many passive participants (i.e., lurkers) who observe rather than actively engage (Lantz-Andersson et al. 2018). While passively reading others' contributions in a CoP may increase an individual member's knowledge, participating only passively inhibits rich perspective taking among all members and, thus, prevents the full potential of a CoP from developing (Cuthell 2005). Similarly, Stuckey and Smith (2004) highlight the importance of active participation within a CoP and advocate for some members to become “leadership members”; these members not only participate actively themselves but also keep other members involved in the community.

In contrast to CoPs that have few active participants, an online teacher CoP, especially one that is informally developed, may overcome this issue because it may serve as a means of professional as well as emotional support, and members may feel encouraged to take risks and discuss successes as well as failures and challenges without feeling like those struggles are being viewed by one’s day-to-day colleagues (Lantz-Andersson et al. 2018; Williams 2006). In this sense, personal distance in online communities may overcome members’ hesitation to share problems with in-house colleagues (Hur and Brush 2009). Accordingly, the exchange of experiences and support within an online CoP might be particularly important for teachers who are aiming to use the DIALLS resources because the teaching resources are not embedded into formal curricula; embedding them formally would have guaranteed that every colleague in one’s school would use them and that teachers would have to share experiences with face-to-face contacts. Instead, a DIALLS CoP can avoid this drawback and offer a community where members exchange their experiences regarding the subject-specific use of resources to teach cultural literacy.

In sum, research has identified specific elements that are perceived as crucial for the success of online CoPs (Apostolos and Alivisos 2010; Lantz-Andersson et al. 2018; Kastens and Manduca 2017; Kraut and Resnick 2011; Stuckey 2004; Vavasseur and MacGregor 2008). For instance, Apostolos and Alivisos (2010) reviewed 38 journal articles on CoPs and identified an extended list of potentially relevant characteristics for an online-mediated CoP: (1) structural characteristics (e.g., active members of a CoP or the quality of collaboration and interactivity actions), (2) motivators (e.g., peer relations/social networking and reuse of resources), (3) success factors (e.g., the acceptance of communication rules or common understanding), and (4) barriers (e.g., lack of communication norms and tools, asynchronous communication, or a high competitiveness). In this context, Kastens and Manduca (2017) highlighted the relevance of similar aspects when referring to an actual CoP for GeoScience education. Additionally, they emphasize the importance of time and dynamic development to increase the benefits intended for individuals or for the collective.

With an integrative perspective, Stuckey (2004) outlined six common frameworks of CoPs and derived common guidelines and principles that are considered relevant to develop, implement, and sustain an online-mediated CoP. In Table 11.1, we show these guidelines as adapted to the development, implementation, and sustaining of a DIALLS CoP (for more information on the frameworks, see Stuckey 2004). Table 11.1 summarizes aspects related to the common ties (the domain) of the CoP, the members of the CoP, the members’ social interaction, and areas within the CoP that are considered relevant for the success of the DIALLS CoP.

What is particularly important in most CoP research, however, is how to encourage effective social interaction in the form of effective collaboration and communication among the CoP members (Lantz-Andersson et al. 2018; Vavasseur and MacGregor 2008). In general, research has indicated that effective online-mediated communication in CoPs is positively correlated with feelings of belonging, trust, support, and

Table 11.1 Adaptation of common guidelines for the development, implementation, and sustaining of an online-mediated CoP to achieve a CoP for DIALLS

	Design	Implement	Sustain
Common ties	• **Situatedness**: Offer meaningful authentic tasks and discussion spaces • **Target members**: Concentrate on teachers teaching cultural literacy via argumentation and dialogue • Define transparently the **CoP's purpose** (i.e., teachers' needs and exchange with colleagues)	• Reinforce continuously the **community's focus** • Focus on **values** (e.g., exchange of tips of DIALLS materials) and adaptation	• Focus on **topics** important to the DIALLS teachers only
CoP's members	• Consider different **roles** (e.g., expert, novice) • Get key thought **leaders** involved (e.g., clarification on difficult topics) • Create **executive awareness** (e.g., consider teachers' needs) • Make sure people have **time and encouragement** to participate (e.g., involve principals; promote benefits) • Collect and use recurring **feedback** from DIALLS teachers about their needs	• Find a well-respected DIALLS teacher to coordinate the community (**leadership** may change over time to distribute effort and to consider different perspectives) • Overview **members' profile histories** (e.g., active or passive participation; teachers may be familiar with specific topics) • Develop a **core group** of teachers that help to develop the CoP • Acknowledge the **voluntary nature** of participation in the CoP	• Harness the power of existing and new **personal connection** • Play on **motives** for participation (e.g., informing, get in contact with colleagues, or share experiences) • **Avoid judging** (e.g., engage in consensus-oriented discussion, see Sect. 10.1.2)
Members' social interaction	• Support **transactivity** (e.g., think reflectively; consider others' perspectives, see Sect. 10.1.2) • Create a **rhythm** and integrate teachers' life **rituals** • Combine **familiarity** and **excitement** • Support **new teachers in CoP** (e.g., keep content up to date and instruct on how to orientate in CoP)	• Invite different **levels of participation** • Provide tasks for **collaboration** (not only within but also among classes from different cities and countries) • **Easy contribution and open access** • Rely on the **fun factor** (e.g., share cultural artifacts)	• **Actively generate content** (e.g., by asking monthly for a relevant topic) • **"Prime the pump with communication"** (see Sect. 10.1.2) • **Etiquette** (e.g., easy-to-access communication rules in CoP) • Create dialogue about **cutting-edge issues** (e.g., on topics currently relevant)

(continued)

Table 11.1 (continued)

	Design	Implement	Sustain
Areas within the CoP	• Form **communities around people**, not applications (i.e., the use of mediating technology might change over time) • Create **forums** for thinking together and sharing information (see Sect. 10.1.2) • Design for **evolution** (i.e., sustainability of DIALLS; CoP may adapt to progresses in communication technologies or in society)	• Fit **tools** to the community (e.g., asynchronous communication) • Develop **public and private spaces** (e.g., open-access DIALLS resources and team teaching assembles) • Open **dialogues between inside and outside** (e.g., share experiences)	• Facilitate **teacher-run subgroups** (e.g., sub-spaces for self-chosen topics)

Source Adapted from Stuckey (2004)

community (Williams 2006). As a result, the more effective the discussions, sharing, and support are, the more the CoP contributes to teachers' professional development (Tseng and Kuo 2014). In this sense, teachers that are part of a CoP for DIALLS need to be engaged in reflective and collaborative conversations about the efficacy and the meaningful use of the CLLP. While collaborating and communicating effectively in an online-mediated CoP offers various opportunities, there are many obstacles as well.

11.1.2 Opportunities and Obstacles of Collaborative Argumentation Among Teachers Online

Drawing on social constructivist theories, collaborative learning approaches in education are based on the idea that knowledge and skills are co-constructed through social interaction (Knowles et al. 1998). Extending this to the form of social interaction in online CoP approaches, a key learning activity in an online CoP that could promote outcomes such as critical reflection, problem-solving skills, and learning about a particular topic might be *computer-mediated collaborative learning* (Chinn and Clark 2013; Namdar 2017; Noroozi et al. 2012). In these learning environments "learners [namely, teachers who are learning in the context of their professional development] communicate with each other via text-based [...] discussion boards [and] are supposed to engage in argumentative discourse with the goal to acquire knowledge" (Weinberger and Fischer 2006, 71). In this sense, collaborative learning is more than merely working together. Collaboration is considered a learning process with "co-elaboration of conceptual understanding and knowledge" (e.g., Baker 2015, 4).

Thus, collaborative learning involves those communicative activities that are also intended in the DIALLS learning program and that should be encouraged by DIALLS teachers when involving their students in dialogues about cultural themes. These communicative activities are geared toward explaining and understanding ideas, representing knowledge and concepts, gaining multiple perspectives from learning partners, as well as arguing collaboratively (Asterhan and Schwarz 2016; Chinn and Clark 2013). The latter, *collaborative argumentation*, is also considered important for teachers who take part in the DIALLS CoP (e.g., Apostolos and Alivisos 2010; Namdar 2017). Teachers' collaborative argumentation would occur when teachers exchange statements and questions, make claims about their teaching perspectives and approaches, support these claims with arguments, and question other arguments critically.

Although, collaborative argumentation is important, it should not replace teachers' emotional exchanges. Rather, collaborative argumentation has the potential to overcome superficial consensus-building in discussions. For instance, when discussing pedagogical strategies, teachers may take part in a discussion by more deeply considering each other's perspective or critically questioning their own arguments and adapt their pedagogical strategies accordingly.

Further, as collaborative argumentation can result in agreement or disagreement among teachers, it must be distinguished from any competitive assertion of one's own opinion (Chinn and Clark 2013). While the aim of argumentative discourse can either be to persuade or to reach a consensus, a consensus-oriented type of discourse may increase the benefits of collaborative argumentation while opposing any barriers due to competition (Apostolos and Alivisos 2010) because the teachers in a CoP would be able to interactively use arguments originally introduced by other members and more critically challenge their own arguments (Felton et al. 2015). In particular, teachers may substantially benefit from collaborative argumentation because it can be used to successfully *integrate multiple perspectives* (Veerman et al. 2002), it can promote interactions among teachers in a transactive way, such as *challenging the partner's knowledge and arguments* (Mayweg-Paus et al. 2016; Vogel et al. 2016), and it can involve high-quality argumentation strategies such as *critical questioning of the arguments* (Mayweg-Paus et al. 2016). In this sense, collaboration among teachers per se describes an interactive process that enables teachers with diverse expertise to work together as equals and engage in reasoned decision-making toward pedagogical goals. Hence, a consensus-oriented discourse would support the aim of a DIALLS CoP to provide collegial support to coequal members.

However, because it is not natural for humans to critically question or to hone skills related to arguing collaboratively, teachers would benefit from instructional support on how to argue and critically reason when engaging in consensus-oriented discourse (Mayweg-Paus et al. 2016; Noroozi et al. 2012). Accordingly, any uninstructed communication among teachers in online CoPs tends to be rather superficial, seldom leads to in-depth discussions about the corresponding instructional or pedagogical issues, and can lack reflection as well as the critical sharing of practices (Lantz-Andersson et al. 2018). This is perhaps unsurprising though, since teachers rarely connect their pedagogical and conceptual knowledge with their own and other teachers' teaching practices in a transactive way (Hawkes and Romiszowski 2001). Nonetheless, if teachers could meaningfully reflect on existing practices that have been shared by the other teachers, this reflection could help them critically examine the practices and identify whether they could synthesize a different perspective into their own teaching, thus supporting the development of their own teaching practices (Danielowich 2012).

In contrast to synchronous online communication among teachers (i.e., at the same time without delay), asynchronous forms of communication (i.e., at different times, which can lead to a delay in transactive responses) may inhibit the immediate exchange and interactivity of communication and, hence, may make teachers less willing to exchange personal experiences and situations (Loving et al. 2007; Lantz-Andersson et al. 2018). However, as the interactions in an online-mediated CoP for DIALLS hinge on teachers' critical reflection, as this may help teachers collaboratively discuss the DIALLS topics in a consensus-oriented way, the process of writing a non-immediate response may stimulate forms of reflection and self-analysis that would not be evident in face-to-face meetings (Unwin 2015). For example, Choi and Morrison (2014) found that compared to discussions had by teachers who met in person, asynchronous online discussions by those same teachers were more reflective and featured a more diverse range of perspectives.

To sum up, patterns of communication in a CoP can have several functions, all of which are relevant in the context of professionalization. For example, while exchanging practical hints and tips or sharing one's experiences may directly serve the purposes of emotional relief or obtaining support, these forms of communication do not necessarily require deeper critical reflection and elaboration through collaborative argumentation. On the other hand, understanding one's own teaching practices and another person's perspective requires teachers to critically question arguments and to transactively engage in discussions that may allow for deeper learning and may apply to other educational situations. Accordingly, encouraging teachers to engage in collaborative argumentation in a CoP will help promote long-lasting professional development of their teaching skills.

11.2 Implications Gained from the Insights of an Emerging Community of Practice for DIALLS

In this final section, we give examples on what the spaces for collaboration among teachers in DIALLS look like. In this vein, we offer a comprehensive picture of what the DIALLS teacher could actually learn and value from a DIALLS CoP and describe how their collaborative argumentation can help to achieve a DIALLS CoP and, thereby, to sustain the impact of DIALLS.

During the DIALLS project, an online discussion forum was implemented that gave the teachers a space to collaboratively work together without time or local restrictions. As one of the main goals in DIALLS is to promote students' dialogue and argumentation so they can better consider other perspectives on cultural themes, the teachers involved in a DIALLS CoP also need to collaborate with colleagues and, hence, may experience similar opportunities and obstacles that their students may experience during a DIALLS lesson. Accordingly, encouraging teachers to work collaboratively and to express their opinions while listening to and respecting the opinions of their colleagues may, in turn, help improve their ability to teach students how to argue. This forum also offered teachers who taught DIALLS the opportunity to find and collaborate with self-reliant colleagues who also taught DIALLS and who might be interested in bringing their classes together to conduct the DIALLS lessons that were particularly designed to have students from different cities or countries exchange experiences. In the following we will provide a selection of teachers' comments representing their perspectives and needs. Based on this, we will highlight the central requirements of the DIALLS CoP and how they were addressed by the implementation of design principles (see Table 11.1). Finally, we will draw conclusions on the role of a long-lasting CoP for sustaining the impact of DIALLS in the future.

From the German teachers' feedback ($N = 16$; those who took part during the implementation phase) on the usefulness of online discussion forums, the teachers underlined the potential such forums in the context of DIALLS. Regarding the common ties of the DIALLS CoP, one teacher expected that "if everyone contributes their plans and applications [of the DIALLS materials], it can help [future] teachers". This exemplary expectation is reflected in the DIALLS CoP's purpose and its value, as members' exchange of materials could be a long-lasting outcome of their collaboration. Similarly, the teachers further emphasized the need to exchange with colleagues, receive tips from them, to discuss how they adapted lesson plans toward the specific needs of their students, and the importance of exchanging ideas about "how to deal with challenges during lessons". All the teachers expressed their future willingness to contribute to the CoP. Having contributions to the CoP from both expert teachers who are familiar with teaching DIALLS and novice teachers who are looking for some guidance can help keep the CoP going and will likely infuse the CoP with diverse values. With regard to the members of the DIALLS CoP, this means that novice and expert DIALLS teachers have been invited to take part in the CoP. Novice DIALLS teachers in particular could benefit from the expertise of those who are familiar with DIALLS. While such novice teachers may benefit from posts by expert teachers and may be more passively involved in information consuming to increase their personal knowledges and skills, the expert teachers could take on the role of vocationalists who share tips and expertise and keep an eye on the needs of the CoP itself (Prestridge 2019). In this sense, one teacher highlighted that expert teachers "could act as moderators for further professional reflections on the use of DIALLS materials". Accordingly, the experts could occasionally take on a moderating role and may stimulate the manner of social interaction between the members, for instance, by supporting new teachers with instructions on how to find certain topics within the CoP.

Finally, here we offer examples of topics that emerged in the DIALLS online discussion forum and describe how they relate to the intended values of a DIALLS CoP. In line with the value creation framework (Wenger et al. 2011) described above, the space for discussion and exchange in the DIALLS online discussion forum allowed teachers to harness the immediate, potential, applied, realized, and reframing values and, thus, can be considered helpful for achieving a long-lasting CoP for DIALLS. First, we highlight the forum topic "Delights and frustration: My experiences with the DIALLS learning program" wherein teachers exchanged their personal experiences; this exchange many have provided the immediate value of sharing and receiving support from colleagues (e.g., about any challenging teaching situation). Within the forum topic entitled "What I personally have learned from DIALLS", teachers could, for instance, discuss whether any DIALLS teaching materials influenced their own perspectives on European values. Such discussions may relate to the applied and realized value of the DIALLS CoP, as teachers here reflected not only on how they taught a specific DIALLS lesson but also on how this teaching impacted them personally. Other forum topics addressed the reframing values of the DIALLS CoP (e.g., "Help to create our community!", in which teachers could express their wishes for other forum topics or the CoP itself). In addition to addressing teachers' needs and, hence, continuously assessing what they expected from the CoP, the form also offered a *netiquette* on how to communicate meaningfully. Displaying such forms of communication rules (e.g., instructing the teachers to ask each other questions, encourage them to read others' posts in order to check whether something similar was posted before) are considered important not only for reducing redundancy but also for encouraging teachers to actively take part in the CoP and to react transactively to what their colleagues contributed. Furthermore, teachers could also easily view the CoP's own values, which helped increase teachers' awareness about the intended benefits and aims of the online discussion forum and the DIALLS CoP. Importantly, sustaining the CoP and, thus, the impact of the entire DIALLS project, relies heavily on having an actively ongoing community of practice (e.g., The California Center for College and Career 2013).

In this sense, continuously promoting the values of the DIALLS CoP as well as providing pleasant and easy-to-access spaces for meaningful collaboration among teachers that allow members to learn and redefine their own CoP in a self-determined way will help sustain the impact of DIALLS in the future. DIALLS addresses highly relevant topics for education and for our society. Establishing and maintaining a DIALLS CoP will make a meaningful contribution to keep DIALLS practices alive, as it flexibly allows teachers to react to the demands of this ongoing changing society and to adapt DIALLS to it.

References

Apostolos, K., and S. Alivisos. 2010. Internet-mediated communities of practice (IMCoPs): A meta-analysis of critical elements. *International Conference on Intelligent Networking and Collaborative Systems* 2010: 1–7. https://doi.org/10.1109/INCOS.2010.23.

Asterhan, C.S.C., and B.B. Schwarz. 2016. Argumentation for learning: Well-trodden paths and unexplored territories. *Educational Psychologist* 51: 164–187. https://doi.org/10.1080/00461520.2016.1155458.

Baas, M., W. Admiraal, and E. van den Berg. 2019. Teachers' adoption of open educational resources in higher education. *Journal of Interactive Media in Education*, 9. http://doi.org/10.5334/jime.510.

Baker, M.J. 2015. Collaboration in collaborative learning. *Interaction Studies* 16: 451–473. https://doi.org/10.1075/is.16.3.05bak.

Bandura, A. (1977). *Social learning theory*. Englewood Cliffs, NJ: Prentice Hall.

Chinn, C.A., and D.B. Clark. 2013. Learning through collaborative argumentation. In *The international handbook of collaborative learning*, ed. C.E. Hmelo-Silver, C.A. Chinn, C.K.K. Chan, and A.M. O'Donnell, 314–332. New York: Taylor & Francis.

Choi, D.S.-Y., and P. Morrison. 2014. Learning to get it right: Understanding change processes in professional development for teachers of English learners. *Professional Development in Education* 40: 416–435. https://doi.org/10.1080/19415257.2013.806948.

Cox, M. D. 2004. Introduction to faculty learning communities. *New directions for teaching and learning*, 5–23. https://doi.org/10.1002/tl.129.

Cuthell, J.P. 2005. What does it take to be active? Teacher participation in online communities. *International Journal of Web Based Communities* 1: 320–332. https://doi.org/10.1504/IJWBC.2005.006930.

Danielowich, R.M. 2012. Other teachers' teaching: Understanding the roles of peer group collaboration in teacher reflection and learning. *The Teacher Educator* 47: 101–122. https://doi.org/10.1080/08878730.2012.660373.

De Laat, M. F., and B. Schreurs. 2013. Visualizing informal professional development networks: Building a case for learning analytics in the workplace. *American Behavioral Scientist*. https://doi.org/10.1177/0002764213479364.

Felton, M., A. Crowell, and T. Liu. 2015. Arguing to agree: Mitigating my-side bias through consensus-seeking dialogue. *Written Communication* 32: 317–331. https://doi.org/10.1177/0741088315590788.

Hawkes, M., and A. Romiszowski. 2001. Examining the reflective outcomes of asynchronous computer-mediated communication on inservice teacher development. *Journal of Technology and Teacher Education* 9: 285–308. https://www.learntechlib.org/primary/p/8425/. Accessed June 17 2020.

Hur, J.W., and T.A. Brush. 2009. Teacher participation in online communities. *Journal of Research on Technology in Education* 41: 279–303. https://doi.org/10.1080/15391523.2009.10782532.

Inel Ekici, D. 2018. Development of pre-service teachers' teaching self-efficacy beliefs through an online community of practice. *Asia Pacific Education Review* 19: 27–40. https://doi.org/10.1007/s12564-017-9511-8.

Kastens, K.A., and C.A. Manduca. 2017. Using systems thinking in the design, Implementation, and evaluation of complex educational innovations, with examples from the integrate project. *Journal of Geoscience Education* 65: 219–230. https://doi.org/10.5408/16-225.1.

Knowles, M., E. Holton, and R. Swanson. 1998. *The adult learner: The definitive classic in adult education and human resource development*. Houston: Gulf Publishing.

Kraut, R.E., and P. Resnick. 2011. *Building successful online communities: Evidence-based social design*. Cambridge: MIT Press.

Kyndt, E., D. Gijbels, I. Grosemans, and V. Donche. 2016. Teachers' everyday professional development: Mapping informal learning activities, antecedents, and learning outcomes. *Review of educational research*. Advance online publication. https://doi.org/10.3102/0034654315627864.

Lantz-Andersson, A., M. Lundin, and N. Selwyn. 2018. Twenty years of online teacher communities: A systematic review of formally-organized and informally-developed professional learning groups. *Teaching and Teacher Education* 75: 302–315. https://doi.org/10.1016/j.tate.2018.07.008.

Lave, J., and E. Wenger. 1991. *Situated learning: Legitimate peripheral participation*. Cambridge: Cambridge University Press.

Lin, N. 1999. Building a network theory of social capital. *Connections* 22: 28–51. http://faculty.washington.edu/matsueda/courses/590/Readings/Lin%20Network%20Theory%201999.pdf. Accessed June 17 2020.

Loving, C.C., C. Schroeder, R. Kang, C. Shimek, and B. Herbert. 2007. Blogs: Enhancing links in a professional learning community of science and mathematics teachers. *Contemporary Issues in Technology and Teacher Education* 7: 178–198.

Macià, M., and I. García. 2016. Informal online communities and networks as a source of teacher professional development: A review. *Teaching and Teacher Education* 55: 291–307. https://doi.org/10.1016/j.tate.2016.01.021.

Mayweg-Paus, E., M. Thiebach, and R. Jucks. 2016. Let me critically question this!—Insights from a training study on the role of questioning on argumentative discourse. *International Journal of Educational Research* 79: 195–210. https://doi.org/10.1016/j.ijer.2016.05.017.

McKellar, K., K.B. Pitzul, J.Y. Yi, and D.C. Cole. 2014. Evaluating communities of practice and knowledge networks: A systematic scoping review of evaluation frameworks. *EcoHealth* 11: 383–399. https://doi.org/10.1007/s10393-014-0958-3.

Namdar, B. 2017. Preservice science teachers' collaborative knowledge building through argumentation on healthy eating in a computer supported collaborative learning environment. *The Turkish Online Journal of Educational Technology* 16: 132–146. https://www.learntechlib.org/p/189616/. Accessed June 17 2020.

Noroozi, O., A. Weinberger, H.J. Biemans, M. Mulder, and M. Chizar. 2012. Argumentation-based computer supported collaborative learning (ABCSCL). A synthesis of 15 years of research. *Educational Research Review* 7: 79–106. https://doi.org/10.1016/j.edurev.2011.11.006.

Prestridge, S. 2019. Categorising teachers' use of social media for their professional learning: A self-generating professional learning paradigm. *Computers & Education* 129: 143–158. https://doi.org/10.1016/j.compedu.2018.11.003.

Stuckey, B. 2004. Making the most of the good advice: Meta-analysis of guidelines for establishing an Internet-Mediated Community of Practice. In *Web based communities: Proceedings of the IADIS international conference*, ed. P. Kommers and P. Goikoetxea, 4–26. Lisbon, Portugal.

Stuckey, B., and J. D. Smith. 2004. Sustaining communities of practice. In *Web based communities: Proceedings of the IADIS international conference*, ed. P. Kommers and P. Goikoetxea, 4–26. Lisbon, Portugal.

Trust, T. 2015. Deconstructing an online community of practice: Teachers' actions in the Edmodo math subject community. *Journal of Digital Learning in Teacher Education* 31: 73–81. https://doi.org/10.1080/21532974.2015.1011293.

Tseng, F.-C., and F.-Y. Kuo. 2014. A study of social participation and knowledge sharing in the teachers' online professional community of practice. *Computers & Education* 72: 37–47. https://doi.org/10.1016/j.compedu.2013.10.005.

UNESCO. 2002. Forum on the impact of open courseware for higher education in developing countries: final report. http://unesdoc.unesco.org/images/0012/001285/128515e.pdf.

Unwin, A. 2015. Developing new teacher inquiry and criticality: The role of online discussions. *British Journal of Educational Technology* 46: 1214–1222. https://doi.org/10.1111/bjet.12194.

Vavasseur, C.B., and S.K. MacGregor. 2008. Extending content-focused professional development through online communities of practice. *Journal of Research on Technology in Education* 40: 517–536. https://doi.org/10.1080/15391523.2008.10782519.

Veerman, A., J. Andriessen, and G. Kanselaar. 2002. Collaborative argumentation in academic education. *Instructional Science* 30: 155–186. https://doi.org/10.1023/A:1015100631027.

Vogel, F., I. Kollar, S. Ufer, E. Reichersdorfer, K. Reiss, and F. Fischer. 2016. Developing argumentation skills in mathematics through computer-supported collaborative learning: The role of transactivity. *Instructional Science* 44: 477–500. https://doi.org/10.1007/s11251-016-9380-2.

Weinberger, A., and F. Fischer. 2006. A framework to analyze argumentative knowledge construction in computer-supported collaborative learning. *Computers & Education* 46: 71–95. https://doi.org/10.1016/j.compedu.2005.04.003.

Wenger, E. 1998. *Communities of practice: Learning, meaning and identity*. New York: Cambridge University.

Wenger, E. 2002. *Cultivating communities of practice: A guide to managing knowledge*. Boston, MA: Harvard University Press.

Wenger, E. 2012. Communities of practice and social learning systems: The career of a concept. http://wenger-trayner.com/resources/publications/cops-and-learning-systems/. Accessed 30 August 2015.

Wenger, E., B. Trayner, and M. de Laat. 2011. *Promoting and assessing value creation in communities and networks: A conceptual framework*. Netherlands Ruud de Moor Center Rapport.

Williams, D. 2006. On and off the net: Scales for social capital in an online era. *Journal of Computer-Mediated Communication* 11. https://doi.org/10.1111/j.1083-6101.2006.00029.x.

Elisabeth Mayweg-Paus is Junior Professor for Digital Knowledge Management in Higher Education at the Humboldt University of Berlin and at the Einstein Centre Digital Future since

2018. Her research interests are in the field of collaborative learning, digital communication and the development of digital skills in formal and informal education.

Maria Zimmermann is a Postdoctoral Researcher at the Humboldt University of Berlin and teaches pre-service teachers since 2014. In her research she is interested in how to promote learning in online learning environments and focuses on the potential of collaborative communication among learners and teachers to acquire the so-called digital skills.

Printed by Printforce, the Netherlands